THE PSYCHOLOGY OF RELIGIOUS EXPERIENCE

THE PSYCHOLOGY OF RELIGIOUS EXPERIENCE

BY

EDWARD SCRIBNER AMES, Ph.D.
ASSISTANT PROFESSOR OF PHILOSOPHY
IN THE UNIVERSITY OF CHICAGO

WIPF & STOCK · Eugene, Oregon

Wipf and Stock Publishers
199 W 8th Ave, Suite 3
Eugene, OR 97401

The Psychology of Religious Experience
By Ames, Edward Scribner
ISBN 13: 978-1-60899-377-2
Publication date 01/07/2011
Previously published by Houghton Mifflin Co., 1910

TO MY FRIENDS
THE MEMBERS OF THE
HYDE PARK CHURCH OF DISCIPLES
CHICAGO

PREFACE

THIS work undertakes an investigation of the religious aspect of normal human experience. The point of view employed is that of functional psychology, which is necessarily genetic and social. The method adopted involves the use of much material from anthropology, the history of religion, and other social sciences, but an attempt has been made to organize this material and to interpret it from the psychological standpoint. The hypothesis that religion is the consciousness of the highest social values arose from studies in these fields, and this conception has been strengthened by further investigations. These highest social values appear to embody more or less idealized expressions of the most elemental and urgent life impulses. Religion expresses the desire to obtain life and obtain it abundantly. In all stages the demand is for "daily bread" and for companionship and achievement in family and community relationships.

These cravings constitute the inner continuity and identity of motive in all the diverse types of religion, primitive and modern, Pagan and Christian. The social consciousness arises in every group in the mediation of these needs, in the struggle for existence, and in the aspiration and endeavor to make life more varied, more adequate, and more ideal. In their simpler expressions among primitive peoples these

PREFACE

cravings struggle blindly, being dominated by rigid custom, and by magic. In higher forms they are gradually freed from superstition, are guided by tested experience, and are incorporated in more elaborate symbols.

In this conception of religion as the consciousness of the highest social values, lies a partial justification for the rather ambitious task of bringing together in a single volume an outline treatment of so many problems. Several studies have appeared treating of primitive religion and the religion of particular races; others have dealt with the phenomena of conversion, of faith, of mysticism, and of other special interests with which the current religious reconstruction is concerned. It seems desirable, however, to bring all these phenomena into the perspective of a comprehensive psychological inquiry. Such a treatment, it is hoped, may contribute to a better sense of proportion and to a clearer understanding of the interrelation of the various aspects of the religious consciousness.

During the past year the chapter on "Religion as involving the Entire Psychical Life" appeared in the *International Journal of Ethics*, and the chapter on "Nonreligious Persons" was published in the *American Journal of Theology*. Other material from this book was used in an article published in the *Monist* under the title "The Psychological Basis of Religion."

I wish particularly to acknowledge my very great indebtedness to my colleagues, Professor James H. Tufts and Professor William I. Thomas, not only for suggestions from their published works, but for criti-

PREFACE

cisms and assistance in various ways during the progress of this investigation. I have also much for which to thank those students who have worked with me in this field in the past six years. Acknowledgment is also made of the valuable services of Dr. Ella H. Stokes, who has read the proof-sheets and prepared the index.

EDWARD SCRIBNER AMES.

THE UNIVERSITY OF CHICAGO,
    August 1, 1910.

CONTENTS

PART I. HISTORY AND METHOD OF THE PSYCHOLOGY OF RELIGION

I. THE HISTORY OF THE SCIENCE 3

II. THE PSYCHOLOGICAL STANDPOINT 15

PART II. THE ORIGIN OF RELIGION IN THE RACE

III. THE DETERMINING IMPULSES IN PRIMITIVE RELIGION . 33

IV. CUSTOM AND TABOO 51

V. CEREMONIALS AND MAGIC 71

VI. SPIRITS 95

VII. SACRIFICE 116

VIII. PRAYER 134

IX. MYTHOLOGY 149

X. THE DEVELOPMENT OF RELIGION 168

PART III. THE RISE OF RELIGION IN THE INDIVIDUAL

XI. RELIGION AND CHILDHOOD 197

XII. RELIGION AND ADOLESCENCE 214

XIII. NORMAL RELIGIOUS DEVELOPMENT 236

XIV. CONVERSION 257

CONTENTS

PART IV. THE PLACE OF RELIGION IN THE EX-
PERIENCE OF THE INDIVIDUAL AND
SOCIETY

XV. RELIGION AS INVOLVING THE ENTIRE PSYCHICAL LIFE . 279

XVI. IDEAS AND RELIGIOUS EXPERIENCE 303

XVII. FEELING AND RELIGIOUS EXPERIENCE 321

XVIII. THE PSYCHOLOGY OF RELIGIOUS GENIUS AND INSPIRATION 338

XIX. NONRELIGIOUS PERSONS 355

XX. THE PSYCHOLOGY OF RELIGIOUS SECTS 377

XXI. THE RELIGIOUS CONSCIOUSNESS IN RELATION TO DEMO-
CRACY AND SCIENCE 396

INDEX 421

PART I

HISTORY AND METHOD OF THE PSYCHOLOGY OF RELIGION

CHAPTER I

THE HISTORY OF THE SCIENCE

THE Psychology of Religion, if it may be dated from the first books published under this title, appeared as a distinct subject of investigation only ten years ago, with the pioneer volumes of Starbuck and Coe.[1] Each of these authors distinctly states that the investigations were prompted both by scientific and by religious interests. They shared the new scientific impulse which was extending to all aspects of individual and social mental life. The whole science of psychology, under the lead of the biological sciences, was then undergoing a complete reconstruction, which still continues. It was inevitable that the extensive areas of experience organized in the religious consciousness should ultimately yield themselves, however reluctantly, to a most fundamental reconsideration. The very attitude of sensitiveness and reserve with which these phenomena seemingly withheld themselves from the methods everywhere else employed added intensity of interest to their study when it was begun. The characteristic eagerness of science to discover and treat all the facts of experience could not be abated by the feeling that this set of facts was guarded by peculiar claims and by keen emotional resistance.

[1] A valuable history of the beginnings of this science is contained in a paper by James Bissett Pratt, "The Psychology of Religion," *Harvard Theological Review*, vol. i, 1908.

PSYCHOLOGY OF RELIGIOUS EXPERIENCE

This demand for scientific thoroughness was reinforced by the assumption of the unity of the mental life, and it was of the utmost significance to determine whether this postulate, already so widely justified, could be maintained with reference to religious knowledge and faith. Besides, there was a growing conviction, now well substantiated, that many facts of religious experience might afford assistance in understanding the typical processes treated by general psychology, such as those of habit, attention, and emotion, both in normal and in abnormal forms.

The religious incentive was of a more immediately practical character. Those interested in propagating religion, whether by education or evangelism, began to realize the necessity of understanding the psychological processes in order to control and direct them. Professor Coe expressed this in the preface to "The Spiritual Life," in these words: "There is reason for doubting whether even the spiritual teachers and guides of the people really grasp the mental processes with which they have to deal — the evident decay of the revival, the alienation from the Church of whole classes of the population, the excess of women over men in Church life, the apparent powerlessness of organized religion to suppress or seriously check the great organized vices and injustices of society, the failure of the Sunday-School to make the people or even its own pupils familiar with the contents of the Bible — these facts ought to raise a question as to what, among the matters upon which we have laid stress, is really practical and what mere ignorant blundering."

THE HISTORY OF THE SCIENCE

It would be difficult to find a more striking illustration of the way in which scientific research is ultimately motivated and occasioned by practical interests. The utilitarian impulse in these first publications is also clear in the particular problems treated and in the scope of their inquiry. They deal chiefly, almost exclusively, with conversion, taking that term in its broadest sense. It is in this process of conversion that the whole task of Protestant Christianity has been felt to focus. The work of the Church has been conceived to be that of making converts. Therefore, the understanding of this process with a view to controlling it successfully among all classes attains first importance. The question of methods in religious work turns upon the psychology of religious experience. The relative value of revivalism, and of religious education, depends upon the comparative significance of the different types of conversion and upon the means by which they are occasioned. The demand of the Church, under an increasing realization of tension between it and many developments of modern society, has been for a more efficient method of winning its own children and securing recruits from the "world." The other functions of religion, in evangelical churches at least, appear to presuppose this "experience," and consequently it has been the centre of attention. Investigations have also been made with reference to such problems as the nature of faith, prayer, revelations, and mystical states.

Another and broader demand for the aid of psychology in dealing with religion has grown up with

PSYCHOLOGY OF RELIGIOUS EXPERIENCE

the work of the historians and anthropologists. Comparative religion has brought to attention a great variety of faiths, often with elaborate ritual, theology, and sacred books. Various theories of their origin, interdependence, and relation to Christianity have been advanced. The application of the principles of historical development to these diverse religions has led to the study of their earliest forms, and to the demand for a knowledge of their origins. Here anthropology has taken up the task in connection with the whole problem of the beginnings of human social interests, customs, morality, and art. But the data furnished by this science, while affording much indispensable material, have yet required the aid of psychology in their interpretation. The remains of early peoples and the customs of existing natural races afford some problems which the psychologist alone is prepared to consider. Along with other inquiries concerning this complex life of the race, it is natural that there should be undertaken a psychological study of the origin and character of religion and religious institutions. And it was this interest in something beyond the range of history and anthropology which contributed to the rise of the psychology of religion. This fact is expressly stated by Professor Morris Jastrow in "The Study of Religion": "In order to trace its history, to lay bare its doctrines, to examine its ethical principles, and to investigate its myths, a consistent application of historical methods is all that is required; but when we proceed further and endeavor to determine the causes of its growth, to penetrate to the secret of its influence and to account for its decline, historical research

THE HISTORY OF THE SCIENCE

needs to be supplemented by a study of human nature."[1]

Among the typical problems which emerge for psychology from the results of historical and anthropological research are those of the nature and scope of custom, or social habit, in early society, and the relation to custom of ritual, sacrifice, prayer, taboo, magic, and myth. In connection with these habitual reactions, involved with the maintenance and furtherance of the life-process, much light is shed upon the nature of animism, fetishism, and other theories of primitive religion. The striking uniformity of early man's attitudes, together with a diversity in the content and formal expression of his experience, offers a psychological problem of the greatest importance. Something more is required here than the naïve assumption of the ancients that it is natural and necessary that all peoples have their own religions, or the equally unreasoned attitude of certain developed, aggressive religions, that all peoples have their own religions, but that all are utterly false or merely poor imitations except the one aggressive religion itself. The great number of independent religions which historical and comparative study have made known raise the questions for the psychologist: How did religion arise in the race? What are the psychological grounds of the differences and likenesses which exist?

From still another side there is a demand for a scientific psychology of religion. The philosophy of religion and the related fields of theology and apologetics are forced to deal with such topics as inspiration, faith,

[1] Morris Jastrow, *The Study of Religion*, p. 273.

knowledge, the nature of the soul, personality, religious genius, and the significance of such conceptions as God, free will, the world, evil. All these questions involve the consideration of psychological processes, the treatment of which becomes a necessary stage in any adequate philosophical discussion of religion. The conflicting points of view, the partial and unsatisfying nature of the various attempts to attain a philosophy of religion, force the inquiry back again and again to a reckoning with the results and standpoints presented by the rapidly growing science of psychology. This is characteristic even of those systems of thought which make a radical distinction between the scientific method with which psychology works and the philosophical apprehension and statement of truth. The value of psychology is necessarily felt to be much greater where the metaphysical and ethical problems are held to be simply the further elaboration and explication of certain psychological problems.

A survey of the philosophy of religion abundantly illustrates the inevitable return to psychological problems, just as the course of philosophy itself has been marked by an increasing regard for the underlying facts concerning the states and functions of consciousness. Schleiermacher made religion a matter of feeling. With Hegel it was intellectual. Ritschl and Kant renewed emphasis upon the difference between the theoretical and the practical reason. The religious consciousness is here entirely separated from the sphere of knowledge, and has to do exclusively with value judgments. The "Outline of the Philosophy of Religion," by Auguste Sabatier, attempts to make a psy-

THE HISTORY OF THE SCIENCE

chological justification of the God-consciousness over against both the theoretical and practical phases of experience. The human spirit posits God by an act of faith. Spiritual truths are apprehended by the heart. They do not need and do not permit of any objective demonstration. "To the man without piety it would be useless, to the man who is pious it would be superfluous." Here, then, there is an attempt to base religion upon a faculty or disposition which is distinct from the theoretical and the practical interests, and yet is able to mediate in some way between them. The justification of such a position very obviously depends directly upon the results of psychology.

More recently, the necessity of taking the perplexities of the philosopher to the psychologist has been emphasized by Professor William James and Professor Harold Höffding. The former, in his "Varieties of Religious Experience," has combated the intellectualists in religion, and has been interpreted to stand for a kind of mysticism. Professor Starbuck and Professor Pratt have undertaken to extend the position of Professor James to the point of making feeling an independent source of experience in relation to extra-mundane realities. In the extension thus given it, Professor James's view is not acceptable to many psychologists, even of the pragmatic type, but it has greatly aided in making it clear that the real problems of the philosophy of religion arise in the field of psychology, and are to be understood, if not solved, by the methods of that science.

In the work of Professor Höffding this relation is even more evident, since here philosophy is seen searching for its psychological grounds. "Even if we learn nothing else from our study of the philosophy of religion, it may serve to enlighten us as to the nature of the struggle which rages round the religious question, and to give us some insight into the significance of this struggle in the development of the spiritual life; while, should the religious problem prove insoluble, we may perhaps discover why it is that no solution can be found." The central problem here is the psychological problem concerning the nature and the significance of religious ideas, and whether, if they lose their value as knowledge, they may still retain importance in other aspects of experience, such as may be involved in the conservation of value.

The development of the central problems of the psychology of religion may also be traced in the various definitions of religion which different thinkers have advanced. It is significant that the reflective and self-conscious attitude in which careful definition is sought did not appear with reference to religion until very modern times. In the ancient world, religion was taken for granted. So also were its various forms. Each nation had its own gods, temples, and festivals. Differences in religion were accepted in the same way as differences in language or dress. This was true not only of the tolerant and pliable Greeks, but also of the strenuous Hebrews. The latter, in the best of their prophets, did indeed present vivid comparisons of the superior power and goodness of their religion, but they did not attain any reflective or philosophical consciousness of the nature of religion itself. At times they separated sharply certain observances, such as animal sacrifice, from the more refined and ideal worship of Jehovah. But these reflections were of a concrete, practical character, within the accepted forms of the social tradition, and did not result in distinguishing religion from the political or domestic life. In the later Hebrew as in nearly the whole Christian period, the conviction of the truth of the one religion and the falseness of all others was taken in a complacent way, which could not arouse interest in the intrinsic nature of religious experience.

It was perhaps the Deists and Skeptics of the seventeenth and eighteenth centuries who first attained a critical judgment concerning the religious problem. And it was Lessing who made the significant observation that the Bible contains religion, but that the foundations of faith must be sought in the human mind and in the human heart. The various positive religions he regarded as upward stages in the education of mankind. In his drama, "Nathan the Wise," he brings together the Jew, Christian, and Mohammedan to illustrate his view that religion has as many different forms and grades as human culture itself.

In the great intellectual awakening which followed, religion came to be treated, as were other phases of human experience, with increasing consciousness and reflective analysis. It was natural that the definitions of religion which resulted should bear the marks of the philosophical standpoints of their authors. With the development of scientific thought, the more objective and descriptive treatment which belongs to the true science of religion was attained. Kant, for example, defines religion as "a knowledge of all our duties as divine commands"; Schleiermacher, as "a feeling of absolute dependence"; Hegel, as "the knowledge possessed by the finite mind of its nature as absolute mind."

During the last half of the nineteenth century a more inductive and empirical method prevailed in science and philosophy, which has had profound significance for the understanding and interpretation of religious phenomena. Herbert Spencer collated many facts concerning the religious ceremonies and beliefs of various natural races, advancing sociological and psychological principles to explain them. The definition of the anthropologist, Tylor, is still more directly drawn from intimate knowledge of the race in all stages of development. He gives as the minimum definition of religion, "the belief in Spiritual Beings." Even here, however, there remains in the word "belief" a trace of that speculative and intellectualistic bias which has been a veil over the eyes of many scholars. Professor William James was the first to point out clearly the partiality and abstractness in the definitions of religion. "Religion" is for him a collective name like "government," and therefore does not signify any one specific thing, but comprehends many activities, beliefs, and sentiments. "As there thus seems to be no one elementary religious emotion, but only a common storehouse of emotions upon which religious objects may draw, so there might conceivably also prove to be no one specific and essential kind of religious object, and no one specific and essential kind of religious act." [1]

[1] William James, *Varieties of Religious Experience*, p. 26.

This statement stands in marked contrast to the usual, nice definitions. It is concrete and comprehensive. By contrast with it, the familiar definitions seem narrow or vague. The latter seem to justify the remark of one writer that "the definition of religion is a matter of taste." It is at least a matter of one's point of view. The advantage of such a statement as that of Professor James is that it allows for precisely this variation in the ways of conceiving religion. The search for a definition of a profoundly complex process always ends in such a tentative, flexible statement. It involves recognition of the living reality of experience, and results in a modest effort to describe it, to analyze it, and to gain certain explanations concerning particular features and stages of it. In other words, the science of the psychology of religion proceeds in the same way as does the science of psychology itself. The latter no longer troubles itself concerning a definition of consciousness, but simply seeks to discover the stages of growth, the various types of reaction to different objects and situations, and the functions of the mental life. The psychologist of religion accepts the facts of religion, the temples and priests, the sacred books and ceremonies, the faiths and customs which exist in such profusion throughout the world. He seeks to know the needs, impulses, and desires from which these institutions and activities arise. He inquires concerning the circumstances under which they appear in the race and in the individual. He attempts to trace their development into settled institutions, doctrines, and emotions. He marks the part they play, the function they perform, in the experience of individuals and of society. The justification for conceiving the task of the psychology of religion so inclusively lies in part in the general psychological point of view outlined in the following chapter.

CHAPTER II

THE PSYCHOLOGICAL STANDPOINT

A SUFFICIENT distinctness now attaches to different types of psychology to make it allowable, if not imperative, to indicate at the outset which is to be employed. It is the intention here to treat the phenomena of religion from the standpoint of functional psychology. In order to define this point of view and the method it implies, it seems advisable to outline its main principles.

Functional psychology views the mental life (1) as an instrument of adaptation by which the organism adjusts itself to the environment; (2) hence the emphasis is upon activities and processes directed toward ends or adjustments: (3) this adjustment to the physical or social environment occurs through the psycho-physical organism and is therefore expressed or registered in definite neural activity and in various objective effects. It is important to apprehend clearly these characteristics.

The conception of the mind as an instrument of adjustment and adaptation is a biological conception and marks the radical transformation which psychology has undergone through the influence of the science of biology. This implies the general doctrine of evolution. Mind is the means by which adaptations occur in novel and complex situations, and is therefore the most important factor in the survival of the highest organisms. This is more obvious when it is understood that instinctive and perceptive processes as well as developed reasoning come within the conception of mind. Animal behavior affords abundant evidence of the advantages held by those species possessing elaborate and persistent instincts. The fur-seal returns in the spring, thousands of miles through the stormy sea, to its breeding-place. The female, leaving her young on the shore, goes hundreds of miles to her feeding-grounds, and upon her return after several days finds her own pup among ten thousand others. This serviceability of mind, in the form of instinct, appears in the migrations of birds, in their nest-building, and in their care of the young. The selection of food is also instinctive. The horse will not eat meat, nor will the dog eat grass.

But the instincts of lower animals are limited in flexibility. It is in man that mind effects preservation in the midst of strange and variable conditions, and makes adjustments to larger and more complex areas of nature and society. Man's conquest of cold climates by fire, shelter, and clothing, his cultivation of the desert, his regulation of animal life, and the vast number and ingenuity of his inventions illustrate the prime function of his intelligence, namely, accommodation to new and intricate environments. This power of control is not present in man as a gift or endowment, but as an achievement. Genetic psychology traces the attainment of this mental power from its feeble beginnings in infancy, in the form of a few instinctive reactions, up to the acquirement of a disciplined imagination and efficient volition. In the func-

THE PSYCHOLOGICAL STANDPOINT

tional view, consciousness itself emerges as a phase of the response to difficult and urgent needs of the organism. The child becomes aware of his rattle, of himself, and of the intervening space, in some dim measure, when the desired rattle is beyond his reach. It is the movement, the muscular strain, the cry and call, which conspire to bring about the idea of the object and the self. The growth of consciousness in the adult proceeds in the same way in the endeavor to reach an end, such as the invention of a trap to catch game, or in the development of a social organization for the prevention of graft.

Since it is the fundamental function of mental life to mediate ends, to smooth the way for action, it is to be viewed as a process rather than a static fact. It is true, as John Locke contended, that an idea can be understood only in its history and in its effects. The idea is itself a movement of imagery and feeling. It might even contribute to clearness to drop the terms "idea," "image," "concept," and speak always of reacting, of associating, of habit, of attending, of feeling, of perceiving, of reasoning. It is commonly recognized that perceiving an object is a stage in the use of it. To perceive a tree is to carry on a larger activity into which this particular activity of perceiving is fitted as a helping or hindering process. To perceive the tree is to further one's journey, the tree being a landmark. Or it is a phase of the process of keeping up the camp-fire; of securing fruit, a bee's nest, or a squirrel. At another time, to perceive it may be an activity in the larger activity of building a house, or of securing by the sale of the wood funds for a journey or for shriving one's soul. The perception may be a factor in a vastly larger and more complex process, as, for example, when it is involved in the esthetic contemplation of one interested in impressionistic painting, or when it is the subject of investigation by a botanist whose description becomes available to others for various purposes. That is, the perception is an activity of a specific sort determined by what the object is perceived as. The mental life is thus at every point to be understood not by what it merely is, but rather by what it does. The analogy between functional psychology and physiology is suggestive here. The bodily organs are treated in physiology in terms of the part they play in the life process, and cannot be understood in themselves, taken statically. In psychology, in the same way, sensations, ideas, memories, and the rest are not taken as existences which can be treated primarily as to their own peculiar nature and secondarily as to their combination and operation in experience, but they are primarily phases of a going life, which becomes abstract and artificial when considered in piecemeal, frozen sections.

A third characteristic of the functional psychology is that the activity involved in the adjustment to ends, however simple or complex, practical or ideal, those ends may be, is an adjustment in the psycho-physical organism. It is a mind-body process. The working hypothesis of modern psychology is that of the correlation of mental states and bodily states. Ideas, for example, are dynamic, that is, they are incipient activities. This is illustrated most clearly by ideo-motor phenomena. In the case of well-established habits or

THE PSYCHOLOGICAL STANDPOINT

powerful impulses, the presence of the idea releases immediately a set of movements. The cry of "fire" sets off the nervous mechanism which controls the muscles, and the soothing word "sleep" serves in favorable circumstances to relax the muscles and reduce all the tensions of the body. The investigations of imagery have made it clear, on the other hand, that the very substance of ideas is gained from the sensations or feelings involved in movements and in bodily processes. This imagery may be of the visual, tactile, auditory, or motor type, but in every case it involves physiological processes. In the idea of opening a certain door, analysis shows that the idea is the awakening of definite sensations of muscular strain, the partial reinstatement of actual movement, or of activities in vision, hearing, pressure, or the like. In more complex ideas or concepts, such as justice, truth, evil, eternity, similar content always exists. There is therefore no sharp break between mental and physical activity, between idea and deed. It is impossible to separate the ideational process from the bodily factors. There is consequently a pronounced tendency for descriptions of mental process to eventuate in physiological or biological considerations.[1]

In addition to these specific principles of the functional psychology there are several important implications. For one thing, it puts emphasis upon the will. It is voluntaristic. Ideation and feeling are secondary. Activity, directed toward selected ends, is the inmost nature of the will. The will appears in simplest form

[1] Angell, "The Province of Functional Psychology," *Psychological Review*, March, 1907.

PSYCHOLOGY OF RELIGIOUS EXPERIENCE

in impulses and instincts. In a more developed stage it takes the form of habits, that is, of organized activities which serve in the attainment of similar recurring ends. Again, the will is involved in conflicting interests, or is confused by a new situation which has not been encountered before. In all these instances there is more or less feeling. The satisfactions may be intense which belong to impulsive, instinctive, and habitual action, though often there is a minimum of feeling of any kind, where the act is immediately successful. There is a corresponding heightening of emotion where the tension is great and prolonged. The ideational processes, such as perceiving, remembering, reasoning, are also most vigorously called into play when the will, or activity, is frustrated. When one is driving through the country, the small stream is crossed on the accustomed bridge, with no thought of it. But when the stream is swollen and the safety of the bridge is uncertain or quite impaired, one examines, tests, and judges it with extreme care and may inquire for a larger, stronger bridge at another place. The intellectual processes arise when the impaired or faltering activity needs them, and the emotion is an accompaniment of the hesitancy, testing, issue, or inhibition in the action. The mental life is in this way approached from a different side than in the older rational psychology. There the question seemed to be, What is pure thought, pure mind, pure feeling? Functional psychology inquires, What is the organism, the mind-body, doing, and what is the mechanism by which it operates? In other words, What is the will, or purposeful activity, accomplishing, and what

THE PSYCHOLOGICAL STANDPOINT

are the means, such as instinct, imitation, habit, attention, association, perception, and reasoning which it employs? The voluntaristic psychology gives a new sense of the depth of the mental life, revealing as it does the instinctive springs of action, the subtle power of imitation, of suggestion, and of the vague half-conscious elements. In contrast to these, the clear, intellectual, rational elements, important as they are, appear as the surface outcroppings of formations whose numerous stratifications and vaster masses lie far below.

A second consequence of the functional psychology, important for the present study, is the meaning it gives to the word "consciousness." The attempt to define this term has long been given up by psychologists, but there is still a tendency to use it in a very general and abstract sense. David Hume was perhaps the first to realize fully that there is no "pure" consciousness. He pointed out that what one discovers when he looks into himself is always something specific. One is never just thinking, but is thinking of a particular journey or of journeying, of the manufacture of shoes or of the habit of wearing shoes. Memory resolves itself into memories, perceiving into perceptions, feeling into feelings. One cannot merely feel, but one may feel cold, or pain. In the same way, consciousness is actually of this or that kind, and there is no more a consciousness in general than a tree in general. Just as little is there a unique art consciousness which is not a consciousness of art forms, of technique, or of subject-matter. There is much discussion of ethical or moral consciousness, or religious consciousness, which seems to imply that these are ultimate faculties or powers, rather than general terms for very concrete and definite particular experiences.

The functional psychology here shows its pragmatic tendencies. Consciousness grows. It is very slight in the infant, somewhat greater in the child, and it may become relatively vast in mature age. But this growth is to be thought of as an increase in the wealth of particular experiences, in their diversity, and in their organization for the guidance of action. One man may develop one kind of consciousness, and his neighbor a different kind. One gives attention to the diseases of the human body and their treatment. He attends lectures, observes clinics, serves as interne in a hospital, enters upon active practice, and thus acquires what may be called a medical consciousness. Another receives lessons in drawing and painting, reads the history of painting, visits galleries, perfects his own technique, and gradually attains an art consciousness. The second person may have little or no medical consciousness, and the first person may have no art consciousness. It depends upon the run of attention. The same is true of the moral and religious consciousness. Each involves specific content and experience. Neither is inevitable. Persons exist without either, and each is attained, if at all, by gradual development and in degree. Not all business men are equally businesslike, and not all religious people are equally religious. This holds true from a practical standpoint, however religion itself is defined. It is no more a given endowment than is a language, and it is just as little impossible to normal people. The extent and power of

THE PSYCHOLOGICAL STANDPOINT

social influences over the individual ordinarily make it difficult for any one to escape language and religion entirely, though in highly complex modern society astonishing variations occur.

A third problem which the functional psychology treats in a notable way is that of the relation of psychology and philosophy. While psychology may be viewed as belonging to the biological sciences, it is also true that it stands in a peculiar relation to philosophy. All schools of psychology agree in this, but they differ as to the precise nature of the relation which exists. Functional psychology holds that the philosophical studies are elaborations of certain phases of psychology. For example, ethics deals with the nature of the will and the methods of its control and development. But this is precisely the inquiry which the psychology of volition undertakes, in the analysis of impulse, desire, choice, habit, and character. Ethics simply makes these its chief concern, and puts the problems into the perspective of human history and of social relations. The question of the standard of conduct, whether it is conceived as hedonistic, rationalistic, or as utilitarian self-realization, starts with the nature of desire and cannot transcend it. Likewise the problem of the organization of personal activity into a hierarchy of interests or selves is to the last degree a psychological problem. This does not mean a confusion of psychology and ethics, but it frankly admits that ethics is a specialized and elaborated psychological inquiry. Casual comparison of the introductory chapters of texts on ethics with the chapters of a standard text in psychology on desire and volition will illustrate all that is here asserted. Similar statements are applicable to esthetics.

It is, however, in the relation of psychology and logic that the functional view is at once most obvious and most consequential. It is often contended that psychology investigates the intellectual processes simply to see what they are, while logic, dealing with the same phenomena, occupies itself with the further problem of their truth or falsehood. Professor Angell has shown [1] that this distinction is not radical, and that the functional psychology of reasoning and logic are essentially identical. They are one in treating ideation in reference to practical activity. Psychology insists that the movement of interest and action in which an idea occurs, throws light upon its nature. Apart from such a setting it has no meaning. Any existence attributed to an isolated or detached idea involves the height of abstraction. The real ideas are bathed in the full stream of concrete experience, and retain the quality of life only so long as they are saturated and dripping with its waters. It is the function of the idea to mediate and to adapt. It points onward to ends. This characteristic of ideation is precisely the problem of logic. Even the old formal logic did not make all its tests of truth just within the ideas themselves. Its ultimate reference was to the objective world of practical experience. This is still truer of modern inductive logic, which through modern science has been directly concerned with the discovery and control of concrete conditions. It has sought to understand the actual

[1] Angell, "The Province of Functional Psychology," *Psychological Review*, March, 1907.

THE PSYCHOLOGICAL STANDPOINT

workings of the mind in attaining practical results. The analysis and descriptions of these mental operations form alike the substance of important chapters in the texts of both psychology and logic. The books on logic simply select parts of the whole field of psychology, namely, the cognitive processes, and proceed to give them a more elaborate treatment and to develop special problems.

The distinction between psychology and ethics or esthetics is similarly provisional. It is justifiable as a convenient device for indicating the differentiation of the whole field, but if taken as anything more ultimate, it becomes misleading. The texts often make much of the fact that psychology is a natural science, while the others are normative sciences. But it is interesting to see that the author is usually careful to insist that by normative he means not primarily the application of the norm, but merely its discovery and the recognition of its function. In this sense it deals with what is and only secondarily with what ought to be. The difference is then quite eliminated, for psychology treats in the same way of ideals or norms, their function, and their fruitfulness in experience.

This conception of psychology extends still further and includes a vital and determining relation to epistemology and metaphysics. Epistemology as theory of knowledge involves, like logic, a consideration of the nature of the cognitive processes and their value in attaining truth and escaping error. Indeed, it becomes increasingly clear that the problems of epistemology are precisely the problems of logic, just as these in turn are the problems of a developed functional psychology. The same is also true concerning metaphysics. If this is regarded as the science of reality, it does not thereby escape from the fact that it is bound up with knowledge and therefore with logic. In attempting to understand the nature and function of consciousness, we are inevitably plunged into the consideration of the nature of reality, not indeed as something over against consciousness, but as involved in the knowledge process itself. The thoroughgoing functional, or pragmatic view tends in this way to obviate many of the sharp oppositions between psychology and philosophy, and between special philosophical disciplines such as epistemology and metaphysics.

This conception of the central importance of psychology has important consequences in the sphere of religious thought. The psychology of religious experience becomes the conditioning science for the various branches of theology, or rather, it is the science which in its developed forms becomes theology or the philosophy of religion. If reality is given in experience (and where else could it be given?) then the science of that experience furnishes the reasonable and fruitful method of dealing with reality, including the reality of religion. The psychology of religion possesses, therefore, the greatest possible significance. It does not merely prepare the way for theology, but in its most elementary inquiries, it is already dealing with essentials of theology and the philosophy of religion. On the other hand, the philosophy of religion in its most ultimate problems and refined developments does not transcend the principles of psychology. The idea of God, for example, which is the central conception of

THE PSYCHOLOGICAL STANDPOINT

theology, is subject to the same laws of the mental life as are all other ideas, and there is but one science of psychology applicable to it. Modern psychology emphasizes the fundamental unity of mental life. The psychology of religion is only the application of the principles of the one science of psychology to religious experience. It does not limit itself to certain phenomena, such as emotion, or to the working of particular "faculties" or instincts, but attempts to deal vitally with the totality of human nature as involved in religion, and with every stage of the religious development.

Further, it has been pointed out that the functional psychology employs the genetic and historical method. This may be illustrated by the way in which the history of religion is employed in working out the psychology of religion. The illustration will serve at once to emphasize the general conception of the functional psychology and to introduce the discussion in the succeeding chapters. The history of religion is employed in working out the psychology of religion in order to present these psychical states and processes in their concrete setting. If ideas and emotions are vitally related to practical interests, a knowledge of those practical interests should aid in understanding the ideas and emotions. In seeking to appreciate the mental life of primitive peoples, it is necessary to know something of the general conditions under which they live. In a sense, the outward, objective life of primitive people is preëminently important, since they are constantly occupied with it, and are relatively little given to introspective and subjectively complicated reflection. Their mentality is more overt and is therefore more clearly expressed in bodily habits and reactions than is true of more highly developed, complex minds.

The early stages of religion are also valuable for the understanding of religion because of their relative simplicity and because of the course of development which they present. The following statement concerning the advantage of studying morality in its earlier stages applies equally to religion: "History gives us these facts in process of becoming or generation; the earlier terms of the series provide us with a simplification which is the counterpart of isolation in physical experiment; each successive later term answers the purpose of synthetic recombination under increasingly complex conditions."[1]

These early forms of religion are not more important than later stages. They are not of greater value merely because they are primitive. Their importance consists partly in the fact that they are simpler and therefore more easily understood, just as the mind of the child shows in simpler form the workings of attention and association which in mature life become highly complicated and hidden. The ground patterns of interest, elicited by reactions to the natural environment under the pressure of hunger and other dangers of pain and extinction, remain essentially unchanged.

[1] John Dewey, "The Evolutionary Method as Applied to Morality," *Philosophical Review*, vol. xi, 1902, pp. 123 f. Cf. William James, *Varieties of Religious Experience*, p. 382: "Phenomena are best understood when placed within their series, studied in their germ and in their overripe decay, and compared with their exaggerated and degenerated kindred."

THE PSYCHOLOGICAL STANDPOINT

The objects which satisfy hunger may be multiplied and the protection and guarantee of life may be greatly increased, but the general process of adaptation to the world in which man lives has not been fundamentally altered. The quest for food may call into play new weapons and inventions, it may accumulate supplies beyond immediate necessities, and it may become refined, but it is still a quest for food. Even under the conditions of a complex society, it operates by energy and cunning, by swiftness and prudence. But the importance of the early stages of mental development consists chiefly in making clear the processes through which the differentiation of consciousness arises, the course by which they move forward, and the relations which the various aspects bear to one another. It is by taking wide surveys of these phenomena as they appear in different races that one may be able to dissociate the permanent principles of religion from its accidental content, and gain a perspective in which the developed, historical religions may be interpreted. Thus may be ascertained the moving impulses of religious ceremonials, the nature of the ideas which accompany them, and the effects to which they give rise.

PART II
THE ORIGIN OF RELIGION IN THE RACE

CHAPTER III

THE DETERMINING IMPULSES IN PRIMITIVE RELIGION

It is generally recognized that in primitive life religion was a matter of social custom. The fact that the individual had not emerged from the tribal consciousness has been reiterated to the point of exaggeration, and the assumption of social solidarity may be made here without argument.[1] It is also unnecessary to prove again that what have come to be known as the religious observances of primitive peoples were concerned with all the vital interests of the social group. It is difficult, and in fact quite impossible, to distinguish sharply and finally in primitive life between law, morality, art, and religion. The conditions were relatively simple and undifferentiated. Social life was more nearly a single process than it is in advanced stages, and therefore it reveals with greater clearness the working of the fundamental life impulses in the whole social fabric. It is the task of this chapter to consider these original driving impulses which result in social customs and institutions.

Food and sex are the great interests of the individual and of society. These may work out in various secondary forms, but the "ground patterns" of man's life are determined by these two elemental forces. The very existence of the individual depends upon his food. He

[1] Warner Fite, "The Exaggeration of the Social," *Journal of Philosophy, Psychology, and Scientific Methods*, vol. iv, 1907, p. 393.

must satisfy his hunger at all costs, and the perpetuation of the race rests upon the individual's sex instinct. The absorbing human interests, even in leisure and contemplation, in art and religion, are those of securing a livelihood and those which spring from the love of woman, including the protection and care of children. These basal instincts are so characteristic of the whole range of sentient life preceding man and now existing below him in the biological scale, that it involves no daring assumption to infer that he possessed them from the most rudimentary stage of his existence. Complexities of custom, law, art, religion, and science which have sprung from these roots in the deep soil of human nature have required vast periods of time and the high pressure of dire necessity. Lewis H. Morgan suggests [1] that if 100,000 years be assumed as the measure of man's existence upon the earth, the first 60,000 years must be assigned to the period of savagery and only the last 5000 years to civlization. Or if the total period is twice as great, the same proportion between savagery and civilization remains. He holds that probably the great occasions of progress have been the enlargement of the sources of food caused by the invention of various arts. He indicates five such epochs in the following order: fruits and nuts; fish, — fire perhaps being first used for cooking fish; farinaceous food, through simple cultivation; meat and milk, involving the domestication of animals; unlimited subsistence, by means of field agriculture in which the plow is drawn by animals.

[1] Lewis H. Morgan, *Ancient Society*, chapter xi, p. 19.

IMPULSES IN PRIMITIVE RELIGION

This statement has only the value of a suggestion, and needs in any case to be supplemented by a recognition of the way in which the division of labor between the sexes and the sex instinct itself enter into the whole social process in connection with the problem of the food supply.[1] To a certain extent the nature of the food secured and the mental type developed in getting it and in making adjustment to the physical and social environment, depend upon sex. In primitive life man and woman had to a great extent different food, different occupations, and also different mental types and social attitudes. These differences have, however, been constantly acting upon each other and coöperating in producing the composite whole of the social life. The conditions which the instincts develop in the life of the sexes differ appreciably. Woman, with the care of children, is less free to move about. Her abode is more fixed and stationary. This necessitates finding food close at hand. She therefore digs roots, gathers berries and fruits, and cultivates them. Man, on the other hand, does not feel the same immediate physical and sympathetic constraint to remain in a settled habitat. Driven by hunger, he is free to rove far and wide in the pursuit of game, and he is also strong to fight other men for their women and for the spoils of war. Man is essentially a hunter even in his wooing. When he is exhausted by the chase and gorged upon the captured game, he sits about the camp, uninterested in the drudgery of the women and quite willing to leave all domestic burdens to their care. He is strong, cunning,

[1] Otis T. Mason, *Woman's Share in Primitive Culture*, p. 2.

and masterful, for these are the qualities developed by hunting and warfare. She is passive, patient, and obedient, for these are the qualities of the mother and of the toiler. There is ground for saying that the masculine type of life is primarily correlative with the food-process, for even man's sexual life takes on the form of the chase and capture. The feminine type, on the contrary, seems primarily conditioned by sex, for woman's food must be of such a nature and accessibility that it can be secured under the exigencies of child-bearing.

This relatively stationary and permanent character of woman's life and the more regular and routine nature of her daily habits have tended to make her the centre of society. The little children must look to her for food, and, in the circle of which she is the central figure, they associate with one another. Man is also drawn back into this group after adventures in hunting or warfare. He is impelled by his sexual desire to seek the companionship of woman, and is attracted to her for the preparation of food taken in the chase. It must also often happen that he is unsuccessful in catching game or exhausts his supply; but her food, while perhaps less to his taste, is more to be depended on and is ready to hand. Naturally, the women of a clan live more or less in common, and the men of the group find companionship with one another in and about the women's quarters. The fundamental social bond is then the tie between the mother and child. Man is attracted to her also, and thus all the elements of the human world cohere by powerful forces in a rudimentary social whole. "We can hardly find a

IMPULSES IN PRIMITIVE RELIGION

parallel," says Professor Thomas, "for the intimacy of association between mother and child during the period of lactation; and, in the absence of domesticated animals, or suitable foods, and also, apparently, from simple neglect formally to wean the child, this connection is greatly prolonged. The child is frequently suckled from four to five years and occasionally from ten to twelve. In consequence we find society literally growing up about the woman. The mother and her children, and her children's children, and so on indefinitely in the female line, form a group."[1]

The primacy and far-reaching significance of these social bonds centering about woman in early society appear in three notable ways. First, descent is reckoned in the female line. The children belong to the mother's line and not to the father's. Among the American Indians, the Blacks of Australia and Africa, the ancient Arabians and Hebrews, Chinese and Japanese, the predominance of woman in the family system is clear. In many cases the husband goes to live in the family of the bride, and " a man's own son is only the son of his wife." Second, through her settled life and labor, woman is the creator and owner of property and on this account often controls the social processes. Her husband is dependent upon her.[2] Third, the cohesive, sympathetic quality necessary to a genuine social consciousness springs from the woman and the mother. The group consciousness is felt most

[1] W. I. Thomas, *Sex and Society*, p. 56.

[2] The portrayal of the virtuous woman in the Book of Proverbs, chapter xxxi, is in point here.

powerfully by the relatively small number which experience immediately the common bond of kinship within the same gens or clan. They live close together, dependent upon each other, and the attitude developed between the mother and child is radiated and reinforced by various experiences. All share in the famine or in the abundant harvest. The dangers from wild beasts, from storms, floods, drouths, and enemies weld the group together as do success in the chase, triumph in battle, and the joys of the feast. It is probably these actual common experiences, rather than the mere fact of physical kinship, which establish the firm coherence of the family or tribe, and produce the gregariousness of the race.

Indirectly, the centripetal, unifying influences of woman's world required the development of quite different qualities in man. The strength of the tie between mother and child expresses itself in an instinctive antipathy to whatever threatens it. Hence the suspicion of strangers and the fury against enemies. It is a matter of common observation that the hatred and revenge of the female of all species when aroused are more ferocious and relentless than the same emotions in the male. This fact aids in understanding the influence of woman in developing the sterner qualities in man. Woman in her weakness and in her peaceful, quiet pursuits, needs protection for herself and child. She depends upon man for this. He is freer, more muscular, and trained to habits of combat and adventure. Nature has enabled that type of male to overcome its enemies and therefore to propagate itself. The very affection and sympathy which

IMPULSES IN PRIMITIVE RELIGION

operate within the domestic circle demand radically different qualities in man as the protector of the group. Consequently, in the selective process of the sexual instinct, feminine favors and honors go to the individuals of strength, prowess, and masterfulness. Sensitiveness to this femininely moulded public opinion is one of the strongest forces in primitive society, or in any society.[1] In many tribes the youth must prove his quality by killing his man, capturing game, or even by providing food for his sweetheart's whole family for a year, before he is allowed to take her as his wife and become a full member of the tribe. Men come to esteem these qualities among themselves and display excessive vanity over their achievements or chagrin at their failure. Woman's influence is therefore twofold. Through her sexually determined manner of life she becomes the centre of the social group. Within itself this group tends to be dominated by sympathy and mutual aid. It has an intimate, personal, and sentimental character. But the exigencies of its existence necessitate an attitude of enterprise, struggle, and warfare with the elements of the environment. Man is affected by both tendencies. Woman herself, together with the domestic atmosphere which she creates by the attractive and suggestive products of her labor, elicits from man the gentler, companionable attitudes. This is seen in all animals in the mating season. But by her helplessness and dependence man is also compelled to a life of strife and adventure against the enemies of the group or in the natural process of extending territory

[1] W. I. Thomas, *Sex and Society*, pp. 111 ff.

and supplying increasing needs. In primitive societies, and for the most part among civilized peoples, man has been more of a fighter than a lover, even though his fighting was so much the outgrowth of his love.

Man's hunger, also, like his love, drove him to a life of adventure, craft, and combat. In him, as in woman, the food and sex impulses conditioned and reinforced each other. He hunted and fought for food much as he hunted and fought for women. The two great springs of his activity drove him to a life of prowess and conquest. Man was free to get food anywhere in a wide range, and his physical and muscular structure were so developed that he could hunt and catch animals as woman could not do. Besides, there is more stimulus and excitement in obtaining animals than in getting herbs or fruits. So important is the manner of getting food that it is regarded by many scholars as the factor which has determined the nature of man's mind. Professor John Dewey makes this statement with reference to the psychological significance of occupations: "The occupations determine the chief modes of satisfaction, the standards of success and failure. Hence, they furnish the working classifications and definitions of value; they control the desire process. Moreover, they decide the sets of objects and relations that are important, and thereby provide the content or material of attention, and the qualities that are interestingly significant. The directions given to mental life thereby extend to emotional and intellectual characteristics. So fundamental and pervasive is the group of occupational activities that it

IMPULSES IN PRIMITIVE RELIGION

affords the scheme or pattern of the structural organization of the mental traits."[1]

The same author holds, accordingly, that it is permissible to speak of the hunting type of mental life, and of the pastoral, the military, the trading, and the manufacturing types. He has shown in some detail what kind of mind results from the hunting life. It develops intense immediate interests. There is no carrying out of a series of activities toward a remote goal. In other words, there is no *work* as the civilized man or as primitive woman knows it. But under the stimulus of his immediate need, as when in pursuit of game to satisfy hunger, the savage is capable of remarkable endurance, patience, inhibition, and self-control. The savage of Australia, for example, hunts when he is in need of food; but he does not provide for the future by drying the meat or saving the skins. He gorges himself and is satisfied until the pangs return. His weapons are of the simplest sort, like the club or spear, which are secured at the moment of need. Much of his fish and game he catches by hand. He does not use set traps or nets. He makes bark boats and even his hut at the moment and on the spot where he needs them. Such a life develops personal resourcefulness, keen sense-perception, quickness, dexterity, and skill. It lacks, however, the power of generalization, of abstraction, of implication necessary to the more complicated routine and remote achievements of the civilized man.

The hunting life develops also a characteristic emo-

[1] John Dewey, "Interpretation of Savage Mind," *Psychological Review*, May, 1902, p. 217.

tional quality. It is full of the most exciting conflict situations. The hunter driven by the pangs of hunger is goaded to the highest pitch of desire and expectancy. He takes desperate risks, the success or failure of which brings the acutest satisfactions or the most gnawing misery. The power and range of his emotional life is well illustrated in the fact that the hunting activities still furnish the recreations of civilization. All games of ball are modeled on the chase, the ball taking the place of the animal. Modern warfare, business enterprise, and even the scientific "pursuit of truth" show how far the hunting process and its terminology hold control over the various interests of civilized man. The readjustment to the necessities of new industrial conditions began in so recent a time, relatively, that the mental type belonging to the older order still persists, and furnishes important clews to many features of modern as well as of primitive social life and institutions. The destruction of game and the increase of population have forced a change of occupation which in time must have its natural effect upon all human ways of life, though the social and cultural changes are effected slowly and against great inertia. These changes, it is important to note, emphasize more and more the typically feminine manner of life, with its sympathetic social attitudes and routine labor; while a different direction is given to the masculine tendencies to organization, combat, and venturesome achievement.

"The primitive, motor type of life evidently continued for an immense stretch of time," writes Professor Thomas, "and it was but as yesterday, especially in the white race, that population became dense, or game exhausted, and man found himself obliged to adjust himself to changed conditions or perish. Instead of slaughtering the ox, he fed it, housed it in winter, bred from it, reared the calf, yoked it to a plow, plowed the fields, sowed seeds, dug out the weeds, and gathered, threshed, and ground the grain. This was disagreeable, because the problematical and vicissitudinous element was eliminated or reduced to a minimum. Under the artificial system in which he was forced to obtain his food, sudden strains were not placed on the attention, emotional reactions did not follow, and the activities were habitual, dull, mechanical, irksome. This was labor, but while the labor itself was disagreeable, its products represented satisfactions, and the habits of the race adjusted themselves to what was from the standpoint of the emotions a bad situation."[1]

It is not difficult to show that the habits and temperaments in both sexes, expressed and built up in their occupations, are reflected in the religious ceremonies and institutions as well as in other forms of culture. Among primitive peoples the notable thing in their religion is the ceremonial or cult. It happens quite universally that the men have charge of these ceremonies, while women are usually forbidden to witness them even at a distance. Though it is through woman that the nucleus of society is begun and though the powerfully cohesive qualities of large societies remain essentially feminine, still the representation of this

[1] W. I. Thomas, "Gaming Instinct," *American Journal of Sociology*, vol. vi, 1900–01.

social solidarity in ceremonials is largely masculine. This indicates that the organizing, directing, executive power is due chiefly to man.[1] He is active, aggressive, and given to leadership. In some tribes, even where the social and political organizations, like the council, are made up of women, the final authority and leadership rests with a small group of men. The dominant influence of the motor male is often seen in violent form within the maternal organization itself, and in the course of social progress the outward mould of the collective organism is determined by the men of the group. An analogous case occurs in reference to occupations. The cultivation of grains and fruits, the weaving of vegetable fibres and wool, making pottery, and possibly the use of domestic animals were at first the work of women. But in time, owing to exhaustion of game and the need of more abundant and certain food, man brought his initiative and mastery to bear upon these occupations and developed them far beyond what woman had done. The content was hers, but the form was his. A similar development has occurred in religion. The content — the social attitude of sympathy, of dependence, of solidarity is woman's; but the form — the dance, the incantation, the symbols, and the priesthood — is chiefly his. It is true man developed certain types of social organization in his own enterprises. He had to coöperate and do team work in catching big game and especially in carrying on warfare. In this, submission to leaders and enthusiasm for the common interest, symbolized by the tribal mark or totemic emblem, tended to

[1] W. I. Thomas, *Sex and Society*, pp. 145, 230.

IMPULSES IN PRIMITIVE RELIGION

create social feeling. Such organization was socially valuable, however, chiefly on the side of technique. It gave mobility and power for deeds of skill and violence. Its great significance was in providing objective, dramatic, permanent, ceremonial expression for his own activities and especially for the deeper spirit of kinship, fraternity, and tribal unity which sprang from the mother in her more settled and peaceful group. It is not to be supposed, of course, that there was in the earlier religions, any conscious intention of producing this result. It was rather the effect of controlling habits.

It was the masculine influence which effected the organization and development of ritual, but the processes reflected in the ritual were those of the occupations of women as well as those of man. The ceremonials were patterned upon food-processes, courtship, war, and migration. Where totemism exists, the totems are both animals and plants. They represent the subsistence of both sexes. Among the Australians the totems are such animals as the kangaroo, emu, wildcat, and such plants as the hakea flower, plum tree, and grass seed. All the ceremonies are in charge of the men, and all show the dramatizing, motor quality of the masculine, hunting mind. Whether the totem is a flower or a fish, the ceremony consists of dancing and mimetic movements typical of the habits of the species. The leader wears a head-gear and his body is painted to make him resemble the totem.

Spencer and Gillen give the following description of the initiation ceremony of the eagle-hawk totem in Central Australia. It was performed by two men, supposed to represent two eagle-hawks quarreling over a piece of flesh, represented by the downy mass in one man's mouth. "At first they remained squatting on their shields, moving their arms up and down, and still continuing this action, which was supposed to represent the flapping of wings, they jumped off the shields and with their bodies bent up and arms extended and flapping, began circling round each other as if each were afraid of coming to close quarters. Then they stopped and moved a step or two at a time, first to one side and then to the other, until finally, they came to close quarters and began fighting with their heads for the possession of the piece of meat. This went on for some time, and then two men stepped out from amongst the audience and took away the Churinga (sacred sticks used in the head-dress), which were a great weight and must have caused a considerable strain on the head, especially in the great heat of the afternoon sun, for it must be remembered that it was now well on into the summer. Then once more they began going round and round each other flapping wings, jumping up and falling back just like fighting birds, until finally they again came to close quarters, and the attacking man at length seized with his teeth the piece of meat and wrenched it out of the other man's mouth."[1]

The ceremony of the plum-tree totem was performed by four men. "First of all one man came up to where the audience was sitting by the *Parra* (a mound of earth). He pretended to knock plums down and to eat them, and after a short time he sat down

[1] Spencer and Gillen: *The Native Tribes of Central Australia*, p. 296.

IMPULSES IN PRIMITIVE RELIGION

amongst the audience. Then two others came up, one of whom remained standing, while he knocked down imaginary plums, which were eaten by the other man, who seated himself on the ground. This over, both of the men went and joined the audience, and the fourth man came and went through the same pretence of knocking down and eating plums." [1]

Similar mimetic ceremonies occur among all peoples, gaining their content from the objects upon which the life-processes focus attention, and having the organized and often highly elaborated form due to masculine control. Seal and fish are the means of life to the Eskimo, and these are the central objects in his religion, the activities involved in their capture and use being the models of his rituals. The Indians of North America are in contact with the bear, deer, and buffalo. Their women cultivate corn and rice. Their ceremonials reproduce in dramatic form the life centering in these. Rice is the great staple of the Malays, and they have extensive rituals in connection with its planting, harvesting, and use. In West Africa special ceremonies attend the eating of the new yams. Among the Arabs the date palm is a determining factor. Every great interest of a people is reflected in its religion. There are therefore many religious objects and observances belonging to a given group. But "there are no tiger-gods where there are no tigers," and no rice-gods where there is no rice. Migration and conquest, decadence and survival, may obscure and confuse this principle, but in undisturbed natural races the main fact is clear, while even

[1] Spencer and Gillen, *The Native Tribes of Central Australia*, p. 320.

in mixed and shifting races the outlines of old customs and traditions give it confirmation.

The Todas, a small tribe in the Nilgiri Hills of southern India, furnish a striking illustration of the economic determination of religion. "The milking and churning operations of the dairy form the basis of the greater part of the religious ritual of the Todas. The lives of the people are largely devoted to their buffaloes, and the care of certain of these animals, regarded as more sacred than the rest, is associated with much ceremonial. The sacred animals are attended by men especially set apart who form the Toda priesthood, and the milk of the sacred animals is churned in dairies which may be regarded as the Toda temples, and are so regarded by the people themselves. The ordinary operations of the dairy have become a religious ritual, and ceremonies of a religious character accompany nearly every important incident in the lives of the buffaloes." [1]

The Semites were originally nomadic, and this accounts for the conspicuous place which animals hold throughout their religion. "The main lines of sacrificial worship were fixed before any part of the Semitic stock had learned agriculture and adopted cereal food as its ordinary diet." Therefore cereals and fruits never had more than a secondary place in Semitic ritual, but those which were most conspicuous in religious ceremonies "were also the chief vegetable constituents of man's daily food," namely, meal, wine, and oil.[2]

[1] W. H. R. Rivers, *The Todas*, p. 38.
[2] W. Robertson Smith, *The Religion of the Semites*, pp. 219, 222. Cf. Barton, *Sketch of Semitic Origins*, chapter vii, "Yahwe."

IMPULSES IN PRIMITIVE RELIGION

These differences of ceremonial detail, varying totems, myths, and institutions should not obscure the underlying unity of primitive religion. Such variations really confirm the principle of unity, which may be expressed thus: religion in its first form is a reflection of the most important group interests through social symbols and ceremonials based upon the activities incident to such interests. The activities and symbols necessarily vary with the environment and with the people, but they are everywhere conditioned by these factors. The religious consciousness is a most intimate phase of the group consciousness. Taken in this way primitive religions present a remarkable unity, which is not lost even in highly developed faiths. The theories which sought to explain this unity by means of direct revelation, or by some special "instinct" or "sense" encountered insuperable historical and psychological difficulties. These difficulties are further increased for such theories by the fact that it is not only the unity of religion which needs to be explained, but also the unity of law, morality, and art; and not merely the unity of each of these with itself in various manifestations, but of all these together in a comprehensive social process. Brinton has pointed out that, "Wherever we turn in time or in space to the earliest and simplest religions of the world we find them dealing with nearly the same objective facts in nearly the same objective fashion, the differences being due to local and temporal causes." [1]

Sociologists recognize a law of parallelism in devel-

[1] Brinton, *Religions of Primitive Peoples*, p. 9.

opment, by which is meant the fact that different groups follow essentially the same steps in their mental and social progress. "It is recognized that the human mind and the outside world are essentially alike the world over; that the mind everywhere acts on the same principles; and that ignoring the local, incidental and eccentric we find similar laws of growth among all peoples." [1] The differences are due to the different directions given to attention by the exigencies of life and by the influence of social suggestion.[2] The recognition of the facts that religion reflects the fundamental life-experiences of man and that the driving impulses in these experiences are the most elemental instincts, such as food and sex; and that the reactions arising from these instincts present a fairly uniform development, varied only incidentally by environmental conditions and occupations concerned with these, by contact with other races, by arrested development of social habits, — the recognition of these facts invites a psychological investigation of the typical phases of the religious consciousness as it unfolds in the life of mankind.

[1] W. I. Thomas, *Sex and Society*, p. 273.

[2] Irving King, *The Development of Religion*, chapter iv, has given an excellent account of these variations.

CHAPTER IV

CUSTOM AND TABOO

IT was maintained in the last chapter that the forms of social life are determined in their main outlines by reactions upon the environment under the stress of the nutritive and sexual impulses. These forms of social life — occupations, relations of the sexes, various ceremonials, and folk-ways — tend to become fixed, and to secure themselves against change by many natural safeguards. Observers of primitive peoples constantly note their minute and slavish subjection to set forms of conduct and the heavy penalties which follow any violations. If Rousseau had known the life of natural races as they are known today, he would not have sought freedom by trying to get "back to nature." He would have found primitive customs far more exacting than the conventions and fashions of modern life. From his birth to his death, the savage lives in a world overgrown with practices which infold him all the more surely because he follows them quite unconsciously and without question.

The force and rigidity of these customs may be seen in the penalties attending their violation. The only crime in primitive society is the transgression of custom, the normal consequence of which is death or exclusion from the tribe. "In Tonga, for example, it was believed that if any one fed himself with his own hands after touching the sacred person of a superior chief or anything that belonged to him, he would swell up and die." [1] Frazer gives the instance of a slave who unknowingly ate food left from the meal of a chief, and who, when told what he had done, "was seized by the most extraordinary convulsions and cramp in the stomach, which never ceased till he died, about sundown the same day." If one touched the dead or were a mourner for the dead, he was excluded from the camp for a fixed time until certain rites were performed. Among some peoples such persons could not touch food with their hands and had to be fed by others. The name of a person may not be spoken aloud, for if this is done, the person named is liable to severe sickness and death. Strangers are likely to convey pollution and cause sickness, famine, and death. Irregular and novel conditions are always dangerous. All departures from custom are therefore taboo. Taboo is just the negative side of custom. They are correlative terms. Neither exists without the other. The taboo is not originally something forbidden by enactment or by authority of any kind. Evil consequences flow immediately from the conscious or unconscious, intentional or unintentional, violation of custom. The customs are the thou-shalts and the taboos the thou-shalt-nots of primitive life.

The question at once arises, How do customs come to possess such inviolability and authority? What is the source of the taboos, the restraints and penalties? Various answers have been given. It was formerly

[1] J. G. Frazer, *Golden Bough*, vol. i, pp. 319, 321.

CUSTOM AND TABOO

held that they were artificial inventions in the interests of the nobility and the priests. J. G. Frazer's position is this: "The original character of the taboo must be looked for not in its civil but in its religious element. It was not the creation of a legislator but the gradual outgrowth of animistic beliefs, to which the ambition and avarice of chiefs and priests afterward gave an artificial extension." [1] Frazer concerns himself almost entirely with the descriptive facts concerning taboo and says relatively little about its origin. F. B. Jevons [2] holds that taboo is an original "sentiment" native to the mind and underived from experience. It is a given datum of consciousness such as the Intuitionist school of moral philosophers conceive the Moral Sentiment to be. The taboo sentiment "is prior to and even contradictory to experience." "How primitive man settled what things were not to be done there is no evidence to show." According to this author taboos become identified with religion by being conceived as the rational, purposive requirements of a divine being. "As soon as a taboo is taken up into religion, its character is changed; it is no longer an arbitrary fact, it becomes the command of a divine being, who has reasons for requiring obedience to his ordinances." [3] The same psychological objection holds against Jevons's explanation of taboo as is made against the general position of the Intuitionist school, namely, that it furnishes assertions where one seeks further analysis, and stops with phenomena concern-

[1] *Encyclopædia Britannica*, "Taboo."
[2] F. B. Jevons, *Introduction to the History of Religion*, pp. 85 f.
[3] *Ibid.*, p. 92.

ing which a genetic account may reasonably be demanded.

Ernest Crawley [1] has shown that the attempt to explain taboo in terms of social functions and practical activities is not futile. He does, however, seem to share with Jevons and Frazer the tendency to distinguish religious from other forms of taboo, and to rest this distinction, as they do, upon the idea of supernatural beings. He wishes to deal with the "ideas underlying taboo," and thus commits himself to the formula if not to the actual meaning of an intellectualistic explanation. A psychology which starts with the search for the underlying ideas of social customs and taboos is apt to fail of results for the reason that these customs do not spring from ideas. They are reactions to felt needs and are non-rational. They develop into habitual activities, acquiring stability through repetition and efficiency, and gaining the powerful sanctions natural to long-standing habits. There is abundant evidence that primitive customs and taboos do not arise from ideas or from systems of belief, and modern psychology has made it possible to account for such usages upon other and far more convincing grounds. Many lines of proof support this view. For example, the replies of savages themselves to inquiries concerning their customs are good evidence that their conduct does not issue from "ideas" nor depend upon "reasons." They simply say, "It is our custom." "One soon gets tired of the everlasting answer that meets your questioning at every turn, 'It is our custom.' No doubt in very many cases it is all a

[1] Ernest Crawley, *The Mystic Rose*.

CUSTOM AND TABOO

Kafir could tell you, even if he wished to be very communicative. You might as well stop a well-dressed man in Pall Mall and ask him why he wears a silk hat with a coat of a certain cut and not with others. If he stopped to answer you at all he would probably tell you that he did so because it was the custom. If an enormous amount of our life is a mass of custom, much more is it so in the case of the Africans." [1]

Spencer and Gillen relate their experience in trying to discover the origin of the *Churinga* or sacred sticks of the natives of central Australia.[2] They were unable to get any other answer than that the ancestors of the natives, the *Alcheringa* men, had them. "Once we ventured to inquire whether there was no story relating how the Alcheringa men came to have them, but the mirth which the question provoked showed us that to the mind of the Arunta native the idea of the possibility of anything before the Alcheringa was a ridiculous and an incomprehensible one. In this tribe 'It was so in the Alcheringa' takes the place of the more usual form of expression: 'Our fathers did it, and therefore we do it,' which is so constantly the only reply which the ethnological inquirer receives to the question: 'Why?'"

How little custom is in the sphere of rational ideas is also seen in the fact that many different myths or stories will be told by the same savage at different times to account for it. The savage has no definite theory with reference to his customs, and has a tendency to reply in harmony with anything suggested by

[1] Dudley Kidd, *The Essential Kafir*, p. 66.
[2] Spencer and Gillen, *Native Tribes of Central Australia*, pp. 136 f.

the question asked him. Kidd found that a Kafir would answer in the same breath that he believed in twenty gods and in only one god, the inconsistency not being felt by him because he had no clear ideas upon the subject. "Out of his mental fog arises a belief which your questions have suggested." [1]

The non-rationality of custom is further proved by the fact that it is not greatly susceptible to modification by more reasonable and efficient methods of accomplishing given ends. Tylor relates that the Dyaks of Borneo, when shown a more efficient manner of chopping wood with a V-shaped cut, not only refused to adopt it, although admitting its advantage, but fixed a fine upon any one who should employ the new method.[2] As Jevons insists,[3] custom and taboo are mechanical and arbitrary. They inhibit experiment and prevent in large part the derivation of advantage from chance experience. "Even if accidentally and unintentionally he is led to make such an experiment, instead of profiting by the experience, he dies of fright, as did the New Zealand slave who ate his master's dinner; or if he does not die, he is tabooed, excommunicated, outlawed; and his fate in either case strengthens the original respect for taboo."

The motor view of consciousness affords explanations in other than intellectual terms of many phenomena previously referred to ideational processes. It is now seen that habits are often established by direct response to needs, without the mediation of

[1] Dudley Kidd, *The Essential Kafir*, pp. 72 f.
[2] E. B. Tylor, *Primitive Culture*, vol. i, p. 71.
[3] F. B. Jevons, *Introduction to the History of Religion*, pp. 90 f.

cognitive reflection. In this way action runs in the short circuit and does not follow the "loop-line" through reflective consciousness. Reflex, instinctive, and imitative reactions are the chief forms of this type. The infant does not grasp the handle of the rattle and swing it about because of any idea underlying the act. It is a direct reflex, impulsive act. With this experience certain visual impressions may be interwoven in such a way that the sight of the rattle results in grasping and swinging it without any intervening ideas of the objects, movements, or ends. The development of language in the child by largely imitative processes is a striking illustration of the complexity and elaborateness of reactions which are not consciously intended or controlled by the subject. This illustration may be carried over into social terms where speech is seen developed into well-grooved grammatical forms of which the agents are not aware in any reflective way. They await the coming of a missionary or philologist to show them that they possess a language with parts of speech and idioms, though they and their tribe have developed and used it for centuries. The fallacy that uniform and involved conduct which attains important ends must spring from the idea of such ends is well exposed by reference to the conduct of animals whose behavior cannot be attributed to knowledge. Wundt emphasizes the fact that it is a natural mistake to suppose that the attainment of ends presupposes the intention to attain them, and cites cases of animal conduct to show that the discrepancy between the effect actually produced and the reflection which would be necessary for its purposed and intentional production should correct the mistake. Neither man nor beast takes nourishment to repair bodily vigor and to gather force for future labor, "but simply because hunger is a disagreeable and satiety an agreeable feeling." "Migratory birds do not go in flocks because they know that they are in this way less liable to stray from their course or to be attacked by enemies; and ants and bees do not nest and hive in common because of a conviction that they can never attain in isolation the ends that must be fulfilled by all if they are to live." These things are the results of impulses, and certain fundamental impulses which man possesses in common with animals are held by this psychologist "to form the inalienable natural foundation of human society as well as of animal association." [1]

We have seen in the previous chapter that these original impulses are those of nutrition and sex. In the method of trial and error through which these impulses first express themselves there is sometimes success and sometimes failure. Necessarily, those individuals and groups which fail, perish; or at least experience pain and distress sufficient to modify the conduct. In any case, painful, disagreeable consequences are in the long run signs of a lack of adaptation, and acts of such a character tend automatically, it might be said, to defeat themselves. On the contrary, those individuals and groups which secure adjustment to their environment gain satisfactions. These satisfactions are indications of right, that is, of efficient, conduct. Such satisfactions as, for example,

[1] W. Wundt, *Ethics*, "The Facts of the Moral Life," pp. 129 f.

CUSTOM AND TABOO

the enjoyment and vigor following upon a feast made possible by a successful hunting or fishing expedition, tend to fix in well-defined habits the use of certain seasons, places, and especially methods of the enterprise, so that when the needs recur they are likely to be met in the previously successful manner. As Professor Sumner has said: "From recurrent needs arise habits for the individual and customs for the group, but these results are consequences which were never conscious and never foreseen or intended." [1]

Not only does the psychology of habit show how customs may arise unconsciously, but it throws light upon the source of the sanctions which customs manifest. These sanctions are inherent in the habit or custom. The history of dress seems to show that it originated with amulets and ornaments and was fostered by the love of display which it favored, but its establishment resulted in the feeling that it was proper to conceal the body, that is, the habit of having the body covered must not be broken. This is the ground for saying that the custom of wearing clothing created modesty. W. I. Thomas has applied this psychological principle fruitfully to the explanation of exogamy, the custom of marrying outside one's tribe. "When for any reason there is established in a group a tendency toward a practice, then the tendency is likely to become established as a habit, and regarded as right, binding, and inevitable: it is moral and its contrary is immoral. When we consider the binding nature of the food taboos, of the *couvade*, and of the regulation that a man shall not speak to or look at his mother-in-law

[1] W. G. Sumner, *Folkways*, pp. 4 f.

PSYCHOLOGY OF RELIGIOUS EXPERIENCE

or sister, we can understand how the habit of marrying out, introduced through the charm of unfamiliarity, becomes a binding habit."[1] Habitual actions establish themselves as the lines of least resistance. They are familiar and put the subject of them at ease. He is at home in them. So much is this the case that in moments of leisure, the successfully thrilling events of the chase or battle are often reënacted, and this is undoubtedly an important factor in the origin of ceremonials. They serve to reinstate the emotional experiences of the real events. How closely the savage is held to the form of his original successful activities is shown by his insistence upon reproducing features of those activities which in reality are incidental. But apparently these incidental and irrelevant factors have as strong "sanctions" as those which are necessary. "A party of Eskimos met with no game. One of them returned to their sledges and got the ham bone of a dog to eat. As he returned with the ham bone in his hand he met and killed a seal. Ever afterwards he carried a ham bone in his hand when hunting."[2] Among the Malays,[3] those who work in the mines are required to wear special clothing and speak a particular language, as those who first worked in them. Success in securing the ore is apparently as dependent upon the use of the ancient coat and speech as upon skill and labor.

The fact that habits and customs gain sanctions or sacredness with age is further evidence that the force

[1] W. I. Thomas, *Sex and Society*, p. 196.
[2] Quoted by W. G. Sumner, *Folkways*, p. 25.
[3] W. W. Skeat, *Malay Magic*, pp. 253, 257.

CUSTOM AND TABOO

or strength of habit is the essence of its sanctity. When particularly important things are to be done, the tendency is to employ older instruments or methods, although the newer ways may be easier and more efficient. Among the Central Australians, for example, the firestick is used in the ceremony of circumcision after stone implements become known.[1] Frazer[2] gives many instances in which stone instruments were used in sacred rites after iron was discovered. A Hottentot priest would use a sharp splint of quartz rather than a sharp knife in sacrificing an animal or in performing circumcision. It is common to find the older method of making fire by friction employed in temples and rituals long after it has been discarded in ordinary matters. In times of defeat or disaster, when the most powerful means of success and safety were needed, ancient customs, such as human sacrifice, were revived.[3]

Those customs which have the greatest importance are those which concern the whole group most vitally. Such are the customs which have to do with procuring and distributing food, birth of children, initiation of youth, marriage, death, war. In all these things the life of the whole group is involved, and the maintenance of such customs springs from the powerful, unreasoning "will to live" of the entire group. Any irregularity on the part of an individual is met by the full force of the entire group. This protection of these highly socialized interests is psychological in so far as

[1] Spencer and Gillen, *Native Tribes of Central Australia*, p. 401, note.
[2] J. G. Frazer, *Golden Bough*, vol. i, p. 345.
[3] *Ibid.*, vol. ii, pp. 39 f.

PSYCHOLOGY OF RELIGIOUS EXPERIENCE

it is due to the unquestioning obedience and superstitious fear of the primitive mind, but there are also established official methods for punishing the violation of custom. The old men, the chiefs, or the council guard the traditions and in many cases fix and authorize the execution of the penalty. Often the whole group, as in the stoning of a culprit among the Jews, or in lynching criminals on the early American frontier, becomes the custodian of its customs. The sanctions for these customs are most vital. They are practical and emotional, for they have developed through generations and constitute the inmost core of the common life. Thus, from many sides, there is evidence that it is the nature of custom to develop and accumulate to itself authority and inviolability.

This furnishes the basis for a psychological explanation of taboo. The very disposition to act in a certain way affords resistance to any deviation from that course. There is abundant proof that anything new, strange, or unusual fills the savage with fear. In some countries the equivalent word for taboo denotes all things unusual. In the Marquesas anything different from ordinary custom is called taboo. There is fear of strangers and of unexpected events. When animals act contrary to their ordinary habits the Kafirs regard them as omens. Upon going into a new country, starting a war expedition, planting a crop, or building a house, ceremonies are performed to avoid evil consequences.[1]

The absence of any adequate knowledge of causes and the extreme suggestibility of the savage mind

[1] Ernest Crawley, *The Mystic Rose*, pp. 22 f.

CUSTOM AND TABOO

confirm the aversion to innovation, for when calamity does occur it is not difficult to discover some novel element in the situation to explain the disaster. White men, at their first contact with lower races, are thus the cause of pestilence, famine, and drouth. On the Nicobar islands some natives who had just begun to make pottery died. The art was given up and never again attempted.[1] Experience seems therefore constantly to operate toward strengthening the established custom. The familiar habit preoccupies the mind so that its bad effects are not noticed, while all evils resulting from, or coincident with, the novel events are magnified.

In the light of the foregoing psychological data, it is possible to suggest more definitely the basis upon which taboos have arisen and to account for the various objects around which the taboos cluster or from which they radiate. Crawley has presented many facts concerning social and sexual taboos which contribute to the organization of a conception of the whole subject in a significant way. He himself seems limited in his theory by the assumption that ideas underlie all practices. For example, he puts an undue ideational content into the fear of the savage. That there is an attempt to escape the terminology of intellectualism is seen in his use of the expression, "*physiological thought*, subconsciously arising from and concentrating upon physiological functions." But why still call this "thought"? The expression "instinctive reaction" would perhaps avoid the objectionable implications and yet serve the purpose of

[1] W. G. Sumner, *Folkways*, p. 24.

the author. Although he constantly verges upon the functional explanation of taboo to which his abundant, well-selected materials point, yet he never seems quite to grasp it. The separation of the sexes he attributes to sexual taboos, and then in turn accounts for these taboos by "segregation due to and enforced by human ideas of human relations." [1] The more defensible position would be that the segregation of the sexes was due to natural causes, such as occupation, food supply, capacities, and interests. The characteristic habits of each sex which thus arose brought their natural sanctions and restraints, or taboos. These taboos in turn exercised a reciprocal influence and contributed to emphasize the segregation from which they originally arose.

This view of taboo gets impressive confirmation by putting it in relation to the natural social divisions and groupings which arise in primitive society in the way indicated in the last chapter. Taboos may be classified with reference to the things which possess taboo most powerfully. These are sex; leaders, such as kings, chiefs, priests; strangers; and the dead. It has been shown that the most radical cleavage within the social group or tribe is determined by the habits of the sexes in getting food and carrying on the immediate life-sustaining processes. The sex-industry divisions have been considered with reference to the characteristic habits and temperaments which they foster. The development of such habits tends, upon the psychological principles stated above, to limit each sex to its own peculiar mode of life. Therefore these habits or

[1] Ernest Crawley, *The Mystic Rose*, p. 35.

CUSTOM AND TABOO

customs hold each sex to certain activities which are taboo to the other. Woman comes to have her peculiar sphere and man his. These are not determined by legislation or decrees. Even the tribes in which they are strongest could not give a connected account of them. They are so deep seated, so automatic and unconscious, that they become apparent in their entire scope to the trained observer only after seeing them acted out. Illustrations of the taboos between the sex groups, which are also the industrial groups, are abundant. Among the Todas, men care for the buffaloes, and women may not approach the dairy nor the dairyman. In the Marquesas Islands the use of canoes is prohibited to women; *tapa*-making belongs exclusively to the women. It is quite a universal rule that before and during war and hunting expeditions men are forbidden even the sight of a woman. Indeed, if a woman looks upon the warrior or soldier he is thereby weakened and she may, in many tribes, be put to death. "Woman has generally been debarred more or less from the public and civil rights of men. This is an extension of the biological difference of occupation, sometimes exaggerated into seclusion amongst polygamous races, and into somewhat of inferiority in martial and feudal societies." From this base line of occupations the reciprocal taboos extend to all kinds of activities and possessions. In many tribes the men and women live in separate houses which are rigidly taboo to the opposite sex. They then meet outside the village, in the bush or forest. Family life is therefore impossible. Men and women eat different food. Women worship female and men male deities. Often

PSYCHOLOGY OF RELIGIOUS EXPERIENCE

certain words, especially the names of men and of their own husbands, are forbidden to women. The usual separation of the sexes is universally more complete and rigid during those periods in which "woman is most a woman," that is, during pregnancy, childbirth, and menstruation.

It is true that the habitual attitude of man toward woman generally involves an assumption of superiority, and he undoubtedly arrogates to himself privileges which she is not allowed. He displays a bearing of haughtiness and disdain, while she is servile and compliant. But it is not so in all stages. In many peoples the woman has the strong hand by the possession of property and by being the head of the family. Where war and hunting develop the motor tendencies of the male and train him to the mastery, there he is most likely to exhibit hauteur toward woman, while in such societies she inclines by habit to acquiescence. It is interestingly true that man and woman in all societies, circumscribed as they are by their functions and habits, remain more or less outside each other's sphere, and are in so far strangers to one another. This element of strangeness, of unfamiliarity, is the essence of that which is taboo.[1]

Another illustration of the development of taboo through habit is found in the way in which kings, war-chiefs, and prominent functionaries generally

---

[1] If we could get back of the rather one-sided development of our social consciousness, due to "the way in which the male sex has practically monopolized the expression of thought," the reciprocal exclusiveness of the spheres of man and woman would be more apparent. Cf. Ernest Crawley, *The Mystic Rose*, p. 57.

become set apart, separated, and consecrated. Kings are evolved chiefs, and chiefs gained their position in early society by actual leadership in war and other exploits, much as, among animals, the leader of the pack wins his place by power and skill. His achievements mark him as different from his fellows, and he proves that he is different by his greater deeds. He habitually stands in a superior relation by natural merit. This high station, sustained by so many surprising deeds, works powerfully upon the imagination, and as society is more highly organized under such leadership, the chief or king is regarded with increasing awe: he becomes more taboo. The more powerful a king, the more taboo he is. It would be the same to say that the greater, more wonderful things he does, the more caution is exercised concerning him. This attitude toward the chief or king is found more highly developed in reference to the great gods where the conception of such gods is attained. Whatever belongs to the god is taboo, — the places where he lives and all the things which his life touches are taboo. The places of the theophanies, like Bethel in Hebrew history, are taboo. Any one entering upon special undertakings makes himself taboo for the purpose by certain rites uniting him with the divine, as did the Nazarite.

Another development of taboo involving the same factor of customary reactions and the correlative restraints is to be found in the treatment of the dead. Without entering into the discussion of the nature of ghosts and spirits, it may be noted that to primitive people the dead are not lifeless. On the contrary, they carry on as many or more activities, and often the same kind, as during their earthly life. The departed ancestors and relatives of the savage simply constitute another society, or at least sustain definite relations to the living which have to be taken into account. The dead must be properly buried, fed, visited. One of the most common requirements is that the corpse must not be touched, but it is also true that the living under many circumstances must not be touched. In some cases the dead are treated as having more power than before death, thus becoming by so much a different order of beings and therefore more taboo.

The primary determinations of taboo are, then, those life-processes which take on relatively stable forms, such as reproduction and tribal organization, including relations with the dead. These are the lines of interest, of habit. The particular objects which are taboo are those in which these processes focus, that is, man over against woman; the king over against the members of the tribe; the dead as contrasted with the living. By the same principle, members of different castes are taboo to each other, as are members of different tribes.

A secondary development of taboo also follows the law of habit, and the objects thus involved may be taken as becoming taboo through association with the main factors in the life activities. In the nature of the case, it is not possible to make a sharp classification here, but taboos seem to appear in areas, radiating from centres in which they more vitally inhere, to marginal objects quite indifferent in themselves. Thus the clothing and discarded food of the king derive the taboo quality from his person. There is, however, no limit to the extent of this radiation or transmission. It is consequently not only what the king touches but what he sees, mentions, points at, and even what he mentally refers to, which becomes taboo. Anything detached from the body, — clothing, nail parings, hair, blood, excrement, — carries the quality of the person and is therefore dangerous. In the hands of enemies who know how to handle such things, they may be used as charms against one.

The dangerous qualities of woman, especially during pregnancy and childbirth, make it necessary to seclude her even more than at other times. Otherwise she would infect everything. The taboo of the infant is apparently derived from the mother. Often the vessels used by her during seclusion must be burned. It is not necessary to cite further details nor to point out that taboo radiates in the same infectious way from the dead, so that in many places even the clothing of the mourners must be burned when their period of mourning is completed.

Another feature of taboo which may be brought under the functional interpretation is the differentiation into holiness and uncleanness. It is agreed among students of the subject that in the earlier stages there was no differentiation. Robertson Smith holds that the irrationality of the laws of uncleanness shows that they are survivals of primitive religion. Holiness is like uncleanness in being contagious and dangerous. He shows, for example, that in the higher Semitic religions swine were taboo, but that it is an open question whether this was because the animal was holy or because it was unclean. The differentiation of taboos into holy and unclean was reached only in the later development of the Semitic religion, and then apparently under the operation of utilitarian influences and of race prejudice. On the whole, those things which were identified with the welfare of society and which were thus closely related to the service of God were considered holy, while acts and objects which were novel or foreign were attributed to evil spirits and to foreign gods and were therefore unclean.

It will have been noticed that little has been said in this chapter concerning the relation of taboo to spirits. The reasons for this will be found in the later discussion of spirits and of animism. The means of overcoming taboos has not been treated here because it is involved in the subject of sacrifice, to which a chapter is devoted.

CHAPTER V

CEREMONIALS AND MAGIC

IN its broadest use the word custom designates all the characteristic life-habits of a people, their language, dress, etiquette, occupations, modes of travel, as well as their festivals, celebrations, and various ritual observances. In this sense custom is equivalent to *mores* or folk-ways. Ceremonials are particular customs of public character and significance, conducted under the authority of the leaders of the group. These ceremonial customs arise in crises where there is great emotional intensity. They acquire the sanction of long usage and tend to become elaborated into highly formal, ritualistic observances. They constitute the cultus and afford the most complete expression of what later comes to be known as religion.

Functional psychology is prepared to accept these ceremonials as the most important factors in primitive religion, for they are just such motor reactions as belong to a relatively simple and unreflective stage of development. The main questions with reference to these ceremonials, in the functional view, do not concern their underlying ideas or systems of beliefs, but rather their practical and emotional significance. The proper subject of investigation is the behavior itself and its effects. Through these, taken in their whole setting, the moving impulses and stimuli may be discerned. Students of animal and of child life no longer search for complex motives and clear ideas as the sources of given actions. They concern themselves more with the motor reactions and the total situation in which these occur. In the same way primitive life and particularly primitive religious life should be investigated. The proper question here is not what is believed or what is thought, but what is done, what is effected. Proceeding in this way, it is possible to deal with the objective, tangible realities of primitive religion and to see these realities in relation to the actual living experiences from which they arise and to which they contribute.

The most important feature of these ceremonials, that which distinguishes them and makes them religious acts, is their public and social character. They belong to the whole group and are conducted by its members. Or, if the ritual is in some sense the property of one or more individuals, its performance is authorized by the leaders of the tribe and eagerly witnessed by the members. In this way the social side is dominant and controlling. It would be no exaggeration to say that all ceremonies in which the whole group coöperates with keen emotional interest are religious, and that all religious acts are distinguished by this social quality. It is because these ceremonials are social and therefore have the massive and corporate value of the entire community consciousness that they attain the distinctive character which entitles them to be called religious. "Religion in primitive society may be regarded as primarily a system for the controlling of the group with reference to the ends which are felt most acutely by the group as a group.

CEREMONIALS AND MAGIC

... All practices designed to do this are religious, whether they are definite forms of worship or not. Among these we should class the complicated initiation ceremonies of many peoples, tribal organization, involving the regulation of the individual's life in the most minute details, his naming, his eating, his hunting, where he may go, whom he may marry, and his conduct toward various members of the tribe." [1]

That the religious ceremonials are preëminently social or group reactions is emphasized by noting the occasions on which they occur. It is found that they are held in connection with the fundamental and crucial biological processes, involving the very existence and welfare of the group.[2] They are dramatic reproductions and representations of these processes and particularly of the crises in nature and in human life. The chief occasions of ceremonials may be classified as follows:

Phenomena in Nature. — These are the recurring events in the cycle of the seasons most intimately connected with human welfare. Here belong the celebrations of returning seed time and of harvest, the opening of the fishing and of the hunting seasons. In sections where the growth of vegetation is obviously dependent upon the rainfall, as among the Zuni Indians, the ceremonies are almost wholly concerned with that event. It is in times of drouth that the ceremonies are most elaborated and most carefully executed. Among the Arabs the fertilization of the

[1] Irving King, *Differentiation of the Religious Consciousness*, p. 39.
[2] Ernest Crawley, "The Origin and Function of Religion," *Sociological Papers*, pp. 245 f.

date-palm sets the season and the pattern for important ceremonials. Many ceremonies which have been interpreted as dramatizations of creation myths are in all probability concerned with the immediate present processes of reproduction of vegetable and animal life. The appropriation of the new grain or fruit is not allowable for the individual until the group ceremonies in reference to the first-fruits have been performed. In the same way the use of the herd is begun by the ceremonial appropriation of the firstlings of the flock.

Birth, Initiation, and Marriage. — Important rites attend the birth of a child and his reception in the camp. How critical and elemental this matter is may perhaps be appreciated best by reflecting that the children are not infrequently put to death because they jeopardize the care of older children and encumber the tribe. The child is named after a prescribed manner and often quite formally. All people have elaborate customs for the initiation of the youth into full participation in the life of the tribe. These ceremonies begin about the age of ten and culminate at the age of eighteen or twenty. They represent to the youth the historic or mythological past of the tribe through symbolic dances, the display of sacred objects of which he has hitherto been kept in ignorance, the revealing of secret names, and the impartation of certain tribal or totem markings.

Marriage is everywhere regarded as a social matter, that is, as an affair of the group. This is seen particularly in the restrictions as to who may marry. It is customary to require persons to marry outside their group or tribe. Even among the low tribes of Austra-

CEREMONIALS AND MAGIC

lia the clan and totem groups are well established and the limits within which selection of mates can be made are rigidly preserved. The establishment of such intimate relations with other families and members of the opposite sex is a matter of such keen social interest and of such hazard that it is safeguarded by various elaborate ceremonies.

Death and Burial. — The death of a member of a primitive group involves definite obligations upon those nearest of kin for the discharge of which they are responsible to the whole group. There are prescribed modes of burial, provision for the welfare and contentment of the deceased, and precautions of various kinds against any unfriendly acts of either the living or the dead. The obsequies, feeding of the dead, care of the grave, and special observances may continue for weeks or months, and among many peoples they extend through years.

War and the Treatment of Strangers. — In carrying out any interest savage tribes usually find innumerable occasions for war. The war ceremonials are therefore much in evidence. They consist of councils, assemblages, decorations, fasts, parades, manœuvres, dances, triumphal processions, feasts. Here as much as, or more than, in any other crisis the sense of tribal unity and power are immediately felt. The tension is great and the value of solidarity is proved in every success or failure. It is consequently to be expected that these war ceremonials should be of great significance in religious history. Contrasted with the hostility of war are the customs of hospitality. These include the signs of greeting which strangers employ, the methods of establishing relations of peace, as by eating, drinking, smoking together, exchanging gifts, and mingling blood.

But when it is shown that the ceremonials are religious primarily because they are social, it yet remains to consider two other facts concerning them. They are magical and have reference to spirits. It is usually maintained by writers upon primitive religion that religion is sharply contrasted with magic, and that its most distinguishing mark is belief in and propitiation of spirits. But the view set forth here is that magic and spiritism are characteristic features of all activities and interests of the savage and are not peculiar to his religion. Not only his ceremonials but all other activities also involve magic and spirits. These cannot, therefore, serve either negatively or positively to delimit religion from other interests. In justification of this view a consideration of magic is first presented.

Many writers put magic and religion in sharp opposition to each other. J. G. Frazer holds that magic signifies the necessary determination of one event by another in a mechanical and invariable manner. Man may gain control of these forces and make them serve his ends. But since the savage confused real causes with all manner of coincident and unrelated factors, his magic often failed and he gradually lost faith in it. Then the powers of nature became occult and mysterious and gave rise to the notion of spirits which man propitiated and worshiped. Thus religion arose.

Lang and Jevons defend the opposite view, that religion was prior and magic a relapse from the

CEREMONIALS AND MAGIC

religious stage. According to Jevons the most primitive attitude is that of an inductive though erroneous reasoning which undertakes to control various processes through resemblances or accidental relations. Then there arises for the more intelligent a distinction between the natural things which can be controlled by man and the supernatural forces which are beyond him. The latter give rise to religion, that is, an effort to form an alliance with these friendly superior powers. The less intelligent members of the group do not understand this distinction and therefore use magic, continuing to employ "for the production of both classes of effects indiscriminately those principles of induction which are common both to savage and scientific logic."[1] Lang explains the origin of religion by man's interpretation of the creation of the world in terms of his own power to build and construct. In this anthropomorphic manner he holds that very primitive people attained the idea of a great god. Magic results, then, as in Jevons' view, from the deterioration of religion to the point where this idea of the great god gives way to a great number of spirits to be controlled by occult means.

William Robertson Smith finds the distinction between religion and magic in the fact that the former is social and the latter individual. "It was the community, and not the individual, that was sure of the permanent and unfailing help of its deity. It was a national, not a personal providence that was taught by ancient religion. So much was this the case that in purely personal concerns the ancients were very apt to

[1] Jevons, *Introduction to the History of Religion*, p. 37.

turn, not to the recognized religion of the family or of the state, but to magical superstitions. . . . Not only did these magical superstitions lie outside religion, but in all well-ordered states they were regarded as illicit. A man had no right to enter into private relations with supernatural powers that might help him at the expense of the community to which he belonged. In his relations to the unseen he was bound always to think and act with and for the community, and not for himself alone." [1]

With this distinction it becomes possible to relate the whole subject of magic to religion in a thoroughgoing way, without attributing to the savage mind such advanced ideational, logical processes as are involved in the view of Jevons and Frazer. It is only necessary to recognize that both the group and the individual undertake to control phenomena without knowledge of their causes and by means of incidental and unimportant factors with which the phenomena appear connected in the naïve association of ideas characteristic of the primitive mind. There does not seem to be any essential difference in respect to the causal principle between the whole group of warriors attacking the image of the enemy with spears during the war dance, in order to weaken or destroy the distant enemy, and an individual in secret thrusting pins into an effigy in order to be avenged upon an absent foe. In both cases it is implied that whatever happens to the image of a

---

[1] W. Robertson Smith, *The Religion of the Semites*, pp. 263 f. For further statements of the social character of religion, pp. 312, 319. R. R. Marett, "Is Taboo a Negative Magic?" *Anthropological Essays*, p. 219, cf. 225, 229.

CEREMONIALS AND MAGIC

person happens to the person himself, unless this mysterious influence is counteracted by some powerful agency. The religious ceremonials, requiring, as they do, the coöperation of the group, may be regarded as collective magic; while those practices which are commonly designated as magic may be distinguished as individual magic. This terminology has the decided advantage of referring to the clear and simple distinction between acts which are social and those which are individual. It does not involve the highly wrought metaphysical discriminations belonging to the classification of spirits into natural and supernatural.

Upon endeavoring to understand the nature of magic, one who approaches it from the functional standpoint will not be surprised to find that the term is quite vague and shifting in its content. Instead of attempting to define magic it is more profitable to indicate some things designated by it without insisting that they exhaust its possible meanings. It is agreed, for example, that when a savage seeks to produce rain by sprinkling water upon the ground he is working magic. We may class such acts as imitative magic, whether performed by one person alone or by many in concert. Another type of savage procedure is to gain possession of something which has belonged to a person, it may be an article of clothing or even some of the earth upon which he has walked. It is felt that the object shares in the life of the person, so that whatever is done to it is done to the person. This also is magic, either individual or collective, and belongs to the special category of sympathetic magic. In other cases a person or a group of persons possesses such powerful qualities that people and things may be directly affected at a distance. For example, the king's gaze or even the intent of his mind may be so powerful as to operate immediately through space, affecting remote chiefs or the sun itself. This may be called direct magic, though it is closely related to sympathetic magic, since it is a part of the king's person which is thus projected by his gaze or by his thought. There are many other uses of the term magic, but these serve the present purpose.[1]

Illustrations of these different types of magic in public ceremonials might be multiplied indefinitely. Frazer cites many cases among widely different peoples showing how the fertilization of grain and trees is effected by ceremonials imitating the process of impregnation. The planting of the crops is accompanied by intercourse of the sexes or in higher stages of development by the symbolic acts of May Day, Easter, and Whitsuntide. In England it was customary on these days for young couples to roll down a slope together. "In various parts of Europe customs have prevailed both at spring and harvest which are clearly based on the same primitive notion that the relation of the human sexes to each other can be so used as to quicken the growth of plants. For example, in the Ukraine on St. George's Day (the twenty-third of April) the priest in his robes, attended by his acolytes, goes out to the fields of the village, where the crops are beginning to show green above the ground, and blesses them. After that the young married peo-

[1] N. W. Thomas, " Studies in Terminology," *Man*, 1904, p. 163. Cf. A. C. Haddon, *Magic and Fetishism.*

CEREMONIALS AND MAGIC

ple lie down in couples on the sown fields and roll several times over on them, in the belief that this will promote the growth of the crops. In some parts of Russia the priest himself is rolled by women over the sprouting crop, and that without regard to the mud and holes which he may encounter in his beneficent progress."[1] It is interesting also to notice that this principle of analogy in procreation may be expressed in just the opposite manner, that is, by the imposition of strict continence, so that the preservation of vigor and energy will also strengthen the crops. Illicit love is in any case harmful for the fields and crops. This emphasizes the point now under discussion, namely, that public acts of the same type are magical, the difference being that the ceremonial acts produce results which are beneficial, while the illicit deeds are disastrous.

Public ceremonials for the production of rain by imitating its fall are widespread; for causing the sun to shine by rekindling its light with fires or by other means of renewing its waning strength; for making the wind to blow by flapping blankets to start a breeze. These ceremonies may be conducted by individuals for the group or by the group as a whole.[2] It is significant that when the stress is greatest, as in times of drouth or during an eclipse, the ceremonies become more completely tribal or social, doubtless not only because the interest in them is more general but also because the greater number of participants, if only as spectators, aids in the efficacy of the performance.

[1] J. G. Frazer, *Golden Bough*, vol. ii, p. 208.
[2] *Bureau of Ethnology, Bulletin* 30, part i, "Handbook of American Indians," p. 959.

The same tendency of the magical act to be most thoroughly socialized where it involves most acutely the common good is also seen in the fact that the ceremonies occupy more members of the group and consume longer periods of time in the performance where nature is most unfavorable. The elaborate rain-making ceremonies of the Zuni Indians confirm this.

Collective, imitative magic is found in war ceremonials. In ancient Peru, when a war expedition was contemplated, they were wont to starve certain black sheep for some days and then slay them, uttering the incantation, "As the hearts of these beasts are weakened, so let our enemies be weakened." [1] Frazer cites similar practices among the ancient Hindoos. "To destroy his foe a man would fashion a figure of him in clay and transfix it with an arrow which had been barbed with a thorn and winged with an owl's feather. Or he would mould the figure of wax and melt it in fire. Sometimes effigies of the soldiers, horses, elephants, and chariots of a hostile army were modeled in dough and then pulled in pieces." [2] This principle of imitative magic may also be used to aid an army. "In the island of Timor, while war is being waged, the high priest never quits the temple; his food is brought to him or is cooked inside; day and night he must keep the fire burning, for if he were to let it die out, disaster would befall the warriors and would continue as long as the hearth was cold. Moreover, he must drink only hot water during the time the army is absent; for every draught of cold water would damp the spirits of

[1] R. R. Marett, "From Spell to Prayer," *Folk-Lore*, 1904.
[2] J. G. Frazer, *Golden Bough*, vol. i, p. 14.

CEREMONIALS AND MAGIC

the people, so that they could not vanquish the enemy."[1] In Madagascar, while the men are at the wars, the women keep up dances continuously. "They believe that by dancing they impart strength, courage, and good fortune to their husbands." Frazer gives other cases where fruits and stones are anointed with oil by the women at home so that the raindrops will rebound from them and thus cause the bullets of the enemy to fall harmless from their husbands; or the women wave their fans in order to direct the bullets away from friends and toward the foe. Another custom is for the women on the day of battle to run about with guns, or sticks carved to look like guns, and taking green paw-paws (fruits shaped somewhat like a melon), they hack them with knives, as if they were chopping off the heads of the foe.[2]

Much of the collective magic characteristic of ceremonials is sympathetic magic. The central element here is the possession of some part of the animal or person in order to derive his qualities. When a Zulu army assembles to go forth, the warrior eats slices of meat which are smeared with a powder made of the dried flesh of various animals, such as the leopard, lion, elephant, snakes, and so on; for thus it is thought that the soldiers will acquire the bravery and other warlike qualities of these animals. It is a common practice to eat the flesh, particularly the heart, and to drink the blood of brave enemies in order to acquire their qualities.[3]

[1] J. G. Frazer, *Golden Bough*, vol. i, p. 31.
[2] *Ibid*, vol. i, p. 33.
[3] *Ibid*, vol. ii, pp. 355, 357.

It is probable that the ceremonies attending the treatment of the first catch of fish or game are cases of sympathetic magic. In the Torres Straits the first turtle caught during the turtle-breeding season was handed over to the men of the Turtle clan, who painted themselves to resemble the turtle and performed dances and certain mimetic acts to insure an abundance of turtles. Here it may be supposed that the treatment of one member of the species proceeds on the notion that what is done to a part is done to the whole of the class. This throws light upon many ceremonials over the first fish or animal or fruit taken. It must be dealt with in the accepted public manner before any others of the species may be appropriated.

"Amongst the Thlinkeet of Alaska the first halibut of the season is carefully handled and addressed as a chief, and a festival is given in his honor, after which the fishing goes on. Among the tribes of the Lower Frazer River, when the first sockeye salmon of the season has been caught, the fisherman carries it to the chief of his tribe, who delivers it to his wife. She prays, saying to the salmon, 'Who has brought you here to make us happy? We are thankful to your chief for sending you.' When she has cut and roasted the salmon according to certain prescribed rules, the whole tribe is invited and partakes of the fish, after they have purified themselves by drinking a decoction of certain plants, which is regarded as a medicine for cleansing the people."[1]

Thus the ceremonial eating of the first fish is a

[1] J. G. Frazer, *Golden Bough*, vol. ii, p. 412.

CEREMONIALS AND MAGIC

means of making sure of the species for the season's food, on the principle that what is done to a part is done to the whole. The ceremonial care with which the first fish, animal, grain, or fruit of the season is treated appears to be just the means of securing an abundance of that class of objects. The use of one is the use of all, just as the care of a man's girdle is a care of the man himself. The intimate association of the part and the whole, of the individual and the species, of the first-born and the whole generation is the clue to many practices which are at once religious and magical.

In the initiation ceremonies both mimetic and sympathetic magic appear. Among the Arunta tribe of Australia the first of these ceremonies is the tossing of boys of ten or twelve in the air. The men catch them as they fall, while the women dance round and round the group, swinging their arms and shouting loudly.[1] This ceremony is to make them grow to manhood. Perhaps the tossing up effects this in the savage mind. Frazer gives many instances of swinging to promote the growth of grain; the higher the priests or peasants swing, the taller will the crops grow.[2] In the second ceremony there are features which seem to accomplish the identification of the youth with the tribe, including the dead as well as the living members. The fur-string from a totem animal, the hair girdle, and the pubic tassel are fastened on him to make him one of the totem-class, kangaroo, wildcat, or whatever the totem may be. All these operate magically to

---
[1] Spencer and Gillen, *Native Tribes of Central Australia*, p. 214.
[2] Frazer, *Golden Bough*, vol. ii, p. 33. Cf. Appendix, Note A.

unite the youth with the tribe and to impart to him in very literal ways the life of the group. Thus continuity is achieved for the tribe. A suggestive feature of the ceremony and one which shows the thoroughly social character of it is the conduct of the women, especially the relatives of the youth. While he is in the Bush recovering from the circumcision, the "Mia (a woman whom his father has married or might have married) may not eat opossum, or the large lizard, or carpet snake, or any fat, as otherwise she would retard her son's recovery. Every day she greases her digging sticks and never allows them out of her sight; at night time she sleeps with them close to her head. No one is allowed to touch them. Every day also she rubs her body all over with grease, as in some way this is supposed to help her son's recovery." [1] There is no reason to doubt that the central factors of the initiation ceremonies are any less magical than these peripheral factors which are obviously such. The last of the initiation ceremonies, the Engwura, strengthens the youth by fire ordeals. It imparts courage and wisdom; makes the men more kindly natured and less apt to quarrel. In all these ceremonies the use of blood is common and its efficiency universally consists in binding together and solidifying the group by its magical power. Several times during the ceremonies the performers lie down in a mass upon the

---

[1] Spencer and Gillen, *Native Tribes of Central Australia*, p. 250. In the ceremony which follows circumcision these authors note that a chant is sung which is supposed to have the effect of promoting the growth of the hair, — the mark of maturity. Biting the head and chin are for the same purpose.

CEREMONIALS AND MAGIC

prostrate novice, the pressing together of the bodies having great power of union and inoculation.[1]

Another instance of sympathetic magic is found in the use of the name of an ancestor, divinity, or man. The name is so much a part of the individual or object that to possess the name is to have power over him. It is therefore frequently found that the names of persons and of the divinities are kept secret. "A man's name — or a god's — is part of himself, and therefore invocation and repetition of the deity's name constitutes in itself an actual, if mystic, union with the deity."[2] In some Egyptian prayers there is sometimes added the reminder that the petitioner knows the divine mystic name.

The songs and chants are also magical in character, and the volume of sound in a chorus of voices makes the effect more massive and compelling. One part of the initiation rites in South-east Australia, as described by Howitt, discloses its magical character so clearly and in such a typical manner that it is quoted here at length. The general effect of the ceremonies is to preserve continuity in the tribal life, and this is done by transferring to the youth the mode of life and even the substance of the ancestors. In the ceremonies the ancestors are present, the savage mind making little distinction between a symbol and the reality symbolized. The ceremonies are not make-believe, but to all intents are the embodiment of the actual being and activity of the progenitors of the tribe. In this instance a procession of old men is

[1] Cf. Ernest Crawley, *Mystic Rose*, p. 374.
[2] Jevons, *Introduction to the History of Religion*, p. 245.

represented to those being initiated. "Great age was shown, as in all these representations, by each man walking in a stooping position, supported by a staff in each hand. After circling around the boys twice, the procession resolved itself into a ring in front of the boys, and the men danced the usual magic dance round one who exhibited his *Joïas* in the usual manner. The men, then, ceasing to dance, rushed to the boys in an excited manner, old Yibai-malian leading the way, and for the first time went through one of their most characteristic performances. They all shouted '*Ngai*,' meaning 'good,' and at the same time moved their arms and hands as if passing something from themselves to the boys, who, being instructed by the *Kabos*, moved their hands and arms as if pulling a rope toward themselves, the palms of the hands being held upwards. The intention of this is that the boys shall be completely filled — saturated, I might say, — with the magic proceeding from the initiated and the medicine men, so that '*Daramulun* will like them.'" [1]

Further evidence of the magical character of religious ceremonials is also afforded by viewing them as means of overcoming or producing taboo. Taboo is regarded by many writers as "negative magic," [2] and to the savage the surest way to overcome any magic is by other magic. The things tabooed are dangerous because they are strange, mysterious, and because they possess qualities, such as frailty or weakness, which one might receive from contact. But whatever explanation of taboo is accepted, it is agreed by all that

[1] A. W. Howitt, *Native Tribes of South-east Australia*, p. 535.
[2] R. R. Marett, *Anthropological Essays*, p. 219.

CEREMONIALS AND MAGIC

any taboo may be overcome by one or another ceremonial device. Crawley has made a most thorough investigation of marriage ceremonies, and his conclusion is that they are employed to overcome the taboos involved, among which the sexual taboo is the most important. "Marriage ceremonies neutralize the dangers attaching to union between the sexes, in all the complex meaning of those dangers."[1] It was shown in the last chapter that the sexes are taboo because of their strangeness and mystery for each other, due to the separation between them, arising from different occupations and their attendant social habits. The utmost caution is, therefore, necessary, when they are to be united. This caution is necessary in any cases of ordinary contact between individuals of the same sex, when they eat together or live together in any way. Marriage must overcome these taboos as well as those of sex. Accordingly, these rites are found universally and with a remarkable similarity. Crawley has brought together an elaborate display of customs in support of this view. These are summarized in what follows. That they are magical in character there can be no doubt, and that they are religious in the sense of embodying the highest social sanction is evident. The preliminary marriage ceremonies indicate that something dangerous is about to be undertaken, demanding various kinds of caution. The bride and the bridegroom are accompanied by processions to allay evil influences. Throwing rice, flour, nuts, or sweetmeats had the same purpose originally. In many countries the parties about to wed must bathe, be fumigated,

[1] Ernest Crawley, *The Mystic Rose*, p. 322.

and fast for purification. Weddings take place at night, when female shyness and timidity are more easily overcome and when the evil eye cannot harm. Various means of concealment such as veils and disguises are employed, so that often the bridegroom never sees the bride until the marriage is consummated, and then frequently both are kept shut up within the house for days. In some cases each party is wedded first to a third thing, such as a tree, to insure harmlessness. Restrictions are sometimes maintained after marriage, such as silence, refraining from sleep, and from food. Among many low tribes the husband is protected from the dangers of intercourse by the ceremonial in which the bride first receives other men. Sometimes defloration is performed by the priest. Ceremonial fights and flights signifying sexual opposition and the necessity for caution are common. It is the sex and not the tribe or family from which the bride is abducted. The most important ceremonies in marriage are those in which the union takes place by an exchange between the parties of some part of themselves, a lock of hair, piece of clothing, food, or drink, special gifts, or by the actual exchange of blood. The hands may be joined or the heads pressed together, but the commonest ceremony of union is that of eating and drinking together. Less ceremonial, that is, a slighter amount of magic, is necessary in the marriage of a widow, since most of the danger has been already overcome in her case.

In practically every instance where the ceremonial is employed it apparently involves this removal of taboo as well as the positive furtherance of the life

CEREMONIALS AND MAGIC

process. In these marriage ceremonies the purpose, according to Crawley, is to overcome negative conditions. In the case of planting crops the negative and positive forces of the rite seem more nearly balanced. In ceremonials for sickness and the dead the opposition to negative elements seems greater. This appears also to be true in the case of warriors returning from battle. They must remain a certain time outside the camp, paint themselves, bathe, be fed by others in order not to touch food, until finally the taboo is removed and they are allowed to return into full relations with the tribe.[1]

In all these ceremonials the tendency of habitual activities to become elaborate and more or less symbolic is evident. The Arunta Tribe in Australia, for example, spend as much as four months at a time in this seeming mimicry and mummery. In more advanced peoples the symbolism develops into genuine art. Among the Greeks music and plastic art can be traced back to the dance of the agricultural festivals, where the rhythm and form are direct reproductions of the rhythm and form of real labor.

Ceremonials need also to be considered with reference to the emotional reactions involved. It is now well established that the emotions arise in situations of stress and tension, where the regular, habitual activity is interrupted and is inadequate to the task in hand. Attention flutters between conflicting plans of action, accompanied by depressing, painful feeling when the cause is losing or by expansive, pleasurable

[1] J. G. Frazer, *Golden Bough*, vol. i, p. 331; W. R. Smith, *Religion of the Semites*, p. 491.

PSYCHOLOGY OF RELIGIOUS EXPERIENCE

feeling when victory and safety are at hand. The despair of defeat endures so long as the consciousness of what is lost remains keen, and the joy of the success waxes great while there is a sense of the loss and pain which have been avoided. It has been seen that the occasions of ceremonials are precisely those acute crises which set the most vital interests of the tribe in greatest tension, — hunger, love, war, birth, death, youth, sickness. The rites which arise in these crises share in these tensions and at the same time resolve them. They are not make-believe and they are not remotely symbolical. They actually do work. Accordingly the participants in the dance or corrobboree experience the whole gamut of emotion. So intense does this become in certain ceremonies that special performances are necessary to allay it. Thus Spencer and Gillen relate the conclusion of a certain dance: "the *Nurtunja* (a pole used in sacred ceremonies) was laid on one side, and the performers, taking each a little bit of down from it, pressed this in turn against the stomach of each of the older men who were present. The idea of placing hands upon the performers is that thereby their movements are stopped, whilst the meaning of the down being placed against the stomachs of the older men is that they become so agitated with emotion by witnessing the sacred ceremony that their inward parts, that is, their bowels, which are regarded as the seat of the emotions, get tied up in knots, which are loosened by this application of a part of the sacred *Nurtunja*." [1]

[1] Spencer and Gillen, *Native Tribes of Central Australia*, pp. 285 f.

CEREMONIALS AND MAGIC

It is probable that this emotional excitement, in many cases amounting to frenzy, is of importance on its own account. The subjects of it pass out of their usual state and become for the time strange to themselves and to others. They lose themselves in the totem and ancestor characters impersonated. Just because they appear other than normal and are able to do extraordinary things, such as uttering oracular wisdom, perhaps in a strange tongue, they are regarded as taboo or sacred. Rivers describes a case in which during a funeral among the Todas the buffalo to be killed became refractory and finally lay down and could not be moved.[1] Then a diviner was called who danced to and fro, from and towards the buffalo. As his dancing became wilder, his appearance was strange. "His hair seemed to stand out from his head, although it shook with each of his violent movements; his eyes were abnormally bright and his face gave every appearance of great mental excitement." While in this state he gave directions in a language which at other times he claimed to be ignorant of. These are the phenomena of temporary possession which occur among all peoples and to some extent in all stages of development. The subjects of them are taboo and at the same time are able to exert magical power. It is when the initiation rites have been carried through various preliminaries that the performers attain sufficient fervor or frenzy to accomplish the transfer of the ancestral life to the novice. Likewise all the ceremonies require dances, chants, surprises, explosions of

[1] W. H. R. Rivers, *The Todas*, p. 253; cf. J. G. Frazer, *Golden Bough*, vol. i, p. 131.

energy, before they become effective. The efficacy of the group is greatest in this climax of emotion, and it is then that the magic is wrought. At that moment power is communicated, the processes of nature are enlivened, the youth is transformed into manhood, sickness is expelled, the evil doer is detected, the enemy is smitten, the future is foreseen, and all manner of miracles are wrought.

It is also true that the ceremonials have a genuine educational value. They inculcate self-control, endurance, obedience to the old men, and acquaint the novices with the stories of heroes of the past and their deeds of valor. But such educational effects are not independent of the magical character of the rites. Indeed it is not difficult to see that the more magical they are, the more impressive the instruction becomes.

CHAPTER VI

SPIRITS

THE omission of the term "spirits" in the discussion thus far has been deliberate, but a full consideration of the subject is important at this point. Two statements from Tylor's great work may be taken as typical of the usual doctrine. "It seems as though the conception of a human soul, when once attained by man, served as a type or model on which he framed not only his ideas of other souls of lower grade, but also his idea of spiritual beings in general, from the tiniest elf that sports in the long grass up to the heavenly Creator and Ruler of the world, the Great Spirit." "The general principles of this investigation seem comparatively easy of access to the enquirer, if he will use the two keys which the foregoing studies imply: first, that spiritual beings are modeled by man on his primary conception of his own human soul, and second, that their purpose is to explain nature on the primitive childlike theory that it is truly and throughout 'animated Nature.'" [1]

This characteristic expression of the view of most writers upon the subject of animism or spiritism betrays plainly the effect of the old rational psychology. It made the assumption that man is directly conscious of himself as a spiritual agent, or soul, and the further assumption that this "conception of the human soul

[1] E. B. Tylor, *Primitive Culture*, vol. ii, pp. 110, 184; cf. pp. 109, 209, 247.

is the very 'fons et origo' of the conceptions of spirit and deity in general." Professor James and many psychologists after him have shown how unsubstantial a foundation there is for the earlier conception of the soul as a metaphysical unit. In his actual experience each man is, as it were, many selves, sometimes organized into more or less of a hierarchy, but often dissociated, if not quite at war with one another. One never feels the whole of himself, so to speak, but is in reality conscious of this or that activity; reading, walking, eating, with a thread of "warmth and intimacy" giving a fragile continuity to the complex series. At best this consciousness of self waxes and wanes in vigor and fatigue, in youth and senility. Instead of having a kind of ready-made knowledge of self which he can employ as a type to project upon all the things he meets, in reality he only gradually attains a dim, partially organized sense of personality out of his experiences with other persons and things. The notion of the soul does not precede the idea of objects. There is no individuality in the subject except in relation to individuality in objects. The discriminating and synthesizing processes by which distinctions between the self and objects proceed, and by which unity and distinctness arise for both, do not concern one more than the other. A highly organized personality implies an equally well-ordered world of various persons constituting a social order and a sphere of multitudinous "things" or "objects" governed by "laws of nature." Subject and object arise together in experience. It is therefore a fundamental fallacy to assume that the soul of primitive man

SPIRITS

became aware of its activity and spiritual character in any prior or independent way which would justify the statement that it served as a type or model for framing ideas of all other spirits.

Primitive man is more like the child than he is like the introspective, anthropomorphizing philosopher. If the latter does not really attain the closely articulated and unified self which the term soul formerly signified, it is certainly impossible for the child or the savage. Genetic psychology makes it clear that the infant is not a self, a personality. He is only a kind of candidate for personality. If he attains it in some measure, he does so gradually. It is an achievement, not a gift. Neither is it the necessary and inevitable unfolding of powers within him. It is actually developed through concrete and vital experiences, or if these experiences do not occur, it is not developed at all. It is just as true, therefore, to say that one gets the idea of himself from the objects he deals with, and that he makes them the pattern upon which he constructs the self, as it is to say that the reverse occurs.

The fact seems to be that both self and object are fused in one activity and are not contrasted in the actor's mind. It is not so much a projection of the self to other things as it is the participation of all in one total undifferentiated process, warm with vital interest. A man feels himself hurt when his body is injured and also when his coat is torn or his money lost. This is in fact the basis of that "animation" which is constantly involved in all immediate, unreflective experience. We feel to the end of our walking-stick, and we only set ourselves off from it when it is dropped, lost, broken, or otherwise "objectified." So long as we possess it and employ it in the ordinary way it is part of us and is as little thought of as is a finger of the hand which works painlessly and harmoniously. But when the stick is broken, it is like a sore finger and on that account stands out with painful clearness in consciousness. If, again, the stick becomes useless and the finger extremely infected, both are removed and in time forgotten. We become indifferent to them and they no longer exist for us. A description of this process of animation and its decadence is graphically presented in the following: "If a boy sets about making a boat and has any success, his interest in the matter waxes, he gloats over it, the keel and stern are dear to his heart, and its ribs are more to him than those of his own frame. He is eager to call in his friends and acquaintances, saying to them, 'See what I am doing. Is it not remarkable?' feeling elated when it is praised or humiliated when fault is found with it. But as soon as he finishes it and turns to something else, his self-feeling begins to fade away from it, and in a few weeks at most he will have become comparatively indifferent." [1]

It only needs to be added for the present argument, that the feeling with regard to the self changes with the changing fortune of the boat-making. While the activity is going on, both the self and the boat rise into consciousness, and when it is discontinued, not only the boat but the self which was correlated with it, fades away. The activity developed not only a boat-self but a self-boat, and, when one died, the

[1] C. H. Cooley, *Human Nature and the Social Order*, p. 146.

SPIRITS

other perished with it. Neither could live alone. This conception of the relation of the self and its objects furnishes quite a different psychological explanation of animism from the one quoted from Tylor. Instead of primitive man discovering his own soul within him and then attributing such a soul to all other things, he is indolent and unattentive; or he is absorbed in an intense activity, all parts of which fuse and blend except in moments of unusual, surprising experiences when a conflict springs up between his accustomed round of action and some feature of his environment. Then, at that moment of conflict, his attention is caught by the escaping animal, by a knotted tree, or by a protruding rock which has shielded the game or interrupted the chase. Such an object becomes a determining factor in the urgent, exciting effort and is thrust up into notice in such a way as to become a living thing. Something like this seems to be the meaning of an extremely suggestive passage by Professor Dewey. In the hunting of the savage, "tools, implements, weapons are not mechanical and objective means, but are part of the present activity, organic parts of personal skill and effort. The land is not a means to a result but an intimate and fused portion of life, — a matter not of objective inspection and analysis, but of affectionate and sympathetic regard. The making of weapons is felt as a part of the exciting use of them. Plants and animals are not 'things,' but are factors in the display of energy and form the contents of most intense satisfactions. The 'animism' of the primitive mind is a necessary expression of the immediacy of relation existing between want, overt activity, that which affords satisfaction and the attained satisfaction itself. Only when things are treated simply as means, do they become objects."[1]

Two important facts here are these. First, the object emerges at the point where the attention is arrested. Obviously this may occur anywhere in the process and in the course of various activities a variety of objects are discriminated. Some of these objects recur in successive experiences and attain greater definiteness and individuality. That is, in hunting, the animal, the stream, the tree play their part with sufficient frequency, and at the same time with enough variability to bring them repeatedly above the threshold of attention. Secondly, the objects thus attended to are not abstracted beyond the active process in which they appear. They are warm with the life and movement pervading all the operations of the chase. They are therefore not inanimate. They possess energy and influence which, to the undisciplined mind of the savage, is magnified rather than minimized. In other words, these objects are living agents or spirits to the savage.

These principles simplify many of the problems which have arisen in the interpretation of primitive religion. They account for the great multiplicity of spirits and for their transient, shifting character. They explain why different peoples have different kinds of spirits and also why the spirits of a given tribe are determined so characteristically by their environment and occupations. These and other phases of the

[1] John Dewey, "Interpretation of Savage Mind," *Psychological Review*, 1902, p. 221.

SPIRITS

problem will be emphasized later in the discussion. At this point it is important to indicate some of the anthropological data which have been used inductively in attaining these broad generalizations.

The meaning of the term spirit among savages is extremely vague and uncertain, even if it is conceded that they really possess such a word at all. "How does a Kafir conceive of a spirit (of an ancestor)? They have many ways of viewing the subject; but all are delightfully vague and ill-defined. The nearest English word would possibly be personality, though that would be but an approximation. This word has a very vague connotation to those who have not studied psychology, and its vagueness makes it suitable in this connection. The Kafir idea of spirit is not at all the same as our religious conception of a soul or spirit. Some natives say a man's soul lives in the roof of his hut; you can hardly keep a 'theological soul' there. It would be nearer the mark to connect it with the body, though it is confused with a man's shadow, which is supposed to dwindle as he grows old. A man's shadow is supposed to vanish or grow very slight at death; most naturally so, for the dead body lies prone. This shadow, then, is connected with the man's personality and forms a basis for the ancestral spirit. You may call it a ghost, if you like, but must be careful to strain off most of our European ideas connected with this word." [1]

It is to be remembered that the Kafir does not belong to the lowest known races and that therefore the vagueness in his conception of spirits is only a

[1] Dudley Kidd, *The Essential Kafir*, pp. 82 f.

PSYCHOLOGY OF RELIGIOUS EXPERIENCE

suggestion of the fruitlessness of any search for definite terms or conceptions with reference to the subject among savages. The vagueness of the notion appears also in the wide range of objects to which it is applied. Herbert Spencer has shown that primitive peoples attribute spirits not only to men, but to animals, plants, and inorganic objects.[1] His use of the facts in the interest of the narrow doctrine of primitive religion as ancestor-worship is confusing, but the data he collated show that the term spirit is applied to every kind of object. R. R. Marett finds that the savage believed in an "infinitely miscellaneous collection of spiritual entities."[2] He quotes the following conversation in illustration: "'To whom are you praying?' asked Hale of a Sakai chief at one of those fruit festivals so characteristic of the Malay peninsula. 'To the *Hantus* (spirits),' he replied, — 'the *Hantus* of the forest, of the mountains, of the rivers, the *Hantus* of the Sakai chiefs who are dead, the *Hantus* of the headache and stomachache, the *Hantus* that make people gamble and smoke opium, the *Hantus* that send disputes, and the *Hantus* that send mosquitoes.'" One other quotation confirms the claim that there are no limits to the use of the term spirits. Speaking of the Polynesians and Melanesians, Ratzel says: "The words spirit and soul indicate generally any expression of life. The squeaking of rats, the talk of children in their sleep, is called 'spirit' in Tahiti."[3]

[1] Herbert Spencer, *Sociology*, vol. i, chapters 20-24.
[2] R. R. Marett, "Pre-animistic Religion," *Folk-Lore*, 1900, p. 167.
[3] F. Ratzel, *The History of Mankind*, vol. i, p. 300.

SPIRITS

This last statement should prepare the way for the observation that the term spirit does not mark any such differentiation between material and immaterial things, or between real and ideal existences, as is generally ascribed to it. Crawley has insisted upon this indeterminate character of primitive thinking. "Primitive man," he asserts, "regards the creatures of his own imagination as being no less real than the existences for which he has the evidence of sense-perception, in a sense more real, precisely because they elude sense-perception, though dealt with in the same way as objective reality."[1] He is probably right also in maintaining that the supernatural and the natural are not distinguished; that matter and spirit are undifferentiated.

This blurred and inarticulate character of early man's thought is not likely to be over-emphasized. Souls or spirits are obtrusively corporeal, while the physical body is capable of transformations worthy of the veriest sprite. Tylor observes: "Among lower races, the soul or spirit is a thin, unsubstantial human image, in its nature a sort of vapor, film or shadow." Skeat reports it among the Malays as a manikin about as big as the thumb, corresponding exactly in shape, proportion, and even in complexion, to the body. This realistic nature of the soul appears in the way of thinking of deceased ancestors. The Kafirs associate their ancestors with snakes, perhaps, as Dudley Kidd remarks,[2] because snakes crawl out of the wattles of the kraal where the grave is. The reptile

[1] Ernest Crawley, *The Mystic Rose*, p. 3.
[2] Dudley Kidd, *The Essential Kafir*, pp. 83, 84.

is even regarded as an actual part of the ancestor, for example, it is the backbone or the entrails. Or they identify a man and his shadow, but the latter is not unreal in any sense. To stand on their shadow is to injure them. Again a man and his possessions are considered so much the same that if the shadow of his sleeping-mat grows less it is because the absent warrior himself has been killed in battle. The dead are not regarded as essentially different from the living. They are given food, which is sometimes literally poured down a tube to the mouth of the corpse as it lies in the grave; they are spoken to, supplied with weapons, clothes, jewels, and many other things. They continue to belong to the tribe and are just as much counted on as are the visible members. We have seen how they participate in ceremonials and continue to direct and control the affairs of the tribe.[1]

There is, then, no sufficient ground for believing that primitive people make any consistent distinction between man and his spirit or between any other object and its spirit. Dreams and trances may indeed give rise to the idea of a double, but this double is not essentially different from the original. The limits and possibilities of changes in personality are not known to the savage, and the stories of the transformation of human beings into animals and other forms are not difficult for him.[2] There is no convincing evidence that he has any such conception of spiritual beings or

[1] Supra, pp. 67, 75; cf. A. C. Haddon, "The Religion of the Torres Straits Indians," *Anthropological Essays*, p. 181.

[2] E. B. Tylor, *Primitive Culture*, vol. ii, p. 467; W. R. Smith, *Religion of the Semites*, p. 87.

SPIRITS

supernatural agents as has generally been inferred. The tendency has been to attribute over-nice distinctions to minds unable to make them. The interpretations of the ideas of lower races have been made from the standpoint and with the preconceptions of races in which the power of abstraction is much greater. What Robertson Smith says with reference to the *jinn* or demons of the heathen Arabs is doubtless still truer of lower types. "These *jinn* are not pure spirits, but corporeal beings, more like beasts than men, for they are ordinarily represented as hairy, or have some other animal shape, as that of an ostrich or a snake. Their bodies are not phantasms, for if a jinnī is killed a solid carcass remains; but they have mysterious powers of appearing and disappearing, or even of changing their aspect and temporarily assuming a human form."[1]

It is not necessary, therefore, to suppose that in the more primitive stages any distinction is made between an object and its spirit. The object is itself the spirit. Specific evidence is not wanting for this view. The Malay miner considers "that the tin itself is alive and has many of the properties of living matter, that of itself it can move from place to place, that it can reproduce itself, and that it has special likes — or perhaps affinities — for certain people and things, and vice versa." [2] "The rice itself is addressed as though it were an animated being." [3]

Upon the basis of these facts, — the variety of

[1] W. R. Smith, *Religion of the Semites*, pp. 119 f.
[2] W. W. Skeat, *Malay Magic*, p. 259.
[3] F. Ratzel, *History of Mankind*, vol. i, p. 471.

objects considered as spirits, the failure to differentiate things as material and immaterial, the transformations which are believed possible between men, animals, plants, and stones, the slight difference between living men and dead men, — the suggestion is here made of a psychological interpretation of the whole subject of spirits, in terms of attention, conception, and habit. If what has been said about the identity of object and spirit be kept in mind, then it becomes clear that a spirit is an object, sensation, or image which strikes the attention forcibly. Among the Malays there is "veneration and awe of any tree that is in any way out of the common. On giant trees or such as have got twined together or shelter white ants' nests, one is sure to find a little shrine in which offerings are brought to the spirit."[1] A passage from Marett is particularly pertinent. "Stones that are at all curious in shape, position, size, or color, — not to speak of properties derived from remarkable coincidences of all sorts, — would seem especially designed by nature to appeal to primitive man's 'supernaturalistic tendency.' A solitary pillar of rock, a crumbled volcanic boulder, a meteorite, a pebble resembling a pig, a yam, or an arrowhead, a piece of shining quartz, these and such as these are almost certain to be invested by his imagination with the vague but dreadful attribute of Powers. Nor, although to us nothing appears so utterly inanimate as a stone, is savage animism in the least afraid to regard it as alive. Thus the Kanakas differentiate their sacred stones into males and females and firmly believe that from time

[1] F. Ratzel, *History of Mankind*, vol. i, p. 471; cf. p. 468.

SPIRITS

to time little stones appear at the side of the parent blocks."[1]

Marett cites in this connection the place of importance held by animals which are strange, gruesome, and uncanny. Such are white elephants, white buffaloes, night birds, monkeys, mice, frogs, crabs, and lizards. It is needless to multiply specific instances. All writers agree that those things are regarded as possessing spirits, or as being spirits which are unusual and astonishing. The impression made by delirium, epilepsy, sneezing, yawning, twitching of the eyelids, and other seizures or convulsive movements, are of this kind. So much is this the case that the word spirit might be taken to mean any strange thing, any unwonted, exaggerated or surprising thing. Psychologically there seems good ground for this hypothesis: a spirit is something which strikes the attention forcibly, interrupting an established habit, and demanding the creation of a new conception. A sentence from Professor James emphasizes this operation of attention as fundamental in conception. "Each act of conception results from our attention singling out some one part of the mass of matter for thought which the world presents and holding fast to it without confusion."[2] This holding fast to the object or quality does not, however, according to James, require any great intellectual clearness or tenacity. It is sufficient just to have the vague feeling of identity. "A polyp would be a conceptual thinker if a feeling of 'Hollo,

[1] R. R. Marett, "Pre-animistic Religion," *Folk-Lore*, 1900, p. 174; cf. 169.

[2] William James, *Psychology*, vol. i, p. 461.

thingumbob again,' ever flitted through its mind." We have here, it may be, a psychological account of spirits, an explanation of the fact that anything, the squeaking of a rat, tin-ore, or a deceased ancestor, may be found in this category.

There is thus discovered also an interesting connection between spirits and taboo. It was shown above that taboo expresses just this sense of uncertainty, of fear or inhibition in the presence of a strange object or an unfamiliar situation. The things tabooed are queer, novel, wonderful. That is, that which catches the attention in the moment of surprise is spirit, and the caution which is the natural result is the essence of taboo or sacredness. Both of these phases, showing what constitutes the essence of spirit and that this is the essence of taboo, came out in the conversation of Marett with the Pigmy chief. "His knife acts normally as long as it serves him to trim his own arrow-shaft. As soon, however, as it slips and cuts his hand, there is '*oudah*' in, or at the back of, the 'cussed' thing. Given, then, anything that behaves 'cussedly' with regularity, that is normally abnormal in its effects, so to speak, and a taboo or customary avoidance will be instituted." [1]

This identification of a thing as surprising, something to be attended to, is indicated among the different races by terms of practically the same meaning. With the Fijians it is *Kalou*, with other Melanesians it is *Mana*, with the Malagasy it is *Andria-manitra*, with the Masai it is *Ngai*, with the Zulus it is *Inkosi*,

[1] R. R. Marett, "Is Taboo a Negative Magic?" *Anthropological Essays*, p. 230.

SPIRITS

with the Baronga it is *Tilo*, with the Omaha it is *Wakanda*, with the Iroquois it is *Orenda*, with the Algonquins it is *Manitou*.[1] Others say the object is possessed, bewitched, inspired, sanctified. Whatever it is called, it is everywhere the same, and the essence of it is, as Marett holds, its power to inspire awe. "This is the common element in ghosts and gods, in the magical and the mystical, the supernal and the infernal, the unknown within and the unknown without."[2]

But Marett is not so convincing when he argues that this awe is the distinguishing mark of religion. It would be just as great a mistake to claim that the notion of spirits or of taboo is the thing which differentiates religion on the intellectual side. The fact is that all of these terms are too large, too comprehensive, when taken without qualification, to designate religion. They apply just as well to individual magic. Religion involves certain spirits, namely, those which signify the most important functions and interests of the group, those in which the group reacts with the greatest solidarity and intensity. These, as we have seen, are the occasions of crisis, when in the most acute way, "the tribal nerves are on the stretch." It is these situations which give rise to the ceremonials. Not all surprising, startling experiences become the occasions of ceremonials, that is, elicit social responses, but those which do are of the greatest importance in primitive religion. Likewise not all spirits, but only those which belong to group activities, enter into

[1] A. C. Haddon, *Syllabus of Lectures on Magic and Primitive Religion*, p. 6.
[2] R. R. Marett, *Folk-Lore*, 1900, p. 169.

religion. In the same way, not all magic, but only such as belongs to group activities, enters into religion. By taking the social consciousness, then, in its profoundest and best organized features, as the very essence of religion, a principle is gained which shows what spirits are important for religion, and also what particular expressions of awe are genuinely religious. It is of course admitted that the social consciousness and its adequate expression in ceremonials and in codes of conduct are matters of degree, but this only aids in showing the advantage of identifying religion with these social phenomena. A conception of religion is thus gained which is free enough to include the lower forms and also the various stages of its development, without the confusion and vagueness which have heretofore arisen from attempting to identify it with such an intellectual element as belief in spirits, or with an emotional factor like the feeling of awe. Irving King has given a good psychological statement of the matter. "It will be noted that we have not referred to the common notion that religion develops primarily from the awe inspired by the unusual, from which the idea of the supernatural is first formed. We have held that a religious act of any kind is primarily a practical act designed for the mediation of an end that has become remote or difficult, and that the genuine religious character develops most fully as the act is fixed in the customs of a social group and becomes an important avenue for the expression of the corporate life of the group. In such a way, it seems to me, the notion of sacredness arose, and with it respect, awe, and reverence in the religious sense. The notion

SPIRITS

of the supernatural may well have originated in the way suggested at the head of this paragraph, but it is not a fundamental concept in the development of religion."[1]

It is the central life interests of a group that determine the run of attention and thereby the objects or spirits which chiefly concern the group. The explanation of the diversity and the similarity of these spirits among different races lies here. The question of the origin of religion, when taken in this psychological way, is not whether animism, totemism, shamanism, or any particular form is the original. The question of origins concerns rather the process by which social activities give rise to the group consciousness and group ceremonials. The particular type and character of the spirits which emerge within and symbolize the great interests of the group are determined by the environment and by the trend of the resulting customs and the attendant crises.

Does the savage make a distinction between an object and its spirit; for example, between a tree and the spirit of the tree? In the simplest and most immediate experience he probably makes no such distinction. At this level nothing is carefully analyzed or abstracted from the living stream of interest and action. Everything which catches the attention at all shares in the movement toward some end and is suffused with vitality and power. There is little mediation of remote ends, little regard for things as means. Means and ends are so closely identified that the

[1] Irving King, *The Differentiation of the Religious Consciousness*, p. 28.

securing of a weapon, such as a stone, is part of the activity of capturing the game; and capturing the animal becomes an incident in using it for food or other purposes. At this stage all objects are spirits and all spirits are objects. This is the pre-animism of Marett and the animism of Tylor. In the next stage the spirit is regarded as separable from the object. The basis of this dualism seems to be the usual and therefore less noticeable character of the object as contrasted with its exceptional phenomena. Thus the pigmy chief's knife had a spirit in it when it slipped and cut him, but not when it worked properly. The term Fetishism has been used by some writers to designate this way of regarding certain objects as temporary or permanent dwelling-places of spirits. There is, however, scarcely any uniformity or precision in the use of the term and it does not aid greatly in gaining clear conceptions. Attempts also have been made to distinguish stages in the further development of spiritism into idols and gods, but such terms have a vague and shifting content. The development of the dualism of the thing and spirit, of body and soul, of natural and supernatural, is gradual and uneven. It is impossible to mark off definite periods of human experience and assign specific notions of spirits to them. As Haddon says, "It is these imperceptible gradations which blur all the outlines of the rigid systematist and make an exclusive classification impossible." It is not, however, impossible to indicate with some certainty the general dialectic of the process. The dualism between object and spirit, as in the pigmy chief's knife, arises with a partial organization of ex-

SPIRITS

perience in the use of the knife. This organized, habitual activity constitutes the known, familiar thing, but there play around and through this core of the knife's reality many occasional, unorganized experiences. As this differentiation is more clearly marked, the distance widens between the material object and the spirit. But this separation never becomes complete, the object remains more or less animated and the spirit continues to be to some extent corporeal and spatial. In the case of the most important spirits of a people, such as the maize-spirit of the American Indians and the animal-spirits of the Hebrews, the distinction between the material substance and the spirit which it contains or symbolizes rests upon a long and complex social history. The growth and objectification of the god goes hand in hand with the social experiences and achievements of the nation. The life of the tribe is registered in its sacred object. When the tribe attains some social history, preserved in oral traditions and various monuments, then the god is credited with long life in the past. The sense of the future and of power to plan for it is expressed in the god's knowledge and control of the future. The conquests of other tribes are the conquests of the god, and the unification of the tribes makes the god of the dominant tribe the aspirant to exclusive recognition. All the other gods have been defeated; there is but one god. As the moral experiences of the people grow, the moral character of the tribal spirit improves; or, more accurately, as the moral sense of the controlling, dominant social forces improves, the spirit or god gradually takes on an exalted character. But even at a relatively late stage the presence of the god in his people or in his habitats is most in evidence at times of crises. In general it may be said that the ideality and the differentiation of the spirit or god reflects the degree of social development attained. In psychological terms, it represents the result of generalization and abstraction.

The expression of the social consciousness in the spirits of the group is due to the feeling of society for its tasks and ideals. When several persons work at a common task, they develop more or less rhythm and harmonious adjustment to each other. The rhythmical labor songs of harvesters from antiquity to the present time are expressions of this spirit of the group and are of the nature of genuine ceremonials. But this spirit of the company, — we call it the spirit of the army, the spirit of the party, college spirit, class spirit, — this is usually objectified in some emblem, flag, crest, or hero. Every one knows how much greater is the sense of fellowship and reality, when the symbol is set up or carried in procession. Psychologically, this is the same experience which in an unconscious and literal way registered the clan feeling in the totem, the ancestral hero, or other chosen divinity. The spirit of comradeship, of communal endeavor, fear, hope, reverence, and trust expresses itself through many forms and many degrees of objectification.

It is obvious that when religion is conceived in terms of social activities and the attendant mental reactions, it must directly affect the notion of worship. The fallacy of the intellectualistic view of religion is manifest in the ascription of highly personified and

SPIRITS

idealized deities to minds which are exceedingly limited in their generalizations and intensely concrete and immediate in their interests. The contrast is forcible and even humorous in the interpretations of Lang and Marett with reference to *Daramulun*, one of the deities of the Australians. Lang holds it to be a "high god" whose worship is pure, ethical religion, at a later stage corrupted into magic. Marett, on the other hand, is sure that the prototype of this divinity is nothing more nor less than the well-known material and inanimate object, the bull-roarer. "Its thunderous booming must have been eminently awe-inspiring to the first inventors, or rather discoverers, of the instrument, and would not unnaturally provoke the 'animistic' attribution of life and power to aid." [1]

The practices connected with *Daramulun* appear very different to one who regards that being as an ethical, spiritual deity, and to one who finds him to be the material, noise-making bull-roarer. It is almost as though the Firecracker of the American Fourth of July were regarded in such different ways.

The general conception of worship in primitive religion is to be derived from the nature of the ceremonial or cultus. Taken thus, worship may be further understood when considered in terms of two factors of especial importance in the later development of religion, — sacrifice and prayer. What, then, is their meaning and function?

[1] R. R. Marett, "Pre-animistic Religion," *Folk-Lore*, 1900, p. 173.

CHAPTER VII

SACRIFICE

THOSE writers, like Jevons, who deal with the earliest forms of sacrifice in terms of "worship" attribute too ideal a character to the act. Worship suggests an attitude of reverence and trust toward a "high God," which is quite impossible in the primitive stages of human experience. In fact, a closer acquaintance with the worship of very civilized, modern peoples startles one with the impression of materialistic and utilitarian factors only slightly disguised and softened here and there by a refinement of indirection. It is, of course, possible to misinterpret later forms by approaching them from simpler and cruder types, but doubtless the more common error has been to misjudge the rudimentary stages by viewing them through the presuppositions of more complex and intellectualistic developments. A safeguard against both extremes is to take the subject of sacrifice in terms of the acts involved, recognizing that the meaning attached to these acts is not to be found, for the great masses of mankind, so much in any doctrines expressed as in the results effected.

This undertaking is greatly simplified when it is recognized that the most basic and characteristic act in the ritual of sacrifice is that of eating food. This ritual in its main structure is just the customary manner in which the group partakes of certain kinds

SACRIFICE

of food. Robertson Smith shows that among the Semites the materials of sacrifice are the substances which form the ordinary staple of human food.[1] In the ceremonial of sacrifice the eating is done by living men and by all the members of the group, and the pangs of real hunger are thereby assuaged. To a far later day than is usually recognized the governing impulse in these rites is the desire for food, though this may become refined into the desire for a particular kind of food more potent or spiritual than others. Among the Hebrews every slaughter of animals for food was sacrifice and every meal at which meat was eaten was a sacrificial feast. The food process, as the central feature of sacrifice, is obscured by the elaboration of preparatory rites, by emphasis upon magical and incidental elements, and by strange substitutes for the act of eating which are of the general nature of sympathetic magic. As will be shown, the eating of the sacred object is important because it identifies the eater and the thing eaten. But this identification is effected also by various other forms of contact, such as rubbing the sacred substance into wounds or anointing the body with it. To the end, however, sacrifice retains the character of an act which seems to benefit men in substantial ways. It is a means of relieving hunger and of gaining power; it averts danger from mysterious forces, by removing taboos, or by establishing counter taboos; it is the means of safe intercourse with strangers, with the dead, with the opposite sex; it is the means of returning safely to one's people and to one's normal functions after a journey,

[1] W. R. Smith, *Religion of the Semites*, p. 218.

a battle, a period of mourning, or other unusual experience.

The fundamental importance of the food process in sacrifice may be stated by saying that the sacred objects themselves were sacrificed at first instead of having sacrifices made to them. There is considerable evidence, for example, that in totemism the totems were originally staple articles of food, both plants and animals. Spencer and Gillen hold this view with reference to the Australian tribes. The *Intichiuma* ceremonies were originally elaborate efforts to increase the food supply by increasing the totem. "The object of increasing the number of the totem is, in all cases, such as that of the Hakea or Irriakura or plum tree amongst plants, or the kangaroo, euro, lizard, snake, and so forth amongst animals, in which the totemic animal or plant is an article of food, that of increasing the food supply." "At some earlier time it would appear as if the members of a totem had the right to feed upon the totemic animal or plant as if this were indeed a functional necessity."[1]

They also refer to other accounts indicating that tribes derived their names from the animals and fish upon which they subsisted. There are some features of the ceremonies of these Australians which justify the suggestion that they are of the generic nature of sacrifice. The following, for example, has many points of agreement with the sacrificial feasts of other peoples:

"In the case of the kangaroo totem of Undiara, after the men have allowed the blood to pour out of

[1] Spencer and Gillen, *The Native Tribes of Central Australia*, pp. 207, 209.

SACRIFICE

their arms over the stone ledge, they descend, and after rubbing themselves all over with red ochre return to the main camp, which is always placed at some distance from the rock so as to prevent the women and children from being able to see anything of what is going on. All of the younger men then go out hunting kangaroo, which when caught they bring in to the old men who have stayed in camp. It is taken to the *Ungunja*, or men's camp, and there the old men of the totem eat a little and then anoint the bodies of those who took part in the ceremony with fat from the kangaroo, after which the meat is distributed to all the men assembled." [1]

The taboos against eating the totem probably arose when it became scarce or when the habit of regarding the totem as sacred developed the restriction of its use to occasional ceremonial functions. The growth of the tendency to reserve the totem for ceremonial feasts, and then to partake of it sparingly, accords with the well-known characteristic of habitual activities to develop to extremes, and even to interfere with their original effects. In this way the very awe and regard attached to an article of food because of its life-giving power might naturally enough tend to remove it from common use, when other food was at hand. This would explain the fact that often a clan will not eat its own totem, though other clans are free to eat it.

This conception of the totem as originally an article of food carries the act of sacrifice down to a deeper level of experience than is possible in a view like that of Jevons, where totemism is regarded as degenerate and disappearing when the totem is used for food. His

[1] Spencer and Gillen, *The Native Tribes of Central Australia*, pp. 204 f.

PSYCHOLOGY OF RELIGIOUS EXPERIENCE

position does not explain adequately the origin or the nature of totemism or the ceremonial acts connected with it. It is necessary for him to assume that when objects were regarded as sacred man sought to get into relation with them by contact and thus sometimes by ceremonial eating. A simpler and more psychological explanation is that since food was a most insistent and dominant need of man he would be particularly interested in whatever afforded food. On this account the plant or animal or fish which satisfied hunger would fix attention and become an object of intense interest. The mystery and uncertainty connected with the appearance of vegetation and with the ways of animals and fish would contribute to make the food object important. We have already seen that precisely this fixing of attention, heightening of emotion, and recurrent stimulation make things sacred or taboo. The savage, even at a low stage, may be regarded as able to ascribe his strength and high spirits to the object he has eaten. At least it is beyond question that he would recognize the food object as savory, filling, and pleasant. Immediate relief from hunger and pain would be the most powerful factor in fixing attention, creating awe, and eliciting affection with reference to the food object. It is truer then to say that the object was sacred because it was eaten with satisfaction than to say it was eaten because it was sacred and because man sought thus to worship it. Crawley identifies religion throughout with the basic biological impulses, and with reference to food he says: "The food-quest provides the earliest illustration of the way in which he (primitive man) lays hold

SACRIFICE

on life. It is the most engrossing fact of primitive existence. It forms the staple of conversation and takes precedence of every interest. Man's daily bread thus becomes the object of innumerable acts of caution and superstition." [1]

What has been said needs to be supplemented by emphasis upon the social nature of the food process in order to bring out its full significance. Evidence is abundant that the getting and use of food among savages is a social affair. Game may be killed only at certain times prescribed by the tribe and signalized by ceremonies. The new crops are taboo until their use has been made possible and safe by action of the group. The distribution of game taken by the hunter, even to the designation of the proper recipients of various parts of the carcass, is prescribed by custom. Howitt gives an extended account of the rules for the disposal of game and fish among the Kurnai tribe of South-east Australia. A native bear is divided in the following manner: Self, left ribs; father, right hind leg; mother, left hind leg; elder brother, right fore-arm; younger brother, left fore-arm. The elder sister gets the backbone, and the younger the liver. The right ribs are given to the father's brother, a piece of the flank to the hunter's mother's brother, and the head goes to the young men's camp.[2]

These various social restrictions illustrate the importance of the food object. It belongs to the whole group and is not privately appropriated. This aids in developing the sense of sacredness of the animal or

[1] Ernest Crawley, *The Tree of Life*, p. 217.
[2] A. W. Howitt, *Native Tribes of South-east Australia*, p. 759.

cereal. It comes therefore to be treated with caution, so that before eating it more or less hesitancy, preparation, and ceremony are necessary. Hence arise the ceremonials of the sacrificial feast.

In the simplest and most typical form of sacrifice, attention centres in the sacrificial object and in its appropriation by the participants. The animal or plant is itself the divinity and the act of sacrifice completes itself in the direct appropriation of the food. The sacrificial feast is indeed a commensal meal, as Robertson Smith shows, but the god is not present as a guest or as one of the participants. It is the god itself which is sacrificed and it is not necessary to suppose that reference to any third factor is involved. The circuit is completed when the food is eaten. Great care is taken to devour or otherwise dispose of every particle of the sacred object, so that its magic power may not pass beyond those to whom it properly belongs. A particle of the devoted food would be dangerous on other occasions or might be used for evil purposes by enemies. The primitive manner of sacrificing camels among the Arabs is best understood when it is regarded as the appropriation of the divinity, every particle of which must be taken by the group itself. "In the oldest known form of Arabian sacrifice, as described by Nilus, the camel chosen as the victim is bound upon a rude altar of stones piled together, and when the leader of the band has thrice led the worshipers round the altar in a solemn procession accompanied with chants he inflicts the first wound, while the last words of the hymn are still upon the lips of the congregation, and in all haste

SACRIFICE

drinks of the blood that gushes forth. Forthwith the whole company fall on the victim with their swords, hacking off pieces of the quivering flesh and devouring them raw with such wild haste that in the short interval between the rise of the day star which marked the hour for the service to begin and the disappearance of its rays before the rising sun the entire camel, body and bones, skin, blood, and entrails, is wholly devoured." [1]

The purpose of the feast, so far as it is appropriate to use the term purpose for a customary, vaguely conscious act, is to gain the magic power of the deity thus devoured. In other words the group receives in this way the sacredness or taboo that belongs to the food object. This sanctity of a people is broken, destroyed, or weakened by death, war, sickness, famine; and it is threatened by any unusual, strange phenomena such as an eclipse or earthquake. These are the natural occasions for sacrifice. It is also true that sacrifice often occurs periodically, as at the approach of the seasons, when there is no adverse or threatening circumstance involved except that of the newness itself. Indeed the sacrificial feast frequently has a positively joyous character, due to the increased sense of power thus obtained. "So the Homeric hymns attribute inspiration to food and tell us how men when feasting feel ageless and immortal." This participation in the qualities of objects eaten is everywhere in evidence. Brave and crafty enemies are devoured to secure their courage and intelligence. Cannibal sacrificial feasts are therefore not to be regarded as mere exhibitions of

[1] W. R. Smith, *Religion of the Semites*, p. 338.

PSYCHOLOGY OF RELIGIOUS EXPERIENCE

depravity nor as acts designed to placate demoniacal gods. The interest is more direct and immediate. It centres in taking over the mysteriously powerful enemy into the life of the group. Under the same urgent practical desire the youth at initiation is fed upon ashes of the organs of powerful enemies. The liver gives valor, the ears intelligence, the skin of the forehead perseverance.[1] The same principle is often operative in infanticide. "In the Luritcha tribe young children are sometimes killed and eaten, and it is not an infrequent custom when a child is in weak health to kill a younger and healthier one and then feed the weakling on its flesh, the idea being that this will give to the weak child the strength of the stronger one." [2]

Frazer has gathered a profusion of examples of the eating of human beings, cereals, and animals to gain their qualities. The North American Indians eat venison to gain swiftness and sagacity, and avoid the flesh of clumsy bear, tame cattle, and heavy swine, lest they should become weakened by them. The Indians of South America eat birds, monkeys, deer, and fish, rather than the tapir and peccary, because of the greater agility of the former. African tribes eat the flesh and drink the blood of lions and tigers to make them brave in battle. Health and old age may be attained by those who are sick by eating the bone of a very old animal. The bile of tigers and bears gives courage; the heart of a wolf or lion makes one bold; the tongues of birds help a child to learn to

[1] J. G. Frazer, *Golden Bough*, vol. ii, p. 357.
[2] Spencer and Gillen, *Native Tribes of Central Australia*, p. 475.

SACRIFICE

speak. One of the most common customs is the drinking of blood to absorb the qualities of men and animals.

Other means than eating these substances are also used to gain their power. Any method of contact is effective. Sometimes wounds are made in the body of the "worshiper" and the powdered ashes of the magical substance are rubbed in. The practice of scarification may thus be a means of inoculation. In other instances the body is smeared or anointed with blood, fat, excrements, or ashes of the sacred object. In all such cases the principle of sympathetic magic is operative, that is, he who eats or otherwise is in contact with the sacred thing partakes of its nature.

There is still another form in which this principle of identification through contact is basal, but one which is easily mistaken for something quite different. The widely prevalent custom of leaving articles at sacred places illustrates it. Offerings of hair, garments, valuables of various kinds are laid on the altar, placed upon or before an image of a god, thrown into sacred wells or hung upon trees. On the same principle the devotee may drop some of his own blood or shed his tears upon the sacred object. In their simplest, primitive form these are not "gifts," nor are they made over "to" a deity. They are rather just the means of identifying one with the sacred object. This identification is effected by leaving a part of one's self in contact with the divinity as well as by taking a part of the sacred thing to eat or to carry about on the person. If a Kafir's sleeping mat touches a woman, it is as though she had touched him. In either case she pollutes him. Clothing put upon a corpse makes the owner languish away as his clothing moulders in the grave. Beneficial relations are established in the same way. "The practice of throwing pins into wells, of tying rags on bushes and trees, of driving nails into trees and stocks, of throwing stones and sticks on cairns, and the analogous practices throughout the world, suggest that they are to be interpreted as acts of ceremonial union with the spirit identified with well, tree, stock, or cairn." [1] Robertson Smith has shown that among the Semites also such acts are not gifts but means of binding together man and the sacred object. He further insists that this unification through contact is the central fact in "sacrifice," and that sacrifice does not therefore primarily involve the death or pain of the victim, nor shedding of blood. The instructiveness of the customs of offering hair, garments, and such objects is that they make transparent the act of "sacrifice" and disclose its fundamental character, namely, the possession of an object's potency by contact with it. Killing a victim is originally only an incident in the process of appropriating its magical properties. By placing one's hair upon the sacred object the same result is attained as by eating the god. In such ceremonies the simple contact experience is not obscured or confused by the death of the victim or by any penal satisfaction to the deity. These things were at first only incidental to the use of animals. When it is seen that the essence of sacrifice is contact, then the material and the manner of the contact become relatively unimportant, and the

[1] A. C. Haddon, *Magic and Fetishism*, p. 8.

SACRIFICE

student is prepared to find the widest variation and yet an underlying unity in the ceremonials of all peoples. Sacrifice may then be regarded as a universal custom. The use of blood is just one form of it. Anything else connected with the person may become the bond. Various offerings may accomplish the purpose. The important fact is that "the physical link which they establish between the divine and the human parties in the rite binds the god to the man as well as the man to the god."[1]

The occasions on which sacrifices are offered make it clear that sacrifice is a ceremony in which union with the powerful sacred object is effected in order to strengthen the group against calamity or to renew bonds which have been broken by tabooed conduct. We have seen that all novel, unusual activities are taboo, such as journeying into an unknown country or meeting enemies or strangers. But such things are often necessary, and therefore a set of customs arise by which taboos may be overcome. The effect of these customs is to possess one's self of more powerful qualities than are present in the thing to be dealt with. Therefore the savage makes himself immune, as it were, from approaching dangers by filling himself with the magic of his totem or other divinity. Or, after he has been surcharged with the qualities of tabooed objects, as in battle, he renews his alliance with his familiar deities by various ceremonies. Illustrations of these two types of sacrifice are plentiful. To the first belong the feasts which warriors hold before going to battle. Here belong the ceremonials

[1] W. R. Smith, *Religion of the Semites*, p. 337.

PSYCHOLOGY OF RELIGIOUS EXPERIENCE

preparatory to building houses, planting crops, undertaking journeys. In principle, the initiation of youth is of this kind. It involves bringing an outsider into the group and inoculating him with its life, without breaking the sanctity of the group itself. The union of the sexes in marriage is likewise dangerous and requires caution. Any event which promises strange developments, such as an eclipse or a sudden, violent storm, requires sacrifices — not primarily to placate angry gods so much as to get into relation with the powerful agencies.

The second class of occasions for sacrifice are still more important in the history of religion. They are the occasions when taboos have actually been broken and the evil consequences have to be dealt with; or when natural taboos have to be overcome. As instances of this may be cited the ceremonies when women return to the camp after childbirth, when warriors and travelers return home, when the sick regain health, and when mourners return from the burial of the dead. These are known as rites of purification, but the purifying process is usually interpreted with too modern a meaning. One of the commonest methods of overcoming taboo is by the use of water. This is not because water cleanses in a hygienic sense, but because it is full of magic power. It is sacred. Its ways are full of mystery. It comes and goes in the strangest manner. As rain, it transforms the face of the earth. As drink it refreshes man and beast. It is ever moving in the stream or lake and is by every token a wonderful divinity. By sprinkling, bathing, drinking, or otherwise coming into contact with it one

SACRIFICE

renews a powerful alliance. Water is seemingly used just as blood is. The latter is smeared over the body or it is drunk. Fat and oil are often employed in the same way. In India and Africa, where the cow is sacred, the floors, walls of houses, beds, and food baskets are cleansed with cow dung. It is the mysterious sanctity of the object which makes it important in purification, and this quality is transferred to any person or thing by contact. Fire ceremonies may be interpreted in the same way. Fire is itself sacred and therefore imparts sacredness to all it touches. Smoke and incense are great cleansers, not so much because they remove the taboo as that they establish a more powerful one. In many cases the taboo is treated as a physical thing to be got rid of by literally putting it aside. But it is not always possible to decide whether the contact takes off uncleanness or simply brings in greater magic. For example, "if a man ate food with tabooed hands, he avoided dangerous results by putting the foot of a chief on his stomach." In such a case, does something pass out of the man to the chief, or does the magic of the chief flow into the man? Robertson Smith puts the matter clearly thus: "In the most primitive form of the sacrificial idea the blood of the sacrifice is not employed to wash away an impurity, but to convey to the worshiper a particle of holy life. The conception of piacular media as purificatory, however, involves the notion that the holy medium not only adds something to the worshiper's life and refreshes its sanctity, but expels something from him that is impure. The two views are obviously not inconsistent, if we conceive impurity as the wrong kind of life, which is dispossessed by inoculation with the right kind."[1]

When, then, sacrifice is examined in order to answer the question, What is done? rather than What is believed? it becomes clear that it must be said, a contact is established with a sacred object in order to become possessed of its sanctity. Sacredness and sanctity here mean mysterious power, for everything which manifests mysterious activity is sacred to the savage mind. Sacrifice is chiefly accomplished by eating the sacred thing because that is the surest way of securing its qualities. But sacrifice may also be effected by a variety of methods of contact, as has been shown. With the development of social customs and organization the mysterious forces come to be identified with certain objects or persons preëminently, and these make the choicest sacrifices, because they are most completely filled with magic power. Such objects are periodically distributed to the people to sanctify and strengthen them. In many instances the ceremonies of sacrifice are preceded by fasting, so that counter influences may not hinder the attainment of the full force of the sacrament, and also, doubtless, in primitive times in order to enable one to appropriate the largest possible amount. In this view every stage of the history of sacrifice continues the original act of participating in the divine life. The victim is not sacrificed when it is slain but rather when it is eaten. The killing is incidental and preparatory. The body and the blood are for the worshipers — not for the god. It is the god which has been slain in order

[1] W. R. Smith, *Religion of the Semites*, p. 427.

that his followers may share his life. The idea of the victim being "offered" to the god is a late development. Even the interpretation of Robertson Smith that the offering is shared by the worshipers with the god is not the original significance. He himself shows that the victim is the most sacred thing in the sacrificial ceremony. The altar does not consecrate the sacrifice, but the animal offered makes the altar holy. When the altar evolves into the altar-idol, it is still the sacrifice which makes the idol sacred. The victim is the source of holiness and there is nothing more holy "to" which it is offered. It is not difficult to understand the psychological processes conducive to the discrimination and objectification of individuality — as in barter and in covenants — by which at a later time the relations were reversed and the god abstracted from the ceremony and set over against it, but this appears to have been an incident in the total history of sacrifice. "It is the sacred blood that makes the stone holy and a habitation of divine life ... and the place where blood has once been shed is the fittest place to shed it again." [1]

It is now possible to deal with the conception of sacrifice as an atonement for sin. The idea of sin as the individual or national transgression of moral law is extremely modern. In primitive times there was no such individual act and no such moral law. The only misconduct was a breach of custom, the violation of taboo. The atonement necessary was therefore something which would counteract the evil influence and offset the effects of disintegrating, poisonous forces by

[1] W. R. Smith, *Religion of the Semites*, p. 436.

beneficent, recreative powers. "At this earliest stage the atoning force of sacrifice is purely physical, and consists in the redintegration of the congenital bond of kinship, on which the good understanding between the god and his worshippers ultimately rests." The piacular sacrifices of the Hebrews seem to perpetuate just this fundamental function. They retain in later Judaism a prominent place because they are survivals of earlier nomadic conditions of life and consequently have the greater sanctity which goes with older customs. They are used, not as inventions to express a new idea of sin and to effect a corresponding atonement; but in an agricultural period they survive as ceremonies which are particularly effective because they are ancient. The seemingly exceptional character of the piacular sacrifices is due to their great antiquity rather than to their novelty, and they preserve their character as the most powerful means of overcoming taboos rather than appearing as agencies for the removal of a new sense of sin.

The continuity of sacrificial ceremonials is emphasized by this fact. Heretofore by identifying sacrifice with atonement for the sense of sin alleged to be peculiar to the Hebrews, it has been easy to deny that the ceremonies of various primitive peoples are sacrificial in character. But when it is seen that sacrifice is ceremonial contact with sacred objects, then the act is presented in a perspective sufficient to include the rites of the American Indian, the Australian, and the African as well as those of the Asiatic, Indian, and European. All have purificatory rites for the removal of taboos and for the prevention of pollution. These

SACRIFICE

ceremonies agree also in their habitual, customary, non-rational nature. The ritual of purification is not hygienic. The ritual distinction between clean and unclean things coincides by accident, if at all, with the contrast between the wholesome and the unwholesome. Sometimes the ritual of purification interferes with the welfare of the group. Such was the case of the North American Indian tribe which was extirpated because it needed a month to wipe off the stain of a single conflict, while their enemies needed only a week for that purpose and therefore had the advantage of three weeks' start in preparing for the next attack.[1]

The real value of the sacrifice lay in its power of consolidating the social life of the group. The suggestive, mimetic drama developed an intense emotional state, the central element of which was the sense of identity in the participants with one another, with their ancestors, and with the mysterious beings which were eaten in the feast or otherwise secured. The actual physical strength derived from the flesh and blood of the victim was multiplied by the psychical impression which it conveyed. Thus the warriors gained courage for battle, the fear-ridden found peace. If the suggestion of having eaten forbidden food is powerful enough to cause sickness and death, then the participation in divine food which is believed to possess the highest possible magical potency should induce hope and energetic effort.

[1] L. R. Farnell, *The Evolution of Religion*, p. 94.

CHAPTER VIII

PRAYER

PRAYER occupies a secondary and relatively subordinate place in primitive religion. This is indicated superficially by the fact that treatises such as Tylor's "Primitive Culture," Smith's "Religion of the Semites," Jevons' "Introduction to the History of Religion" scarcely contain the term prayer and give almost no consideration to it. Yet prayer, if the word is used broadly, is almost as universal as sacrifice in primitive religion and persists in later faiths in refined and ideal forms when sacrifice has ceased.

Prayer at first sight seems very obviously and inseparably bound up with ideas of spirits. It appears therefore to justify more than anything else the intellectual view of religion. Why, it may be said, should the savage pray, if he has no definite idea of a being or beings to whom he prays? Is there not here evidence that the act of prayer presupposes necessarily belief in supernatural beings? The approach to the subject of prayer lies through the phenomena of speech. But speech itself is for civilized man a product so highly wrought that it is difficult to estimate its early forms properly. In its beginnings language is a matter of gestures and of inarticulate cries and calls.[1] These expressions are older than words, which arose subsequently as aids to the earlier and more natural form

[1] E. B. Tylor, *Primitive Culture*, chap. v; *Anthropology*, chap. iv.

PRAYER

of communication. Gestures are more elemental and more universally understood than is any spoken language. How serviceable gestures are may be seen in such a list of signs as Howitt gives from the usage of the tribes of South-east Australia.[1] Articulate speech in modern times still depends to an appreciable degree for vividness and power upon facial expression and other bodily signs. It continues to be one element in a complex whole. In its simple form the process may be thought of in terms of nervous energy overflowing into various motor centres and thus producing muscular reactions. In this system of movements are those of the vocal organs, which under the inhalation and expulsion of air produce sounds, — the rudimentary vocalizations from which speech is gradually developed. The cry of pain and the grunt of satisfaction are the beginnings of the vocabulary and these are shared by man with the lower animals. They are thoroughly instinctive and relatively unconscious reactions which occur in response to stimuli of different kinds, often without reference to communication with other beings.

Articulate speech does not justify the assumption that the speaker has in mind any clear conception of the nature of the one addressed. The child certainly does not construct a notion of the personality of his parents before communicating with them. His prattle is quite submerged in his instinctive and imitative activities and proceeds in the vaguest way with reference even to his own wants and satisfactions. Language may reach high development with the child

[1] A. W. Howitt, *Native Tribes of South-east Australia*, p. 727.

PSYCHOLOGY OF RELIGIOUS EXPERIENCE

or savage without introspection or careful reflection. Exclamatory speech and indeed extended and elaborate utterance may occur under emotional stimulation or in habitual experiences without denoting any such depth of awareness or insight as is often attributed to them. It is therefore utterly fallacious to suppose that speech is always directed to definitely apprehended persons. Gestures and words are so wrought into complex motor reactions that they occur incipiently, at least, wherever there is vivid consciousness. They tend to become automatic in the same way as do other activities. Civilized man reacts quite automatically with vigorous speech upon many occasions when his words do not have any clearly conceived object. He talks to inanimate objects, to tools, machines, trees, and stones. Our tirades against chairs we stumble over are instructive illustrations of the tendency of intense emotional states to release torrents of words. It is therefore to be expected that speech will often be found to occur among primitive people as a kind of explosive accompaniment of emotion and as an attendant phase of common actions. These actions involve the whole motor zone and involve the speech centres as well as those of the eye and hand. The chatter of monkeys, the prattle of children, and the talkativeness of uncultivated men indicates how language is entwined with the total activity of the organism. The relatively numerous sound-words in every language are also suggestive of the imitative and immediate character of speech. Language only attains relative independence and becomes indicative of a high degree of intellection when considerable power of

PRAYER

abstraction is attained. Even written words remain for a long period incidental to picture-writing, just as articulate sounds are long secondary to gestures.

The social origin and the social significance of language is not disregarded in the foregoing. It is undoubtedly true that speech is interlocutory in form, and this form is due to its nature as social discourse. But it is quite another thing to insist that it therefore carries a constant and definite reference to other persons or selves in any such sophisticated way as would justify the conclusion that the speaker always has in mind some conception of the fact or the meaning of personality. The speech reaction may be regarded as elaborating itself below the threshold of consciousness of the self speaking or of the self addressed. The notes of distress, of warning, of solicitation among birds and other animals involve a social situation and imply a reference to others, but this is not sufficient ground for concluding that these creatures consciously address their kind or that their use of such communication depends upon recognizing personality in those influenced. In the same way the fact that human speech grows up in societies of human beings is not evidence that the members of such societies have any clear consciousness of their own nature. Speech, that is, some form of communication, is so constant and habitual an atmosphere for human beings that it is taken for granted without reflection. It is as far removed from conscious analysis as walking or breathing. The child acquires it literally before he knows it. And even if experience forces him later to take account of differences in the languages of different tribes, or of individuals in his own group, he is still far short of such psychological or metaphysical questions as those which relate to the concept of personality. Language grows up as social habit, under the stress of practical needs, and is carried on in a thoroughly objective way. The social origin and the naïve use of speech are not incompatible. It is therefore fallacious to infer that its social character is evidence of the presence of notions of ego and alter or of any idea of personality.

The use of personal pronouns is therefore to be estimated cautiously in this connection. They designate immediate concrete phases of experience rather than organized generalizations. The terms "I," "me," and "mine," even at advanced stages, have shifting, vague emotional contents. Professor James has shown how concrete and unsteady such conceptions are.[1] And yet these forms of expression are so much a part of language and answer so surely to vivid mental images that they are inevitable. The talk of children at their play is typical. "R., beginning when about three years of age, almost invariably talked aloud while he was playing alone — which, as he was a first child, was very often the case. Most commonly he would use no form of address but 'you,' and perhaps had no definite person in mind. To listen to him was like hearing one at the telephone, though occasionally he would give both sides of the conversation. At times again he would be calling upon some real name, Esyllt or Dorothy, or upon 'Piggy,' a fanciful person of his own invention. Every thought seemed

[1] William James, *Psychology*, chap. x; cf. C. H. Cooley, *Human Nature and the Social Order*, chap. v.

to be spoken out. If his mother called him, he would say, 'I've got to go in now.' Once when he slipped down on the floor he was heard to say, ' Did you tumble down?' 'No, *I* did.'"[1] The narrator of these observations is right in saying that such conversations are not merely occasional and temporary, but are characteristic and underlie all thinking. "It is true of adults as of children, that the mind lives in perpetual conversation." But such conversation does not imply any speculative or metaphysical notion of the self. The personal pronouns used are just those of "common speech and workaday usefulness" without ulterior reference or implication.

These observations suggest the point of view from which prayer is treated. No more than speech does prayer presuppose some theory concerning the nature of that to which it seems to be directed. Neither does it involve any doctrine of the nature of the self. In many cases it satisfies itself immediately as impulsive expression and at other times as a factor in establishing contact with sacred objects or in otherwise controlling them. The fact that the sacred objects are spoken to does not prove the presence of any definite notion of their spiritual nature. Many facts in primitive religion may be cited in support of this position.

The various forms of articulate speech in connection with religious activities are imbedded within the ceremonial rites and are subservient to them. In many instances, as in songs, chants, and prayer formulæ the words seem quite incidental accompaniments. They merely assert that certain actions are taking place.

[1] C. H. Cooley, *Human Nature and the Social Order*, p. 53.

Here is an example from a magical ceremony of a Kafir chief. He is warding off evil magic and turning the scales on his enemy. After washing himself, he takes a vessel and churns medicines in it, saying to himself all the time, "Now I am overcoming my enemy: I have overcome him, in fact: he is here in my vessel: he is vanquished: I am treading on him: I am conquering him just now: in fact, he is killed already by my magic: I can see this by the churning of my vessel."[1] Every one occasionally has analogous experiences of accompanying the deed with the word. For example, the boating party sings, "Merrily we roll along o'er the dark blue sea." Harvest festivals with the songs of the reapers, warriors with their chants, athletes with their slogans asserting prowess and strength illustrate the principle. Marett expressly recognizes this feature in many prayer formulæ. He says: "Such a verbal accompaniment will either be purely expletive, or it may be what I call 'descriptive,' as when a child making a picture of a man says aloud to himself, 'I am making a man.'"

This exclamatory or descriptive character of simple prayer formulæ is confirmed by Rivers' account of the Toda prayers. He summarizes the words of the dairy ritual thus: "May it be well with the buffaloes, may they not suffer from disease or die, may they be kept from poisonous animals and from wild beasts and from injury by flood or fire, may there be water and grass in plenty."[2] Rivers' comment on these prayers is that there is no evidence that they contain any sup-

[1] Dudley Kidd, *The Essential Kafir*, p. 308.
[2] W. H. R. Rivers, "Toda Prayer," *Folk-Lore*, 1904, pp. 168, 178.

PRAYER

plication. "The gods are not directly invoked: the name of no god is ever mentioned in vocative form, and in some prayers there may be barely mention of a god at all." He shows that these formulæ are used in exactly the same way in the case of a god as in the case of a buffalo, a place, a dairy vessel, or other even meaner object. This is precisely what would be expected upon the view we have been considering, for it shows that the "god" is the same as the sacred object, — buffalo, dairy, dairy vessel, or whatever it may be. The ceremonials express the natural desire that it may be well with these most important objects and that they may continue their beneficent influence. It is as possible to have prayer which is not prayer "to" some person or thing, as to have sacrifice which is not sacrifice "to" some person or thing.[1]

This conception of speech as an accompanying expression is well illustrated in the chants and songs of the ceremonials. Often the words used are quite meaningless in themselves. But perhaps the non-rational use of the words in such rhythmical sounds reveals most clearly the relation of such expressions to the main activity. Kidd says of the Kafirs, "They have endless chants. As the Machilla boys carry a traveler they keep up a sing-song chant all day. Natives sing as they row their canoes, and chant as they run with a load: yet all the time their words are practically devoid of meaning."[2] He reports the following song

---

[1] In the article referred to, Rivers is puzzled to account for the lack of the definite reference of prayer "to" the gods, but upon the above mentioned principles that difficulty disappears.

[2] Dudley Kidd, *The Essential Kafir*, pp. 333 f.

PSYCHOLOGY OF RELIGIOUS EXPERIENCE

which a missionary heard some women chanting as they walked off to hunt for a lost cow: —

> We say, let her come, let her come, we are calling her:
> Our cow, let her come, we are calling her:
> Let her come to me, then let her come:
> Our cow, let her come, we are calling her.

Spencer and Gillen give many chants used by the Australians in their ceremonies. During one of the initiation performances, while the performer was being decorated with an elaborate head-dress, "the men sitting around sang of the hair-knot of Kukaitcha, the latter being a celebrated man of the Alcheringa associated with the plum tree totem, the top-knot having reference to the manner in which the hair is worn previous to the boy's passing through the ceremony of circumcision. Time after time some such simple refrain was repeated while the down was fixed on to the performer's head-dress and body." [1] Of the same character apparently are the songs of the North American Indians. Their mystery songs are said to have originated in times of need, "when healing plants were gathered and when the medicine was administered: when a man set his traps or hunted game: when he desired to look into the future or sought supernatural guidance or deliverance from impending danger."[2]

That the prayer or kindred expressions, such as chant or song, is not something primary and independent is seen in the fact that prayer seldom, if ever,

---

[1] Spencer and Gillen, *Native Tribes of Central Australia*, p. 290.

[2] Alice Fletcher, *Indian Story and Song from North America*, pp. 27, 114.

PRAYER

occurs alone. It is always part of some ceremony or, at least, accompanies an objective act of some kind. Even in the most rationalized and ethicized religions, the bodily attitude of kneeling or bowing, that is, the action, is maintained with scrupulous care. The same words said in other attitudes are felt to be inefficient and may even be regarded as impious. The improper use of prayer is regarded as dangerous. It is likely to recoil disastrously upon the offender. The action thus remains in control, and the prayers are contributing elements to the larger, more objective ceremonial or practical element.

But the prayer does not remain a mere accompaniment. It has power and does work. It exerts magical influence. It "forms an integral part of the rite since it helps the action out." The magical power of words is seen in the charming of a bone, stick, or spear by "singing" it. It is thus supposed to be endowed with magical, poisonous properties. Any native who believes himself to have been struck with a charmed spear will be almost sure to die.[1] The power of words is felt to be mysteriously projected through space. Thus in West Africa the women at home help their husbands on the distant battlefield by singing as they dance: "Our husbands have gone to Ashantee land: may they sweep their enemies off the face of the earth." In the Kei islands the women wave fans and say, "O golden fans, let our bullets hit, and those of the enemy miss." Marett observes in reference to this instance that we must not make too much of such a change from impersonal mention to personal address. It

[1] Spencer and Gillen, *Native Tribes of Central Australia*, p. 537.

implies no more than a slight increase in vividness of idea.

Yet he goes on to argue that prayer proper involves the process of personification. The impersonal form he designates a "spell." But it is not difficult to show that the element of compulsion, of magical control, persists long after the sacred object seems to be quite definitely personified and even idealized. This may be shown by the use made of the name. The name of a thing is regarded as a part of the thing itself. Accordingly the name is a kind of handle by which the object may be controlled and compulsion exercised.

This compulsion appears in all its crudeness in the abuse visited upon idols and fetishes when they do not grant what is desired. Tylor recounts stories of worshipers in China who address a faithless idol thus: "'How now, you dog of a spirit, we have given you an abode in a splendid temple, we gild you and feed you and fumigate you with incense, and yet you are so ungrateful that you won't listen to our prayers.' So they drag him in the dirt, and then if they get what they want they clean him and set him up again with apologies and promises of a new coat of gilding."[1]

The use of blessings and curses throws light upon the nature of prayer in its compelling character. Westermarck cites many instances which are in point. "A poor man is able not only to punish the uncharitable by means of his curses, but to reward the generous giver by means of his blessings." "Among the early Christians those who brought gifts for the poor were specially remembered in the prayers of the

[1] E. B. Tylor, *Primitive Culture*, p. ii, 170.

PRAYER

church," the implication being that these prayers operated as blessings of a definitely magical sort. The words of a holy man, a magician or priest, are considered more efficacious than those of ordinary mortals, although certain mystic formulæ or spells are effective, whoever uses them. The literal physical influence of the blessings and curses can scarcely be overestimated. "The curse of Moses was said to lie on mount Ebal, ready to descend with punishments whenever there was occasion for it. The Arabs, when being cursed, sometimes lay themselves down on the ground so that the curse, instead of hitting them, may fly over their bodies. According to Teutonic notions, curses alight, settle, cling, they take flight, and turn home like birds to their nests." [1]

When words come to be written they still retain their magical character. The written prayer has the form of address to a deity, but it is employed at least by the vast mass of the people not as the best expression of their desires in an effort to reach the judgment or will of a deity, but as a powerful magical device for necessitating him to produce the required results. The prayer wheel is one of the commonest contrivances of this kind. The prayers, written on parchment or paper, are placed inside a cylinder, by the rotation of which the sentences are repeated. A large part of the Buddhist prayers consist of this mechanical use of the magical formulæ. The Jewish Pharisees in the time of Jesus apparently used quotations from the Law in a similar way, and the rosary of Christendom is

[1] E. Westermarck, *The Origin and Development of Moral Ideas*, pp. 57, 562.

of the same nature. Tylor regards these mechanical formulæ as stiffened reproductions of prayers which were at first "utterances as free and flexible as requests to a living patriarch or chief." But while it is doubtless true that writing may have aided in petrifying the verbal forms, yet it is a mistake to regard the earlier stages of religion as possessing more freedom and spontaneity than later ones. In any case the earlier prayers were in reality charms operating magically, and lacking for the most part the elements of conversation between persons in the way it is usually interpreted. A further evidence that the efficacy of prayer is felt to emanate from the form as much or more than from the content is seen in the use of ancient forms of speech. The older usages are generally held to be more sacred, and accordingly it is quite generally true that terms other than those of common use are employed in all the ritual, including prayer. The "Thee" and "Thou" and the ending "eth," for example, occur in the language of prayer in present day Christianity more than in ordinary speech.

Two things, then, seem clear with reference to primitive prayer. It is one factor in the larger ceremonial activity, and it shares the magical character of the ceremonies. In more advanced religions prayer still occupies a relatively secondary and dependent place, that is, it does not occur to any great extent as the expression of direct, personal need. Neither does it become highly spiritualized. Farnell, in a most suggestive and comprehensive sketch of the evolution of prayer, states that he has "not been able to find any example of a savage prayer for moral or spiritual

PRAYER

blessings."[1] Even among the cultivated Greeks the public prayers clung to utilitarian levels. The Athenian state prayed "for the health and safety of the people of the Athenians, their wives and children and all in the country," and the formula might include a prayer for the prosperity of their allies, such as Milesians or Plateans. But we have no indications that the blessings prayed for included others besides the material ones. Private prayer among the Greeks did indeed include higher interests. Especially was this true of the philosophers, Socrates and Plato, but in the popular mind the more immediate desires ruled the religious utterances. In a striking degree also the magical character of prayer persists side by side with more ideal elements. To the purest forms of prayer is often attributed the power of the magic spell. "A real spell can accompany a real prayer, and the text of the prayer itself becomes a most potent charm." In the Zarathustrian system, where many exalted prayers are found, the utterances are yet felt to possess peculiar power beyond the meaning conveyed or the attitude induced. They are used as charms, purifying and wonder-working. In the same way the creeds of Christendom and the paternoster are often employed not for their spiritual content but for some mysterious influence supposed to attach to their repetition. The most spiritual and spontaneous prayers usually open and close with references to the name of the deity, which interestingly perpetuates the form at least of superstitious practices. The basis of these superstitions lies in the animism and demonology of

[1] L. R. Farnell, *The Evolution of Religion*, pp. 183, 200.

primitive religion. As these give way before the scientific conception of nature, the magical element in prayer is gradually eliminated, and prayer becomes increasingly meditation and communion. It preserves more or less clearly the interlocutory, conversational form, which in a real sense is the inevitable nature of any thinking whatsoever.

CHAPTER IX

MYTHOLOGY

SCARCELY another subject has received more diverse treatment from the students of primitive religion than mythology. Wundt makes myth primary. "It includes science and religion: it regulates domestic custom and public life."[1] Robertson Smith, on the other hand, says "mythology was no essential part of ancient religion."[2] Others who attach importance to mythology give various explanations of its nature. Max Müller and D. G. Brinton make much of the theory that myth-building is due to the influence of language. The direction of the poetic personifying fancy of primitive man may be determined by a word rightly or wrongly understood. For example, among the Algonquin Indians the words meaning Dawn and Giant Rabbit being similar, occasioned the myth of light to degenerate into an animal fable.[3] Spencer, Frazer, and Tylor agree in the anthropomorphizing character of mythology: but they apply this principle in different ways. For Spencer, myths are distorted stories of remote ancestors. Frazer regards them as attempts to explain the phenomena of nature and the origin of man. "Mythology is primitive man's science and philosophy." Tylor classifies myths according as they are concerned with explanation, descrip-

[1] W. Wundt, *Ethics, Facts of the Moral Life*, p. 55.
[2] W. R. Smith, *Religion of the Semites*, p. 17.
[3] D. G. Brinton, *American Hero-Myths*, p. 27.

tion, legend, metaphor, or instruction. All of these treatments seem to lack unity and reality. They are more satisfying in citation of fact than in interpretation. They fail to relate mythology to other features of primitive life in an organic and adequate way. It remains detached and separate, whether it is made the antecedent of custom or something quite irrelevant. This attitude is expressed in the following characteristic passage: "Myths are not like psalms or hymns, lyrical expressions of religious emotion: they are not like creeds or dogmas, statements of things which must be believed: they are narratives. They are not history, they are tales told about gods and heroes, and they all have two characteristics: on the one hand they are to us obviously or demonstrably untrue and often irrational: on the other hand they were to their first audience so reasonable as to appear truths which were self-evident." [1] What is needed is some principle which will resolve this confusion and uncertainty and discover the vital relation between myths and other forms of primitive experience.

It is important first to determine how the word mythology shall be used. It is often employed as a general designation for all types of folk-lore, legends, traditions, tales, stories, and narratives. In order to avoid confusion mythology will be used here as equivalent to cult-lore as contrasted with the less sacred legendary tales. This is the distinction which Mr. Frank H. Cushing found among the Zuñi Indians.[2]

[1] Jevons, *Introduction to the History of Religion*, p. 250.
[2] *Eleventh Annual Report of American Bureau of Ethnology*, 1889–90, p. 369.

MYTHOLOGY

Their cult-lore is intimately bound up with their most sacred ceremonials and partakes of the ceremonial sanctity. The cult-lore consists of the dramatic stories of creation and other supreme interests. In their ritual observances the events of these stories are not merely represented but are actually reproduced. The actors do more than impersonate the gods. They *are* the gods, and they take on these characters as easily and completely as children transform themselves into their play people. Other stories, not thus vitally interwoven with the ceremonials, such as legends and mythic tales, may be classed as folk-lore. There are several distinguishing marks in the mythology proper, or cult-lore. All these marks are evidences of mysterious sacredness. The cult-myths are not spoken of or repeated on ordinary occasions. An Iowa Indian, when asked about the traditions of his tribe, said, "These are sacred things and I do not like to speak about them, as it is not our custom to do so except when we make a feast and collect the people and use the sacred pipe." [1] When the myth proper is told it is preceded by fasting and prayer. It is usually told in an archaic or other strange language. In some tribes this cult-lore is preserved by secret societies which are the recognized repositories of the sacred possessions of the group.[2] During the performance of the ceremonials these myths are in the minds of the actors, and it is part of the initiation of the novice to hear and to learn them with all due reverence and secrecy. It is the

[1] Dorsey in *Eleventh Annual Report of American Bureau of Ethnology*, 1889-90, p. 430.
[2] Webster, *Primitive Secret Societies*.

mythology which gives psychological unity to the ceremonial. It furnishes the imaginative setting through which the dramatic illusion and emotional rapport become complete. The true myth is highly socialized. In its vivid imagery the whole drama of the tribe is reënacted. The narratives, songs, and prayers in which it is embodied are surcharged with the full measure of sanctity which belongs to the motor, pictorial, and decorative factors of the sacred ritual. On this account the mythology is just as genuine and real a part of primitive religion as is anything else. It carries the social significance and ideal value which constitute the religious character of any activity.

The importance and significance of mythology may be further appreciated by considering its relation to the motor side of the ceremonials. It is not necessary to suppose that the motor activities of the rituals were prior in time to any ideational processes. Neither is it defensible to hold that the mental images of the myth occurred independently and previous to concrete reactions. Both belong in some degree to all human experience. Probably even the higher animals possess rudimentary images or recepts. The dog certainly distinguishes and recognizes objects, and displays appropriate reactions of a selective and determining kind. When remote from the scene of the chase, the characteristic signal or the sight of his master in hunting costume appears to be a sufficient cue to reinstate a series of reactions which it is reasonable to believe are associated with concrete images. In such instances the physical and the psychical are correlative phases

MYTHOLOGY

of the whole activity. With reference to human conduct of a selective sort this is certainly the case. We have seen that the ceremonials are reproductions of occupational and social activities and turn upon a variety of relations of the group to its environment. There are in these ceremonials trains of imagery organically involved with the acts of the ritual. Such images get expression and further definition in speech: in the word-symbols of the narratives. The real basis or cause of such images and such speech symbols is not the mimetic action of the dance. It rather springs up with the dance from the original occupation or social activity itself. The primary reactions sprang from impulse and desire. In establishing these reactions or habits, psychical as well as physical effects were produced: that is, images flowed through the mind while the body experienced the movements of the chase or of the struggle with the enemy. It is just because man has an elaborate and sensitive central nervous system to register his experience that he is capable of sensory and memory images. Man is a psycho-physical unity, every brain state involving some corresponding mental state. Ideo-motor activity is the type. The idea cannot be present without at least incipient action, and the action cannot occur, certainly not in situations where there is inhibition and obstruction, without ideation. The myths of the ceremonials are verbal expressions which disclose the ideational processes of the actors, just as their bodily movements in pantomime express the same meaning. Therefore, both the bodily movements and the verbal expressions of the ceremonial on the one side, and the corresponding mental imagery on the other, are to be understood as simultaneous and mutually determined effects of the underlying biological impulsive actions. We have seen that the kind of bodily ceremonial acts which a people develops depends upon the experiences they have in getting their food, fighting enemies, and maintaining living relations among themselves. Their language and literature are determined in the same way and by the same events, so that the acts and the words correspond. Both record the same story and, in fact, are the opposite pages of the same leaf of the book of man's life. It is not strange therefore that some authors, having noticed this correspondence of the myth and the ritual, have concluded that the ritual is the dramatization of the myth: or, on the other hand, that the myth is the explanation of the previously existing ritual. Doubtless they do interact and support each other, yet the ground of both is deeper and is to be found in those activities and strivings arising from the most elemental needs. Self-preservation, and, with less consciousness, race-preservation are the urgent impulses. Out of these spring the manifold social institutions and ideals, among which are the cults and cult-lore of primitive religion. We have seen how the food and the socialized sex interests mould the cults. It remains to show how they operate in the mythical lore.

The activities and concurrent interests of a group necessarily centre in its adjustment to the environment. The topography of the country inhabited, the fauna and the flora, and the human agents in the drama are of capital importance. The myths deal chiefly with these factors, and are narratives descrip-

MYTHOLOGY

tive of the typical experiences of the tribe attributed to ancestral beings. Some illustrations of this tendency will be given. Spencer and Gillen, in presenting the traditions of the Udnirringita or Witchetty Grub people of Australia, state that they occupy a tract of country about one hundred square miles in extent, through the centre of which runs a range of hills, often lofty and broken by gaps or gorges. There are about forty individuals in this totem group, the largest local group known to these authors. At various places throughout this district Udnirringita people originated in the Alcheringa (the far past) from their animal ancestors, and these Alcheringa people deposited Churinga (sacred stones or sticks) at various spots during the course of their wanderings. Just within the entrance to one of the gorges, "at a spot marked now by a large stone, close to which stands the trunk of an old and long since dead gum tree, the great Alcheringa leader of the Witchetties who was named Intwailiuka sprang into existence.... The stone has since been associated with the spirit not only of the dead Intwailiuka but also with one or two men who have been regarded as his successive reincarnations, the last of whom was the father of the present Alatunja (head man) of the group. A number of smaller stones close by represent men who sat there with him."[1] Near this place is the spot where Intwailiuka stood and threw numbers of eggs of the grub up the face of the rock just as is now done during the Intichiuma ceremony, the object of which is to increase the number of the totem animal. Thus these traditions relate the life of these ancestors

[1] Spencer and Gillen, *Native Tribes of Central Australia*, pp. 424 f.

who lived much as do the present members of the group. During the ceremonies which were originated by the Alcheringa men these traditions are rehearsed, and are not only a means of instructing novices but of heightening the emotional value for all participants. Howitt inclines to attach some historical significance to such traditions. "It seems to me," he says, "that these legends may be taken to be not merely mythical, but rather dim records of former events, such as the wanderings of the early Australians, dressed in a mythical garb and handed down from generation to generation, from father to son, in the sacred ceremonies." [1] Mr. Frank H. Cushing found the same indications of early historical conditions and events in the mythology of the Zuñi Indians. "That thus the Zuñis are actually descendants of two or more peoples, and the heirs of two cultures, at least, is well shown in their legends of ruins and of olden times, and especially in these myths of creation and migration as interpreted by archæologic and ethnographic research." [2] Mr. Cushing finds evidences of two parental stocks of the Zuñis. One ranged the plains north of the arid mountain region of Utah and Colorado. To this aboriginal stock was added the intrusive western branch. From the myths the latter appears to have been more vigorous, though fewer in numbers, and to have contributed to the united people their most distinguishing traits. For example, while other Pueblo Indians in their stories located their ancestral home in the north, the

[1] A. W. Howitt, *Native Tribes of South-East Australia*, p. 482.
[2] *Thirteenth Annual Report of the American Bureau of Ethnology*, p. 342.

MYTHOLOGY

Zuñis placed theirs in the west, whence they themselves had migrated. The west was to them "the place where the human family originated, where the ancestral gods chiefly dwell, and whither after death souls of men are supposed to return anon." Many other features of this elaborate mythology emphasize the way in which geography and the topography of the country become prominent in the ceremonials just as they are important factors in the life history of the group. Animals and plants are still more prominent in the tribal observances than are the cosmic or geographic factors. The interest in these living forms is more immediate. Attention is fixed upon them by the food process. Compared with objects of food all other things have an indirect and secondary interest. On this account totemism takes us into the inner sphere of primitive interests. The animal, plant, or fruit is so closely connected with the dominant biological functions that it has the most immediate hold upon the mind. The habits of animals, their mysterious powers, and experiences in hunting them form constant themes of conversation, song, and story.

Even the great prominence of human heroes in the traditions is derived from the fact that these individuals have been specially successful in exploits with animals, or in repulsing enemies who threatened the common welfare. The achievements which magnify a man in the eyes of his fellows are those which make him a mighty hunter or a man of valor. He is a means to an end. He is a protector, a provider, a leader: and his exploits eventuate in better food supply and in greater comfort for the group. Self-preservation is then the focal point of interest, and the objects and agencies involved with it share this interest. The psychical world of the savage is organized on this basis in concentric circles. He himself and his group are at the centre. The things which serve his needs fall into a well-defined psychical perspective. Many objects which the interest of civilized man defines and illuminates do not appear conspicuously in the universe of the less developed mind. It is through failure to recognize this fact that undue importance has often been assigned to natural objects like sun, moon, stars, mountains, in the sentiment of primitive folk.

At the same time it is true that the attention is increasingly riveted on the means. The leader in battle or in the hunt is found to be the determining factor. His success, his safety, is identified with that of the members of the tribe. He becomes individualized more than others, and the variety, power, and stimulus of his deeds are perhaps the most effective aids to reflection and to the development of consciousness of personality. This consciousness, however, remains vague, inchoate, and shifting, up to very modern times. Before the romanticizing, democratizing era of recent centuries the sense of personality had little stability and little organized content. It is yet relatively feeble for the masses. But the centres from which it has been developed have been the chiefs, kings, warriors, heroes, and saviours of the social group. Naturally, therefore, mythology has given an increasing place to divine men, while attention has been somewhat withdrawn from the divine animals and plants. Self-preservation gradually magnifies human

MYTHOLOGY

agencies as the means of life, and accordingly in the later periods where social organizations are closer and more powerful, mythology turns more and more about human characters. This transition in interest is shown in the traditions concerning the creation of men from animal ancestors, and also in the transformation of the deities from animal to anthropomorphic gods. The development of the bull-god among the Greeks shows the transition. "Dionysos Dendrites is easy to realize: he is but a step back from the familiar, canonical Vine-god. The Bull-god Dionysus is harder to accept because we have lost the primitive habit of thinking from which it sprang. The Greeks themselves suffered the like inconvenience. They rapidly advanced to so complete an anthropomorphism that in Periclean Athens the dogma of the Bull-incarnation was, we cannot doubt, a stumbling block, a faith as far as possible put out of sight." [1] Primitive ceremonials, with their twofold aspect of cult and tradition, are thus determined in their origin and development by human needs and by the habits and interests which are incident to their satisfaction.

From this general point of view light is thrown on many questions concerning mythology. The myth cannot be regarded as peculiarly the product of the personifying activity of the mind. All primitive man's experiences are anthropomorphic so far as they are conscious at all. That is, his experiences are suffused with the warmth and intimacy of his own interests and emotions. But the myth is just one expression of the total drama of his life. It is the speech expression.

[1] Jane E. Harrison, *Prolegomena to the Study of Greek Religion*, p. 432.

Other coördinate, simultaneous expressions of the underlying vital impulses are the pictorial, decorative, and motor forms. These involve personification as much as does the myth. Language is doubtless a more adequate instrument for the complex and subtler imagery, and it may therefore well be the most satisfactory means of registering the elaborations and refinements of the ceremonial symbolism. But this does not prove that the myths are in reality more anthropomorphic than the costume and the dance.

With the advance of a group under contact with other peoples or by the working of inherent forces, changes occur in both the ritual and the myths, and these changes are apparently registered in the myth earlier and more fully than in the cult. This may be attributed to the more flexible character of speech. It is easier to fit a new story to the old ceremony than to create a new ceremony for an old story or even to modify the ceremony. On this account the myth is more variable than the ritual. In the decay of tribal custom the myth may be corrupted and lost while the ritual remains intact. This has been observed among the Todas. "The present state of the Toda religion seems to be one in which ritual has persisted while the beliefs at the bottom of the ritual have largely disappeared." [1] On the other hand, the myths may take on idealized forms while accompanied by essentially the same ritual observance.

The myths of primitive religion are, however, far from possessing the degree of rationality which many writers impute to them. For example, it is a charac-

[1] W. H. R. Rivers, *The Todas*, p. 452.

MYTHOLOGY

teristic statement that the myths are ætiological, that is, concerned with the causes of natural and social phenomena. But it is a gratuitous assumption that primitive man is very curious to obtain rational explanations of his experience. On the contrary, he is notoriously content to accept the traditional narratives without question. He accepts all sorts of jumbled imagery with reference to the most vital things, such as disease or the growth of crops. These trains of imagery have grown up under associations of ideas quite regardless of rational explanations. Chance associations have given prominent place to entirely incidental features, as has been shown in the treatment of imitative and sympathetic magic. These fantastic stories do indeed move within the circuit of the tribal interests, and relate to the social activities and organizations, but interest in explanation satisfies itself with trains of vivid imagery rather than with actual facts or real relations. Such narratives are the work of memory and crude fancy. The mind at that stage prefers vividness to consistency. It is dramatic rather than scientific. An illustration of this tendency to mistake sequence of images for reasonableness is seen in the quotation cited above, in which it is said the myths "were to their first audience so reasonable as to appear truths which were self-evident." Now "reasonableness" of the kind with which "self-evident truths" are connected is not the possession nor the concern of primitive people. It would be true to say the myths were so familiar and so weighted down with tribal usage and sanction that there was no disposition to question them. The principle of habit applies to trains of imagery as definitely as it does to bodily movements. It is not the reasonableness of the habitual activity which makes it powerful and controlling, but just the fact that it is habitual. The myths sprang up in much the same unconscious way as did the customs, and the non-rational character of both sets of phenomena is one of their most striking features. The technique of the dance becomes close knit and automatic, so that when started the series of acts runs off promptly. In the same way, tales, chants, songs, and prayers grow up and transmit themselves without intent or criticism.

Not only in reference to their degree of reasonableness, but with respect to their space and time concepts, the myths have been taken in a too large and sophisticated sense. Students have apparently lacked the power of imagination to move back from the vast universe as it is known to-day to the small contracted world of early man. For the Australians, as for the early Hebrews, the earth is flat, and the sky is a hard vault close down over it. Some Australian legends reflect the belief that the sky rests on poles placed on the mountains. These poles at times become rotten and have to be replaced. Other legends reflect the belief that high trees grow through the sky, on the other side of which is another country like this. By means of these trees the people of the past climbed up through the sky to gather manna. In other legends people ascended above the sky upon the whirlwind. The sun is a woman. The Dieri have a legend that the sun sets in a hole twenty-five miles from Killalpanina, towards Lake Eyre, called the "Hole of the sun." In

MYTHOLOGY

the same way the moon and the stars are people who through some adventure or accident came to live in the sky and to go about as they do now. The seasons are reckoned by the blossoming of the trees, and the summer is also known as "the time when the ground burns the feet." [1] Spencer and Gillen say that the natives have no "idea of the distance away of the sun, believing it to be close to the earth." "The Magellanic clouds they regard as endowed with Arungquiltha (evil spirit), and believe that they sometimes come down to earth and choke men and women while they are asleep. Mushrooms and toadstools they will not eat, believing them to be fallen stars and endowed with Arungquiltha." [2] This is in keeping with the concreteness and nearness of all phases of belief. It is the animals of every-day experience which are sacred. It is the pipe of the Indian, the eagle feather, the rain, or the maize which engages his attention in the ceremonials. In the myths these things are magnified and endowed with greater power than they ordinarily possess, but the ability to conceive things in heroic terms is decidedly limited. When one reads a legend about the sky being lifted up by the magpie, it should be remembered that a very small sky is referred to and not the vastness which we know.

Everything known about the primitive mind supports the inference that to it there is little appreciation of cosmic distances or forces. The myths cannot rise far above the original patterns set by the life interests, nor transcend greatly the proportions of the narrow

[1] A. W. Howitt, *The Native Tribes of South-East Australia*, pp. 426 ff.
[2] Spencer and Gillen, *The Native Tribes of Central Australia*, p. 566.

sphere of practical life. Spencer and Gillen relate how wonderful the Australians are in their perception of tracks. They recognize the tracks of every beast and bird and of particular men and women. They can follow those which would be indistinguishable to white men. But in the more abstract concepts of number and time they display remarkable limitations. "Whilst in matters such as tracking, which are concerned with their every-day life, and upon efficiency in which they actually depend for their livelihood, the natives show conspicuous ability, there are other directions in which they are as conspicuously deficient. This is perhaps shown most clearly in the matter of counting. At Alice Springs they occasionally count, sometimes using their fingers in doing so, up to five, but frequently anything beyond four is indicated by the word okuira, meaning much or great. . . . Their mental powers are simply developed along the lines which are of service to them in their daily life." [1] Rivers made investigations among the natives of the Torres Straits, and became convinced that attention given predominantly to objects of sense, as is characteristic of savages, is a distinct hindrance to intellectual development.[2] Ranke found in his own experience in South America that on account of having constantly to attend to details, he was unable to give attention to the more serious problems of life. In view of such evidence it is obviously misleading to attribute to primitive myths any large concepts or generalizations. To

[1] Spencer and Gillen, *Native Tribes of Central Australia*, pp. 25, 26.

[2] W. H. R. Rivers, *Anthropological Expedition to Torres Straits*, vol. ii, pp. 44, 45.

MYTHOLOGY

people for whom anything beyond four or five is numerically "great" there cannot be for modern thought any very imposing idea of distance in space or of time past or future. Much less could they possess notions of a deity of vast power or high moral excellence.

Probably one reason primitive religion has been so often interpreted in too large and ideal a way is the intense emotional excitement which it produces. The actors in the ceremonials exhibit every mark of the greatest awe, reverence, and affection. We have seen how the simple black fellows of Australia approach the repositories of their sacred objects with solemnity and ritual caution: how they are moved to tears as they handle the precious sticks and stones with which their ancestors are associated. They repeat in low whispers the story of each relic and of the persons to whom it has belonged. All the powers of suggestion — a sacred place, special dress and decorations, an atmosphere of profound mystery and expectation — are employed. The imagery is concrete and conduces to intense social sympathy. Under such influences emotional reactions reach the stage of hypnotism and the trance state. This is true among the American Negroes and Indians at the present time.[1] Such emotionalism is quite independent of any particular intellectual content, except the simplest kind of familiar symbols or images. Great emotion is not evidence of the presence of great ideas among civilized people, much less among savages. On the contrary, intense feeling arises most easily and gains most demonstrative expression where the higher intellectual processes,

[1] F. M. Davenport, *Primitive Traits in Religious Revivals*, p. 50.

such as abstraction and discursive reasoning, are absent or in abeyance. An instinctive sense of awe attends the contemplation of anything which passes the limits of our calculation, particularly if in some way there is at the same time some suggestive sensuous content. Beyond the number four for the Australian, and a million, or whatever the point may be where civilized man loses definite imagery, there is only a confused chaotic blur which both call "great" and with reference to which the same emotion of awe appears. In both cases this sense of mystery may be focused in a definite image or object of sensation, such as the sacred stick of the savage or the relic of the mediæval Christian. But the fact that the savage and the Christian experience comparable emotional states, so far as the observer can detect, is no proof that the range and ideality of the symbols employed in their respective traditions have any corresponding rational content. Taking the experience of each in its entirety, they are remote from one another: and in strict analysis the emotions of the two are as different as are the total worlds of their imagination.

Mythology proper, then, is that body of traditions among a given people which is most closely associated with their ceremonials. Such mythology moves quite at the level of associative trains of imagery and without rationalized form, yet furnishes the psychological *milieu* within which the dramatic action lies. It furnishes literary expression of the background or atmosphere of the dance and pantomime. Above or outside this central body of tradition there were many legends and stories more or less vitally held by each group.

MYTHOLOGY

Among these were the myths from neighboring tribes, which might in time come to be domesticated. Sometimes the rituals would also be adopted. Such syncretism is common among the Greeks and Romans and to some extent among the North American Indians and other still lower peoples. But the similarity in the myths of the different races is more directly due to the similar habits and customs arising in experience with similar environment and racial temper. This hypothesis also accounts for the variations.[1]

[1] F. B. Jevons, *Introduction to the History of Religion*, xviii, "Syncretism and Polytheism."

CHAPTER X

THE DEVELOPMENT OF RELIGION

The origin of religion, as has been shown, is to be sought in the origin of the social consciousness. In other words the religious consciousness is identified with the consciousness of the greatest values of life. This sense of value, as Crawley contends, is the feeling of the worth of life, which expresses itself in the demand for self-preservation. Self-preservation is not an individual matter simply, but at every point involves also the welfare of the group. In the early stages no pronounced distinction is made between individual and social phases of experience, and the values which are felt to be greatest are in reality those social interests in which the individual also finds his fullest life. Primitive religion is therefore social, and is a tribal or group concern. Indeed religion consists in this social consciousness. Religion is constituted by the deepest, most vital interests and ideals. It is most manifest in what is prized most highly; in what society maintains with the greatest energy and caution; in what is defended with the most devotion and with the heaviest penalties. The original and perpetual spring of religion is therefore the life activity itself involved in procuring food, caring for young, acquiring and defending property, and in furthering social welfare. This vital impulse increases with its satisfaction. The craving for life in fuller and more varied forms

THE DEVELOPMENT OF RELIGION

increases with every advance. In the effort to appease his hunger and thirst primitive man was dependent upon blind impulses within and upon an unknown world without. He was therefore largely subject to instinct, to chance association, and to momentary need. Out of his shifting experience arose vague notions of spirits, fanciful myths, the practice of magic, and the observance of customs and cults. In all of these appears the will to live, the sense of value, the unreflective, elemental, communal quest for life. Those spirits, myths, and ceremonials are most religious which express and foster most vitally these life interests, and have therefore the greatest urgency and necessity. Professor Dewey says: "If that necessity is felt to go clear down to his very existence, not merely to his more transitory thoughts; if he feels that those things are so interwoven with his individual life that his very being is dependent upon them, then they are conceded as religious." [1]

By development in religion is meant that change and movement by which the social interests become larger, more inclusive, elaborate, and refined. It means a richer tradition, a more esthetic ritual, and a moralized conception of life. Such changes obviously cannot take place in religion independently of other phases of experience. Unless there is development in social organization, and in methods of controlling nature, there can be no advance in religion. But wherever there are profound changes in economic conditions and in the machinery of the social organism, there changes will occur also in religion. The con-

[1] Unpublished lectures on the Evolution of Morality.

trolling influences are primarily economic. The failure of the food supply through natural causes or through the encroachment of other tribes, the discovery of new lands or resources, the invention of tools or weapons may lead to radical changes in the entire mode of life and, consequently, to changes in that social consciousness with which religion is identified.

Not all groups experience the shock of migration or achieve discoveries and inventions through which progress arises. These experiences may not occur at all, or may come so abruptly that the necessary adjustment cannot be made. The latter has happened with many native races upon the advent of the highly complicated European civilization. Some peoples, again, have apparently maintained themselves for ages at a practically static level. They have made their adjustment to food and climatic conditions, and have elaborated their customs in minute details but without radical changes. This apparently was the case with the native Australian races for thousands of years before the advent of the white man.

An illustration of the radical development of social organization following upon a new instrument for controlling the environment is given in the account of the rise of social institutions among the Snake Indians. The introduction of horses was the event which made social organization possible. These Indians inhabited an almost desert region. "The paucity of game in this region is, I have little doubt, the cause of the almost entire absence of social organization among its inhabitants; no trace of it is ordinarily seen among them, except during salmon-time, when a large number of

THE DEVELOPMENT OF RELIGION

the Snakes resort to the rivers, chiefly to the Fishing Falls, and at such places there seems some little organization. . . . Prior to the introduction of the horse, no other tribal arrangement existed than such as is now seen in the management of the salmon fishery. . . . The organization would be very imperfect, because the remainder of the year would be spent by them in families widely spread apart, to eke out the year's subsistence on the roots and limited game of their country. After a portion of them, who are now called Bonaks, had obtained horses, they would naturally form bands and resort to the buffalo region to gain their subsistence, retiring to the most fertile places in their own, to avoid the snows of the mountains and feed their horses. Having food from the proceeds of the buffalo hunt, to enable them to live together, they would annually do so, for the protection of their horses, lodges, etc. These interests have caused an organization among the Bonaks, which continues the year through, because the interests which produce it continue; and it is more advanced than that of the other Snakes."[1] The reports do not indicate just how this social development expressed itself in religious symbols and ceremonies, but parallel instances from other tribes make it probable that the horse and the buffalo would become conspicuous in the new ritual, and that special ceremonies would occur at the opening of the season for hunting buffalo.

The Hebrew people present one of the most significant developments of religion. They passed through

[1] H. R. Schoolcraft, *History of the Indian Tribes of the United States*, vol. i, pp. 207 f.

the whole range of progress from savagery to civilization. Modern knowledge of their history makes it possible to see how their social advances were expressed in their religious institutions and traditions.

The first and lowest stage from the standpoint of the psychology of religion is that in which anything which catches attention and excites wonder is considered sacred. The Semitic folk-lore and customs show the evidences of such a stage when rivers, springs, trees, stones, caves, and animals, particularly such objects as were unusual in appearance or in value, were sacred. The sacred mountain about which the storm-clouds hung, the rock from which water flowed, the serpents and strange birds, and the flocks tended, were all mysterious and divine. "The religion of the desert is polydæmonism. The *jinn* inhabit every rock and bush, and many of them receive worship from men. To a very late time Israel remembered that it had worshiped the hairy monsters that infest the desert. Totemism is one of the forms in which tribal man attempts to come into relation with superhuman powers. The vestiges of totemism which persist in the tribe names of Israel show that this people formed no exception to the rule." [1]

In the second stage the process of selection which accompanies more definite organization of life brought certain objects more into the focus of attention. The ancestors of the Hebrews, at the earliest point where tradition and the oldest customs give knowledge of them, were nomads and shepherds. Their attention was fixed upon their flocks. The sheep was the most

[1] H. P. Smith, *Old Testament History*, p. 66.

THE DEVELOPMENT OF RELIGION

important object in their experience; hence it was the most sacred. It was a totem animal. The oldest ceremonial, the passover feast, is the survival of that stage. All authorities agree that this is the most characteristic and the best authenticated feature of the ancient religion. We have seen that in this stage the sacrificial animal was the god, and those who feasted upon it thereby gained its magical quality. This nomadic shepherd life and the consequent deification of the sheep were characteristic of the tribes of the steppe. In the restless migratory life of the desert, under the pressure of increasing population and the limited food supply, these tribes were constantly pressing westward to the better pasture lands and more fertile fields along the Jordan river. Such migrations have occurred, wave upon wave, for centuries.

The third stage in Hebrew history is marked by the migration of their nomad ancestors into this richer country to the west. In this movement, perhaps extending over a period of hundreds of years and involving endless tribal wars, they developed the characteristics of fighting people, and their desert gods became war gods. But the most important change was wrought by the new mode of life which an agricultural country required. Cattle were here the great staple possession. These were sacred animals of the land, and in the modification of interests which necessarily followed the adjustment to these new conditions it was not strange that the bull should become sacred to the invading tribes as the sheep had been in the desert. The god of the ancient tribes has become known as Yahweh. The passover feast is evidence that

PSYCHOLOGY OF RELIGIOUS EXPERIENCE

he had the form of the sheep, and when the interests of the people became identified with the care of cattle it was natural that Yahweh should acquire the form of the bull. That the bull was a symbol of Yahweh is clear from the bull images that were set up at various shrines and even in the temple at Jerusalem.[1] It is well known, however, that Yahweh was by no means the only deity of these tribes. That they still deified many natural objects such as rivers, trees, and the tops of hills, is apparent from their history much later than the invasion. The impression that Yahweh was the only deity of the earlier periods is the result of the effort to unify and exalt his influence at a later period.

The fourth stage was the result of the conflict between the desert tribes and the older settlers of the country. This conflict had its deepest ground in the race feeling and prejudice which is as old as tribal life. It is not difficult to understand that these invading tribes would be in constant warfare with those they were seeking to displace. In their struggles they gained reinforcements from some tribes already in the land who had the same traditions and customs of the old nomad life. Gradually the kinship bonds between the desert tribes were strengthened by the rise of leaders of prowess and skill. These leaders were foremost in battle, acted as judges between their people, and were active in the maintenance of the old religion. In time sufficient coöperation was attained to make possible the development of temporary leagues of these tribes and finally of the kingship. This increasing political

[1] G. A. Barton, *A Sketch of Semitic Origins*, p. 299; H. P. Smith, *Old Testament*, p. 181.

THE DEVELOPMENT OF RELIGION

unification was accompanied by a religious consciousness which became ultimately the most remarkable product of the national development. The strife between the nomadic tribes and the agriculturalists was felt as a contest between the nomadic type of divinity, designated as Yahweh, and the gods of the land, known as Baalim. Before the organization of the nomadic tribes into a federation, when the ancient spirit and customs were not protected by a national feeling, there was much fusion of these tribes with the Canaanites. They adopted many of the customs of the more elaborate civilization. It was natural that in seeking prosperity they should be eager to gain the aid of the gods of the land, and should participate in their ceremonials. But when the common interests of the allied tribes were urged, there was a revival of the old nomadic tendency and a consequent desire to renounce the richer and more sensuous customs of the Canaanites for the simple, austere ways of the desert. Three classes were influential in solidifying the religious and national consciousness upon this ancient basis, the priests, the prophets, and the kings. The priests, perhaps originally members of a tribe particularly loyal to Yahweh, scattered through the country and cared for the ritual. The prophets were at first wandering bands of half-mad enthusiasts; and, later, individual statesman-like champions of the ancient ideals. The kings, through prowess and leadership, consummated the formation of the national life, and thus raised Yahweh to supremacy over the gods of the land. Priests, prophets, and kings combined in support of the ancient nomadic ideal in contrast to the customs of the Semitic peoples about them. Out of the same movement which thus produced the monarchy arose ultimately, after a long period, the monotheism of the Jews. With the monarchy a new pattern was given upon which the conception of Yahweh was remodeled. His animal shape was reduced to secondary symbolism, while he took on the anthropomorphic and kingly qualities of an oriental monarch. Among the masses of the people this refinement was of slow growth, and they still maintained in the time of David their local shrines and ancient animal symbols and sacrifices, but every effort was made, especially by the prophets, to substitute Yahweh-worship for Baal-worship.

With the change and humanizing of the conception of God new attitudes arose in the performance of ceremonials and the maintenance of customs. As personality came to mean more in the person of the king and in the conspicuous individuals of the national life, a thought-form was created in which it was possible to enlarge the idea of God. In addition to being some mysterious agency with which it was important to get into relation, God might now be conceived somewhat after the type of a mighty monarch *to* whom gifts could be made in sacrifice, and from whom in return aid and care might be received. Somewhere in this process arose the sense of personal relationship between the members of the tribe and Yahweh, and this consciousness of kinship and identity of interests continually increased in the consciousness of the prophets. In this way the national spirit, the spirit of the united people, grew into the objective and exalted

THE DEVELOPMENT OF RELIGION

personal leader and protector, Yahweh. To him honor and worship were rendered, and his will was regarded as the law of his land and people. In order to fortify the claims of Yahweh, history and tradition were recast in a way to suppress every evidence that Baal-worship ever had been practiced. "It soon came to be regarded as a stain," says Budde, "that Baal-worship should ever have been practiced in these localities, and the endeavor arose to refer back their Yahweh-worship to primeval times. Sacred legends grew up in the bosom of the priesthood charged with the service in these shrines, whose precipitate now lies before us skillfully stratified in the stories of the patriarchs. All sorts of motives coöperated to form them and found satisfaction in them: Israel's claim to the possession of the land of Canaan; Yahweh's claim to its sanctuaries; the wish to bring under the sway of Yahweh even the pre-Mosaic ancestors of Israel, ancient ancestral deities, eponym heroes, and whatever else can be included under this term." [1] At Jerusalem, which had never been the shrine of any Baal, David created the sanctuary of Yahweh and concentrated there the symbols and ritual of his worship. This marked Yahweh's "final possession of Canaan."

The antagonism between the nomadic and the agricultural types of life and religion was not ended, however, with the rise of the kingdom and the erection of the temple at Jerusalem. It only took on a new form. The conflict which was originally between Israel and the Canaanites continued in the national life between the stricter followers of Yahweh and

[1] Karl Budde, *Religion of Israel to the Exile*, p. 107.

those who had adopted more or less of the religion of Baal. This tension between the Yahweh party and the Baal party within the divided kingdom was rife more than a hundred years after David. The Baalizing of Ahab's court aroused the champions of Yahweh anew. "This opposition was headed by Elijah the Tishbite, from Gilead, a country of pasture lands where the forms of nomadic life and the original ritual of the worship of Yahweh were probably less disturbed by the settled life of the Jordan." [1]

Other elements beside abstract loyalty to the ancient religion roused the prophets of Israel. With the introduction of the more indulgent customs of the Tyrian Baal-worship there came also greater luxury at the court, for the maintenance of which the people were oppressed and impoverished. The advocates of the simple nomadic life became indignant at the unaccustomed class distinctions and at the resulting poverty and slavery of the masses. "It is no accident that just at this time Jonadab ben Rechab, the descendant of the ancient Kenites . . . should have founded a sect hostile to civilization. The dangers of civilization were crowding into view at just this time with such overwhelming force as seemingly to justify a pessimism which saw no salvation short of return to the purely pastoral life, in renunciation of all the comforts of civilization." [2] The devotees of Yahweh see the vindication of their cause in the calamities which befall the nation. This is the burden of the two oldest literary prophets, Amos and Hosea. The former

[1] G. A. Barton, *A Sketch of Semitic Origins*, p. 300.
[2] Karl Budde, *The Religion of Israel to the Exile*, p. 120.

THE DEVELOPMENT OF RELIGION

struggled to overthrow the feasts which did not belong to the ancient religion of the wilderness, and Hosea tried to rid Israel of her Baal lovers and reëstablish the old conjugal fidelity to Yahweh. In Amos the intense self-consciousness of the clan spirit reaches the point of belief in the unqualified superiority of Yahweh over all the gods of the heathen. They are regarded as subject to him. Yahweh has proved his power by victories over Canaan, Philistia, and now over the Baal of Tyre.

From this point on, the intense religious consciousness of the literary prophets, which is the expanded and heightened group consciousness springing from the simple nomadic tribal life, is augmented by every outward event favoring the Yahweh party, and is transformed by most significant moralizings due to defeat and suffering. The psychological meaning of the righteousness which Amos and Hosea advocated lies in this group consciousness which had been built up by a long and varied history of conflict and achievement. Their messages were moral in two senses. They put into definite contrast two sets of customs, the simple *mores* of the desert over against the elaborate *mores* of the city and country; and they formulated their own *mores* into general principles as conditioning the welfare of the people and the destiny of the nation. It is obvious that the morality of the prophets was the restatement of the ancient simple life. They used it as a basis of protest. Righteousness consisted in negation of the customs of their political, economic, and religious opponents. The feasts of Baal, the aristocracy of the Baal-worshipers, the tyranny and oppression characteristic of Baal peoples were offensive. They were foreign, modern, and complicated. The desert customs, in which elaborate sacrifices were impossible; in which all members of the tribe shared in the wealth procured; in which expensive and luxurious living was impossible — these were the ancient customs with which Yahweh was honored and by means of which his favor might yet be assured. All experiences of the nation came to be regarded as due to acts of Yahweh directed to the maintenance of the ancient purity and simplicity of his chosen people. As the shifting fortunes of the great neighboring empires brought Israel and Judah into various international situations, the horizon of the writing prophets widened, but they never surrendered the ground pattern nor the broad outlines of the ancient faith. They therefore inevitably extended their conception of Yahweh's jurisdiction. Even the great empires, Egypt, Babylonia, and Assyria, were instruments in his hands. The events of Israel's history were of such magnitude, and the forces operating were so evidently beyond the power of a little nation to regulate or hinder, that the prophets, in whom almost alone the great spiritual conceptions developed, were forced to regard all these events as determined alone by the mighty will of their God. "It was not the tempestuous power of its practiced troops, not the superior might of its gods which led Assyria from victory to victory. It was Yahweh Himself who was bringing it up as a scourge against guilty nations, chiefly against His own people Israel." The outward strength of the chosen people mattered little now. Yahweh did not

THE DEVELOPMENT OF RELIGION

need an independent nation, nor any external ritual, but only such faith as the prophets themselves displayed.

Isaiah carried this conception to the farthest point. Whatever happened, he advocated nothing but faith in Yahweh and conformity to the simplicity of the ancient religion. He advised the kings against any foreign alliance because Yahweh was supremely powerful and could deliver the nation if he would; and unless he willed to do so every effort would be futile. Moreover any such alliance would be proof of distrust which would be punished by calamity. The mysterious good fortune by which Sennacherib was compelled to raise the siege of Jerusalem gave overwhelming support to Isaiah's prophecy that Yahweh would protect and deliver the city and visit disaster upon the Assyrians. Yahweh had indeed allowed all human help to exhaust itself, and then had proved himself alone superior to the greatest foe. Such an event gave tremendous increment to the group consciousness of the Yahweh followers and exalted into new meaning the faith in Yahweh which Isaiah demanded. It probably was partly a consequence of this new confirmation of the supremacy of Yahweh over the gods of the nations which later under Manasseh led to the assembly in the temple at Jerusalem of the gods of the nations as Yahweh's vassals. An accompanying result was the adoption of Assyrian and Babylonian myths and legends into the literature of Israel with the substitution of Yahweh's name for the names of other gods, and the purging of their narratives to accord with the simpler ideals of the Yahweh devotees. "The narrative of the creation of the world, of the oldest families of mankind, of the mighty flood by which all mankind was destroyed save one favorite of the gods, was, in all likelihood, adopted in *this* period by Israel from the Assyrians, and incorporated in its history of the primeval age. The Babylonian cosmology, which now in Genesis forms the opening chapter of the Holy Scriptures, thus took the place of the anthropocentric story of Paradise with the fall of man, which belongs to an earlier time."[1]

Another and more complete movement toward the exclusive recognition of Yahweh, however, followed the syncretism of Manasseh. The extremists of the Yahweh party succeeded in effecting the most drastic reforms under Josiah and in establishing the code of laws set forth in Deuteronomy. Yahweh worship was purged from all images and symbols and from all foreign cults, and the purity of his worship was farther sought by closing all local shrines throughout the country and conducting the ceremonials, such as the Passover, at Jerusalem.

But the capital of the little country of Judah could not withstand the power and intrigues of her powerful neighbors. By rebellion against the Chaldeans the vengeance of Nebuchadnezzar was brought upon Jerusalem; her nobles and warriors were carried away captives; the city and temple were desecrated. Jeremiah was the spokesman of the old religion in the midst of these approaching calamities. He warned the king against alliance with Egypt and urged the surrender of the city to the Chaldeans. After many were

[1] Karl Budde, *The Religion of Israel to the Exile*, p. 168.

THE DEVELOPMENT OF RELIGION

carried into exile he did not encourage them to hope for a return. He attached no importance to national freedom and power. He did, however, preach faithfulness to Yahweh and magnified the consolation and comfort of communion with him. Jeremiah was himself abandoned by relatives, priests, prophets, and royalty. He stood alone in his misfortunes but found his strength in Yahweh. He proclaimed the uselessness of sacrifices and ordinances in the spirit of Amos and Isaiah, and insisted upon true devotion of the heart and will. The new covenant is one written on the heart. Thus once more the ancestral faith in Yahweh is purified and strengthened in defeat by attaining the conviction that national independence and religious ritual are not essential to Yahweh's companionship and aid for the individual. Israel does not need to be an independent people to enjoy Yahweh's blessings. In Jeremiah the individualizing anthropomorphizing tendency is complete. Yahweh is a person with whom the prophet holds dialogues. "He complains, he contradicts Him, contends with Him, defends himself against Him, but is ever worsted by Him." It was this individual piety of Jeremiah which constituted his contribution to the development of the ancestral religion, and this individualism of his inner experience was a natural culmination of the prophetic opposition to all the external forms of religion. It was also a natural refuge from the calamities which had overtaken his nation and city and from the abandonment and persecution which the prophet suffered at the hands of his people.

The fifth stage of this religious history is marked by

PSYCHOLOGY OF RELIGIOUS EXPERIENCE

the exile. It is distinguished by two types of expectation. One is that of Ezekiel, which represents a reversion to the more material hope of Israel and to the priestly conception of religion. He portrays the return of the tribes to their own land and the rebuilding of the temple on its old site. He sees the religion of Yahweh revived with increased precautions for all ceremonial purity and holiness. It is the holiness of remoteness and the correctness of the worship. Elaborate provision is made for ranks of priests to avoid all ceremonial pollution. While this priestly Utopia was never realized, it nevertheless exerted a determining effect upon the history and literature of the subsequent period. "For, in reality, the principles and aims of the priestly law are all in every respect derived from Ezekiel, who has justly been called in recent times the father of Judaism." The code of Leviticus, and the priestly historical document were the direct results of the prophet's influence; while the glowing descriptions of the restored Israel became the basis of many eschatological hopes which find their full expression in the apocalypse of Daniel and the kindred literature of a later time.

But the exile produced in the Second Isaiah a further refinement of the idealizing tendencies which had found such clear expression in Amos, Isaiah, and Jeremiah. In them the course of events had confirmed faith in the power and greatness of Yahweh, but only by compelling them to relinquish all claim to his dependence upon the maintenance of the nation or upon the outward worship of a faithful people. Instead of being crushed by any calamities, the prophetic faith in Yahweh was so invincible as to turn to its own

THE DEVELOPMENT OF RELIGION

support every national disaster. The second Isaiah, through the experiences of the exile, and particularly in the hope of the overthrow of the Chaldeans by Cyrus, added the final development to the universality and exclusiveness of the conception of God. For this prophet Yahweh is the only God. There never has been any other. The others are manufactured by human hands from wood and stone. Moreover Yahweh is really the God of all other nations as well as of Israel. He has chosen Israel as a means of making himself known to other peoples, and when they witness the redemption of Yahweh's suffering Servant, the nation of Israel, they too will bow before Yahweh and acknowledge his rule. Thus the trials of the nation lead to a comprehensive universalism within which the suffering of Israel gains an elevated and ennobling explanation.

A sixth historical epoch in the Hebrew religion was attained in the rise of Christianity. Two conceptions which had long been forming found revival, purification, and increment in the teaching of Jesus. These were the ideals of a divine kingdom and of inward ethical character. Both were directly related to the prophetic conception of God as the God of all nations, and as the God of infinite justice and mercy. In the long and troubled national history the conviction grew that the religion of Yahweh did not depend upon the existence of the state nor upon the maintenance of the ritual of formal worship. In the process Yahweh became superior to the primitive condition in which a god is so dependent upon his group that he degenerates into a demon or disappears entirely when the group life ceases. The writing prophets were repeatedly compelled by political disasters either to admit the defeat of Yahweh or to claim that he was working out plans which proved him to be superior to all outward human aid. They did the latter. In these plans he came to be viewed as guiding the affairs of all the nations, using them merely as instruments for effecting his sovereign will. The conclusion was that the supreme concern should be to gain Yahweh's favor, and that this could be done only through faith and purity of life. Here was attained the reversal of the earliest attitude. In the earliest stages of religion the god is in mutual relation with his people. They support him, give him food and precious gifts, and in turn make demands upon him, threaten, punish, and reward him. But with the great prophets Yahweh receives the utmost reverence. He does not need armies, alliances, and sacrifices. Faith alone is required, and those who possess this "tender, passive individualism" of Jeremiah and obey patiently God's will by walking in his way will receive salvation and become the agents of the divine kingdom. Jesus proclaimed this God of power and holiness with still greater tenderness and compassion. Those who have faith in his Fatherly pity and graciousness will be received with all forgiveness and blessing. That is the meaning of the story of the Prodigal Son. There are no national or outward limitations to this divine favor. That is shown in the conversation with the Samaritan woman. Such believers constitute the religious community, the spiritual Israel, the true kingdom of God. That is the significance of Jesus' assurance that those who have faith shall enter the kingdom of heaven, regardless of their ancestry or nationality.[1]

Many things in the experience of Jesus contributed to his acceptance and enrichment of this prophetic idea of God and of the kingdom as a society of those who have this faith. There was spread out before him the history itself, a history in which the power of Yahweh must be seen, if at all, in the punishment and discipline of his people. In this humiliation of Israel the kings of the nations had been his scourges. In Jesus' own time only such a view could give any meaning to the national history. The foreign hand was still heavy upon the land. God must be more than a God of Israel or he could be no God at all, and since he evidently was not one who depended upon armies and temples, he must be the God of a spiritual kingdom which had no local, outward, or ceremonial limitations. This supra-national character of God was also rooted in the immediate contact of Jesus with men of various races and classes. That which pressed upon his attention wherever he went was the great human need, — poverty, sickness, discouragement, sin, and unsatisfied spiritual hunger and thirst. Redemption from these things demanded a compassionate God of mercy and truth, of righteousness and infinite love. The salvation which the officials of religion in his time offered involved such details of ceremonial observances and such minute legal requirements that they were hindrances rather than aids. Burdens too heavy to be borne were thus laid upon the people, while those who were most faithful devotees of the Law and the

[1] G. B. Stevens, *The Teaching of Jesus*, p. 62. Cf. Matt. viii, 10-12.

Temple were ever busy with mint, anise, and cummin, and neglected the weightier matters. Thus they became bigoted zealots, full of formalism and hypocrisy. From them Jesus turned, as the great prophets had turned from the priests and the popular prophets, and proclaimed a God who is Spirit and who is Love. He felt the need of a God who is approachable by the humblest soul, without ceremonials or ordinances, whose forgiveness and aid are for all who have faith and seek righteousness.

The other notable element in the teaching of Jesus was its ethical inwardness.[1] This is, of course, not separable from his idea of the divine righteousness and of the kingdom of God. The sufferings of the nation had, before the time of Jesus, forced sensitive minds to question whether there was any relation between righteousness and prosperity, between virtue and happiness. It was the problem of Job and it was the burden of the Wisdom literature. The latter taught that the principle held: suffering is the result of sin. If therefore a man's outward life was virtuous, his suffering must be due to some "secret sin." So involved and deep-lying might this hidden fault be that the person himself would be unconscious of it: —

> Who can discern his errors?
> Cleanse thou me from unwitting faults!

The confusion in the Wisdom literature was in regarding such inner qualities as merely subjective, or at most as determining one's relation to God. Pride and a stubborn will were thought of chiefly as something

[1] Arthur O. Lovejoy, "The Origins of Ethical Inwardness in Jewish Thought," *American Journal of Theology*, 1907, p. 228.

which God could not endure. They were not conceived as elements which are inherently and intrinsically incompatible with social righteousness.

Christianity took up this element of ethical inwardness, developed by the Hebrew sages, and connected it with the social conception of the kingdom of heaven. This connection appears in the insistence of Jesus that the feelings and desires of the heart shall not terminate in their mere occurrence in the heart as sentimental emotions, nor yet exist with sole reference to the kind of a heart which the all-seeing eye of God might approve; rather that these feelings and desires of one's inmost nature shall have issue in social relations. The love enjoined is love of one's neighbor, of one's enemy. In the contrasts which Jesus points between his teaching and that of the olden time he transfers the emphasis from the overt act to the motive and intent of the heart, but preserves — and this is his greatest achievement — the organic relation of the purpose and the deed. Anger and hatred are forbidden rather than acts of violence alone, because anger and hatred are the fountains of such crimes. They are the first stages of a continuous process ending in blows and bloodshed. Lustful thought is prohibited because it is the beginning of adultery, and the taking of oaths is sinful because it involves irreverence and untrustworthiness in common affirmations. It was not the outward deed alone, nor the inner desire alone, but the outgoing, objectifying, socially effective attitude of will which proved a man's virtue or sinfulness. And this established itself intrinsically. Virtue of this kind carried its own reward of satisfaction and efficiency.

It possessed its own consolation and peace. It contributed to the creation of an actual social order within which the inherent rewards of right conduct could be experienced, and it provided an assurance that in the fuller development of the social order to which all such effort tended, the rewards of righteousness would be increasingly attained.

In Christianity the development of religion has continued and still continues, under the stress of conflicting social influences ; by the formation of institutions and parties; and by means of the great democratic social awakenings and the rise of the scientific spirit of inquiry. These agencies have created new types of social consciousness in terms of which the conception of personality, human and divine, is undergoing changes, and the ancient demand for more adequate social justice is being pressed with new claims.[1] With the gradual working out of democratic ideals in society and the application of scientific methods and results to the whole round of human interests and endeavor there are hints of the rise of a religion of science and democracy.[2] Viewed in this way, as the expression of the profoundest social consciousness, religion must continue to advance in the future, as in the past, in close relation with the concrete life of mankind.

Parallel development, through certain stages at least, has been traced in other religions. The transformations of Dionysus and other Greek gods in con-

[1] J. H. Tufts, "The Adjustment of the Church to the Psychological Conditions of the Present," *American Journal of Theology*, vol. xii, 1908.

[2] John Dewey, *Hibbert Journal*, July, 1908.

THE DEVELOPMENT OF RELIGION

sequence of economic and political fortunes have been elaborately presented.[1] Probably the reason the Greek religion did not attain a continuous development was that its earlier, cruder forms had become fixed in the writings of Hesiod and Homer and in the popular imagination. There were attempted reforms comparable to those of the Hebrew prophets, but without avail. The result was an independent growth of moral and social ideals which were regarded as sharply contrasted with religion.[2] The Greek philosophers, like Plato, appeared therefore to oppose religion itself, and thus what may be called an accident of history has probably been an influential factor in giving currency to the conviction that religion and philosophy, not to say religion and morality, are incompatible.

One of the most significant features of social and religious development is that of the survival of early customs in later periods. Christianity is full of forms and doctrines which illustrate this tendency.

The oldest feast of the Hebrews, the Passover, determines the conceptions which centre in the Mass or the Lord's Supper. The oldest ideas of sacrifice persist here too. The communicant partakes of the magic life, literally by eating the body and drinking the blood; or ideally by employing the bread and wine as symbols. It is the old process of establishing fellowship and social unity by eating and drinking. In Baptism, also, there continues the form of purgation in which sin is regarded as physical contagion and sub-

[1] L. R. Farnell, *The Cults of the Greek States.* Jane E. Harrison, *Prolegomena to the Study of Greek Religion.*

[2] Dewey and Tufts, *Ethics,* p. 116.

ject to exorcism by the magical power of water and the use of a specific formula. The use of the "name" in prayer, the observance of special days and seasons, the regard for familiar superstitions concerning sacred or evil numbers, days of the week, vestments of priests and services of worship, show how persistent such survivals are. These survivals would have less significance if they were only this, but they indicate the persistence in human society of the cruder types of mind to which such customs are natural and satisfying. Some fashions do continue, like the dead leaves upon the trees in autumn, after all vitality has left them. But the sacramental doctrines and customs of religion spring from the living and perennial superstition of the masses. They exist not merely because it is the fashion to cultivate them, but also because the magic and mystery which they involve are native to unenlightened minds. "As to 'survivals' of primitive speculation and custom into civilized periods, the term is misused when it is implied that these are dead forms, surviving like fossil remains or rudimentary organs; the fact is that human nature remains potentially primitive, and it is not easy even for those most favored by descent to rise above these primitive ideas, precisely because these ideas 'spring eternally' from permanent functional causes." [1]

When human nature rises above primitive conditions into scientific conceptions and into a broader, many-sided civilization, the earlier customs are transformed by new content or entirely discarded. "Our

[1] Ernest Crawley, *The Mystic Rose*, p. 4; Sumner, *Folkways*, chapter v, "Societal Selection."

THE DEVELOPMENT OF RELIGION

pagan ancestors, when they launched a ship, bound a captive to the rollers to propitiate the god of the sea. The bottle of wine broken on the ship's prow to-day is our way of 'reddening the keel' of the vessel to be launched and insuring her good luck. The old form is kept, but what a change in the spirit!"[1]

But the vitality and strength of real religion is only enhanced by the transfusion of the growing social consciousness into new forms and methods of expression. That social consciousness remains the constant, enveloping reality of human experience. Without it individualism becomes anarchy. By means of it the individual is identified with the great movements of history and is able to transcend the momentary and illusive interests of the sensuous and material phases of life. In the organized efforts of his group primitive man felt himself in league with vast powers. The widening scope and increasing control of conscious, coöperative social enterprises has only enhanced that consciousness of the magnitude and marvelous character of the forces with which the individual is allied. If the sense of participation in the tribal wars of desert nomads, or the right to share in the harvest of the little land of Palestine could arouse the religious sentiments of gratitude and awe, how much deeper and richer may be the religious consciousness which holds in imagination the immense universe of modern science and possesses the key to so many secrets of welfare and progress. If the symbols of that little simple human world aroused the devotion and enthusiasm of sensitive men, the symbols of the present

[1] E. A. Ross, *Social Psychology*, p. 142.

world have meaning and value to produce still greater reverence and more efficient service.

We have thus far considered the nature of religion and the processes by which it arises in the social experience of the race. It is important also to view the way in which these organized social values of the group are appropriated by the individual, and to analyze the psychical phenomena which they produce in individual experience.

PART III
THE RISE OF RELIGION IN THE INDIVIDUAL

CHAPTER XI

RELIGION AND CHILDHOOD

SINCE religion is identified with the fullest and most intense social consciousness, the problem of the rise of religion in the individual resolves itself into the question of the origin of his social consciousness. Every human being is confronted from birth with the social customs and sentiments of his group. If he does not respond to them from the first, it is not because they are not present in institutions, beliefs, and practices constantly encircling his life. It is because he does not possess capacity, interests, experience, and imagination for such things. It is, therefore, the task of psychology to investigate the nature of the child with reference to his relation to social and religious ideas and activities, and to determine at what period and under what circumstances the individual attains the capacities and interests which enable him to share fully in the community life.

For this purpose a brief survey of the various periods of childhood is suggestive. The theory of recapitulation in the child of the stages in racial development is not a trustworthy guide here. That theory has been modified by the recognition of "short-cuts" and the influence of the immediate social environment in the development of the individual.[1] The surer

[1] Baldwin, *Mental Development*, p. 20; Thomas, *Sex and Society*, p. 282.

method is observation and analysis of individual children in reference to mental progress and awakening.

The period of infancy extends from birth two and a half or three years. The baby exercises his muscles and sense organs through impulsive and instinctive reactions. This activity is increasingly selective and results in such control of the larger muscles as is involved in creeping, walking, and in the hand-eye movements. The use of the sense organs and usually some proficiency in speech are gained by the third year. The organism, during this period, is chiefly concerned with nutrition and with the larger bodily movements and adjustments. The infant is not positively a member of the human world if judged by his ability to participate in it in a human way. He is more nearly on the level of animal life, though in ability to care for himself, he is inferior to other animals. The actions of the infant, not being guided or conditioned by individual judgment, are non-moral and non-social. The infant is not a person in any proper functional sense. Modern psychology denies to the mature individual the possession of a "soul" in the sense of a substantial and static entity within him, and only accepts the term reluctantly when it is made synonymous with person or agent. It is therefore still less defensible to think of the infant as possessing a soul. He is an active, sensitive, growing organism on the way to become human, to be a person and to grow a soul or character. As an infant, he is therefore non-religious.

The six years extending from infancy to second dentition approximately cover the period of early

RELIGION AND CHILDHOOD

childhood. Here physical activity continues dominant with more attention to details. "The child now likes to play games that test the sharpness of the senses; he likes to experiment with new movements — to walk on tiptoe, to skip and dance, to play finger-games, to draw, to string beads, and so on."[1] Imitation is strong now. The occupations of the persons about him become his models. He plays school, church, and store. Boys ape the manners of their older brothers, and girls delight to wear long dresses and care for their dolls as they see mothers and nurses caring for their charges. The plays are imitative and repetitious. They are marked by predominant interest in persons. Inanimate objects are personified. Mr. Wind, Mr. Rain, and Jack Frost are characters of varying caprice and benignity. All objects of interest are given names. As memory and imagination develop, tales are invented, and there is great interest in hearing stories. "Children's lies" belong to this period where fragmentary, random impressions and imaginative tendencies are not checked by any adequate appreciation of the distinctions between truth and fiction. The child delights in the train of images and in the expressions of shock and surprise which he is able to elicit from playmates and elders by his assertions.

The ends in which the child interests himself up to the age of about nine are immediate and momentary. He delights in nonsense rhymes and jingles largely for the sensuous joy of the rhythm and of the rhyming words. His activities in the same way show the limited nature of his interest. "The child enjoys the action

[1] A. E. Tanner, *The Child*, p. 236.

for its own sake without much reference to any end. Little children who are playing 'Pom pom pullaway,' for instance, may forget all about the goal in the delight of running, and end the game in a chase. So also a little fellow begins to draw the story of the Three Bears, gets interested in making the bear, and covers his paper with bears. The movement or activity is what he enjoys. He does not care for making some *thing* so much as he does for going through the movements of making." [1] Many acts often attributed to childish destructive tendencies are really due to this delight in activity. Knocking down the pile of blocks is much the same as building it up, so far as the exercise of energy is concerned, with the added interest due to the crash which accompanies the collapse. The child does not estimate the consequences of his deed. He strikes matches and delights in the pretty flames of the burning papers without realizing the danger of burning down the house. He finds a loose tile on the hearth and proceeds to pull up one tile after another, and is unable to understand the anger and dismay of his parents upon finding the wreck he has caused. It is the little girl's love of using the scissors which leads her to cut off her own hair or to gash her dress. When reprimanded she does not know why she does such things and is unable to appreciate the full meaning of the prudent mother's extended remarks upon thoughtfulness and economy. The child's experience is piecemeal and haphazard. His extreme suggestibility is further evidence that he does not hold in mind the ends to which acts lead. His interests are momentary,

[1] A. E. Tanner, *The Child*, p. 237.

RELIGION AND CHILDHOOD

only slightly related, and therefore have little sequence or consistency. All phases of his world are of this fragmentary character. He does not hold his images apart from their motor responses. He has no unified and proportioned conception of himself. His passing feelings are the determining factors in controlling his acts. His memory is short, and the corrections and encouragements for conduct must be connected necessarily with his likes and dislikes, even with his sensuous pleasures and pains. These may be of the cruder sort of corporal punishment and sweet-meat rewards, or they may be of the more humane character of disciplinary silence and educative play.

This fragmentary and immediate character of their experience accounts in large measure for the individualism, the selfishness, and the cruelty of children. Their personality is narrow and centered in the feeling of the moment. They do not go beyond delight in their own activity to consider its effect upon others in any personal way. It is the movement and action of the tormented animal or child which they notice. There is a satisfaction in finding one's self able to produce such lively effects. This sense of power, of novelty and curiosity, is quite detached from any adequate appreciation of the feelings of the one tormented. The experience and organized imagery are lacking, without which permanent and comprehensive social attitudes are impossible in any human being, whether child or adult. The intellectual life reflects this chaotic, unorganized state in the chance associations which it makes. Theological ideas are caught up piecemeal and superficially. The delight of children in fairies, sprites, and goblins, whose conduct is more or less capricious and always mysterious, is evidence that children do not demand unity and consistency in the "supernatural" beings of their fancy. They prefer action, cleverness, and spectacular achievements. Sully cites many instances of the tendency of children to assimilate the idea of God to their scale and manner of thinking. In his admiration for the workmanship of the Creator, which he was nevertheless under necessity of putting into terms of human labor, one little boy, on seeing a group of workingmen returning from their work, asked his mother: "'Mamma, is these gods?' 'God,' retorted the mother. 'Why?' 'Because,' he went on, 'they makes houses, and churches, mamma, same as God makes moons and people and 'ickle dogs.' Another child, watching a man repairing the telegraph wires that rested on a high pole at the top of a lofty house, asked if he was God."[1] In his prayers the little child asks earnestly for toys and pleasures, and if they are not obtained, falls out with God as easily as with a playmate. All attempts to inculcate ideas of divine omnipotence, omniscience, and ubiquity inevitably result in confusion and literalism. The mind can only operate on the basis of its experience, and when that is limited all objects are determined and limited accordingly. The little child displays only faint traces of a sense of personality, appreciation of social relations and of ends or ideals beyond the moment. He is, therefore, lacking to a large degree in the attitudes which are essentially social and spiritual. In so far as he does possess such interests

[1] James Sully, *Studies of Childhood*, p. 127.

and values he is moral and religious, but it is a matter of small degree and of slight beginnings. Many things in religious history and practice, however, afford points of contact at this level. Such are the heroic deeds of individuals, the outward customs of dress, food, migration, war, and ceremonial. These materials, woven into story form and set forth in pictures, in dramatic representation, and in manual arts, can be appropriated by the child, but their full significance and their fundamentally religious quality as complex social phenomena are beyond his powers.

In later childhood, which extends from second dentition to early puberty, that is from about the ninth to the thirteenth year, the brain has reached approximately the normal adult weight, and the powers of generalization, comparison, and analysis are attained, but there is a lack of experience and consequently of ability to enter deeply into the social experiences of mature persons. During this period interests gradually widen. The child is able to pursue more remote ends and to employ more complex means to accomplish his purposes. He begins to defer immediate wants for greater future interests, and learns to work somewhat indirectly for the more important ends or ideals.

This tendency may be illustrated in several specific interests. In games, the boy of ten or twelve prefers those which give opportunity for the most vigorous physical activity. This interest is accompanied by increasing skill, involving finer muscular adjustments. In drawing and workmanship, there is more attention to details, though without proportion. A few features in the schematized whole are made prominent, as shown in G. S. Hall's "Story of a Sand Pile." Here the barn gates were worked out with much greater care than other parts of the farm. During these years a marked change is noticeable from a pronounced individualism toward coöperation and social feeling. "When coöperative games are played before eleven, there is little feeling of solidarity. The boy is generally willing to sacrifice the interest of the group to his personal glorification. The earlier interest in such games seems to be proportionate to the amount of opportunity they afford for the exhibition of personal prowess, but the pre-adolescent glories in the fact that it is his club or team that has won." [1]

This nascent social attitude is conspicuous in the intense interest in the organization of secret societies and clubs from the tenth to the thirteenth year. But the purposes for which these groups are formed show that the period is still dominated to a large extent by the desire for physical activity and for adventure. The clubs and societies of this period are the outgrowth of athletic and predatory tendencies. The ends sought are somewhat more complex and more remote than those of earlier childhood, and there is more concerted and sustained effort in their attainment, but they are ends impossible of the highest idealization or socialization. Investigation of a large number of such organizations proved that only seven per cent of children's clubs are formed before ten, and but one per cent at seventeen and later. Eighty-seven per cent are formed between ten and fifteen, and seventy-seven per cent of

[1] Irving King, *The Psychology of Child Development*, p. 192.

RELIGION AND CHILDHOOD

them are athletic and predatory. Military organizations, such as boys' brigades, are popular. Few voluntary organizations are formed in this period for art or literature, and practically none for religious purposes.[1]

The choice of occupation reflects the same growing ability to appreciate more remote objects and to hold in imagination characters and enterprises not close at hand. The results of a study by Earl Barnes[2] shows that children from eight to thirteen rapidly cease to choose characters in the immediate environment as their ideal. At eight years forty-two per cent chose characters close at hand, while at thirteen only fifteen per cent did so. This shift of the centre of interest from a narrow to a wider range is shown in the same study in the fact that the interest in historical and public characters was represented by seventeen per cent at eight years and by sixty-nine per cent at thirteen years.

The interest in making collections of stamps, buttons, coins, stones, and other objects confirms the same point. Before the age of nine the collections are of trivial objects, from the immediate surroundings, and the collections are made in a scrappy manner. There is no attempt at systematic classification. But after the age of nine, the child makes more collections and goes out of his way to get them. The social tendency is seen in trading as a means of increasing these collections, and there are more definite attempts to make careful classifications. The social factor in col-

[1] Irving King, *The Psychology of Child Development*, p. 203.
[2] "Children's Ideals," *Pedagogical Seminary*, vol. vii, p. 3 ff.

PSYCHOLOGY OF RELIGIOUS EXPERIENCE

lecting is seen in the desire to imitate the example of others, and also in the effort to surpass one's associates in variety and quantity.

The results of the varied and minute psychological study of child nature lead to the conclusion that religion is not an instinct in the child, nor a special endowment of any kind. Religion is rather an experience of groups of individuals resulting from their collective and coöperative effort to secure and preserve the ideals which appeal to them as possessing the greatest value. The child up to about thirteen years is capable of only very limited social ideals because his experience is too small to afford him the basis for large generalizations and for complex, comprehensive, social conceptions. He is religious in the degree and to the extent to which his powers and experience enable him to enter into the religious values of his social environment or to find such values in his community life. This religious experience, limited and partial as it is, demands respect and sympathy from all who are in any way responsible for the training of the young. They cannot be required without injury to assume the forms and terms of the religion of their elders. They necessarily live their own life, on the scale of interests which is natural to them, and gradually pass on into an understanding and support of the institutions and activities which growing experience requires. Irving King has stated the morality of the child in relation to the developed social order in terms equally applicable to religion. "It is clear he cannot at first, nor even well-nigh to youth, have a comprehension of the meaning of the complex system of values recognized

RELIGION AND CHILDHOOD

by society. He can learn their meaning only by meeting crises for himself and readjusting his direct and unreflective action to broader settings. Such a process necessitates years of growth mentally and abundant opportunity for interaction with playmates and elders. Until he has thus grown into this complex life, its requirements must always seem external and, in a sense, imposed upon him. . . . On his own plane of experience he has a limited moral code of his own, and the degree of his adjustments of action to these values that he has himself worked out may be counted his real morality." [1] Professor Starbuck remarks in dealing with this question, "Children, like savages, can possess just such a religion as they have minds and hearts to comprehend," and insists that "religion changes its form and content as life changes." [2]

This functional view of mental development and of the growth of religious consciousness in connection with mental maturity and social experience solves some of the theological puzzles and furnishes psychological explanation for many customs with reference to the treatment of children. It has been customary to regard the child as outside the social order, an alien and even an enemy to the interests which adults considered most important. The impulsive, unreflective nature of the child, which puts him frequently in opposition to the settled order of the society about him, makes him appear contrary and rebellious, flippant and devoid of reverence. On this

[1] Irving King, *The Psychology of Child Development*, pp. 137, 138.

[2] E. D. Starbuck, "The Child-Mind and Child-Religion," *The Biblical World*, 1908, p. 101.

account he has been regarded by many theologians as sinful and perverse by nature, and without the capacity for any good thought or deed, until miraculously regenerated by supernatural power. The diary of Cotton Mather tells how he took his four-year-old daughter into his study and "set before her the sinful Condition of her Nature, and charged her to pray in Secret Places every day that God for the sake of Jesus Christ would give her a new Heart." Even at the present day a well-known Presbyterian clergyman writes: "The Presbyterian doctrine concerning the relation of young children to God is this: That by original nature, in their first state, they are in a state of deficiency, needing the touch of divine grace with regenerative power, before they are made the subjects of salvation. This touch of divine grace or regenerative presence in the child life may come at birth, or, as I believe and I think others do, may come before birth or quickly after."[1] Such an opinion may reveal a more human conception of God among theologians to-day, but it is chiefly significant as a survival of an unpsychological notion of childhood and of the manner of its development. Those older theologians who believed that the touch of divine grace was given in the period of later childhood had some basis of fact for their theory, for it is true that the child then begins to display genuine social interests and is able to have some real contact even with the extreme orthodoxy of the old Calvinistic religion. But to suppose that the religious nature is miraculously implanted at birth

[1] Letter to Professor Coe quoted in his work, *Education in Religion and Morals*, pp. 66 f.

RELIGION AND CHILDHOOD

or before birth betrays inconsistent and unscientific ideas, both of religion and of human nature.

Many champions of the child, reacting against the older view that he is irreligious and depraved, have posited a religious nature, instinct, or sense with which the child is endowed and which is capable of awakening and development under proper nurture. But it is not necessary to assume such a religious nature, and psychological analysis does not justify it. All that psychology permits is the conclusion that the infant is non-religious, non-moral, and non-personal; that in early childhood impulsive, sensuous reactions together with absorption in immediate details and fragmentary interests make it impossible for the child under nine years to pass beyond the non-religious and non-moral attitude to any considerable degree; but that in later childhood up to about thirteen years of age he responds to more interests of a social and ideal character, and thus manifests tendencies and attitudes which are religious in character. These beginnings of religious life are the accompaniment of crude coöperative activities. They are the first gleams of the sense of power and opportunity which result from team work and from social organization. But the distance which still separates the individual of late childhood from the adult social and religious world is seen in the tendency of these juvenile organizations to be secret and to cultivate a certain opposition and antagonism to the larger social order. This is notable in the gangs of boys which delight to maintain a kind of tribal life of their own. G. Stanley Hall summarizes the investigations of Gulick on this subject. "Gulick has studied the propensity of boys from thirteen on to consort in gangs, do 'dawsies' and stumps, get into scrapes together, and fight and suffer for one another. The manners and customs of the gang are to build shanties or 'hunkies,' hunt with sling shots, build fires before huts in the woods, cook their squirrels and other game, play Indian, build tree-platforms, where they smoke or troop about some leader, who may have an old revolver. They find or excavate caves, or perhaps roof them over; the barn is a blockhouse or a battleship. In the early teens boys begin to use frozen snowballs or put pebbles in them, or perhaps have stone-fights between gangs than which no contiguous African tribes could be more hostile. They become toughs and tantalize policemen and peddlers: 'lick' every enemy or even stranger found alone on their grounds; often smash windows; begin to use sticks and brass knuckles in their fights; pelt each other with green apples; carry shillalahs, or perhaps air rifles." [1]

The first spontaneous social interests have therefore a certain intense anti-social character, judged from the standpoint of the organized institutions of adults. Consequently the child, even in this stage of pre-adolescence, stands outside the constituted order and easily reacts to it as something quite external to him. It is not strange then that the developed adult world of traditions and inflexible customs should in turn regard the child as an alien. In the most civilized societies one is not formally recognized as a person until after the period of adolescence is nearly completed, that is, at eighteen years for females and at twenty-

[1] G. Stanley Hall, *Adolescence*, vol. ii, p. 396.

one years for males. The minor is a ward, a dependent, a passive being before the law. The same is true among savages. The infant is taboo and dangerous. Among the Kafirs, when the second teeth begin to be cut, the boy is taken from association with the women, but is only allowed on the outer circle of the real world of the men. "Children are thus regarded as negligible quantities until after puberty; they take practically no part in the religious or social rites of the clan. . . . They are not taught religion in any formal way and are freely allowed to break some laws of the clan." [1]

The records of their own childhood experience by mature persons add interesting confirmation to the conclusions of genetic psychology and to the observations of particular children by specialists. The records of more than eighty cases which I have gathered confirm the generalization of Starbuck based upon similar records. He says: "One of the most pronounced characteristics of the religion of childhood is that *religion is distinctively external to the child rather than something which possesses inner significance.*" [2] In the replies I received to the question, What impressions did the church services and the Sunday School make? the most frequent answer was that they made little or no impression at all. "Up to the age of twelve, I know of no definite impression the church service made on me. I took it as a matter of course." "I cannot recall any impressions that church and Sunday School made except that I acquired a definite habit of attendance and reverence." "My memory of the

[1] Dudley Kidd, *Savage Childhood*, p. 14.
[2] E. D. Starbuck, *Psychology of Religion*, p. 194.

impression that Church and Sunday School made upon me is not at all clear." "The impressions made by the Sunday School were very vague." "Cannot recall impression made by church services and Sunday School."

The experience of others was the feeling that the services were not for them. "Church services impressed me as being the 'proper thing' but not particularly applicable to us outsiders." "I always felt that they had no real significance for any one excepting the elderly and most devout church members." Many recall the fact that they were attracted to the services by minor factors, the walk or drive, fresh clothes, meeting other children, the music, stories, etc., elements which would not ordinarily be considered in any sense religious. "Sunday School I liked. I enjoyed the sabbath freshness, wearing my best clothes and meeting with other clean, well dressed children." "Sunday was a delightful day. We had a beautiful drive through one mile of woodland to the Church, and there I met my little friends, and we had such a good time visiting while in the Sunday School class. I cannot recall any of my teachers or any definite impression I received from them, although I must have received something." "The Sunday School impressed me with sacred things, yet the being with other children, especially my cousins, before and after Sunday School was the thing that attracted me." "Sunday School was pleasant because of the hymns and the teacher. Also an interest in learning catechism and Bible verses." Several speak of liking their teachers, enjoying reciting verses, and getting books

RELIGION AND CHILDHOOD

from the library. One seemed to get satisfaction out of his power of endurance. "The Church services were not very impressive, only I thought it was nice and right to stay through a long service because older ones did." The child's unconscious subjection to routine is expressed by another. "I believe I went to Sunday School because it never entered my mind that any other course of action was possible."

CHAPTER XII

RELIGION AND ADOLESCENCE

THE results of the psychological investigations of religious experience by Starbuck, Coe, James, Hall, Leuba, and others agree that the period of adolescence is preëminently the period of the rise of religious consciousness in the individual. Statistical inquiries, which are likely to be extended in a much more comprehensive way by future observations, are already sufficient to show in broad outlines that for the individual religion originates in youth. There are foregleams of it in late childhood and marked developments of it in mature years, but the period of original, spontaneous and vital awakening is the teens. This religious experience is, however, not an inevitable and uniform occurrence in all individuals. It is conditioned by training, environment, physical development, and social influences. Religion is subject to the same determining factors as are other social phenomena — such as language, art, domesticity, patriotism. In any society all persons are likely to experience these to some extent, but it is not due to their native endowments alone, nor to accidental circumstances, but to the operation of social forces within the experience and consciousness of each person. The specific factors and processes involved in this variable development of the religious consciousness in different persons will be treated in other connections. There are two important problems to be considered here. One concerns the evidence that religion arises in the individual during adolescence. The other is the question of the causes which produce this result in this period.

One of the most significant and best-established facts which the new science of the psychology of religion has discovered is that conversion belongs primarily to the years between ten and twenty-five. This is the period of adolescence, and justifies the observation that conversion, or the beginning of religion, is an adolescent phenomenon. Starbuck observes, "that if conversion has not occurred before twenty, the chances are small that it will ever be experienced." [1] Coe brings together the cases of 1784 men and finds that the average age of the most decisive religious awakening or conversion is 16.4 years. This result is made more significant by noting that the 1784 cases are gathered by different investigators from different groups of people, and each set of cases agrees closely with the average age of the whole number. G. Stanley Hall brings together over four thousand cases of men in whom the average age of conversion is about sixteen.[2] He also quotes less accurate observations of evangelists and ministers based upon extended experience. These confirm in general terms the foregoing conclusions. All agree that between ten and twenty religious awakening occurs in far the largest number. Before and after that period

[1] E. D. Starbuck, *The Psychology of Religion*, p. 28. Conversion is here used in the broader sense, signifying no particular type of awakening.

[2] G. S. Hall, *Adolescence*, vol. ii, p. 290.

the number is relatively very small. Professor Coe, in his more recent investigations, considers early adolescence, about the age of twelve, the more important turning point. This is the time when the "gang impulse" is strong, and under proper training it is available for the larger, socializing process of religion.[1] It is probably true that the age of joining the church, especially in many protestant bodies, does not correspond to the time of first religious interest in the child, owing to the very common opinion that a child of twelve is too young to understand the obligations of church membership. This opinion in turn may be ascribed to the practice once prevalent in many communions of requiring all candidates for membership to make an elaborate statement of faith and to subscribe to a difficult creed. When, however, the reception of candidates is based less upon theological doctrine and more upon interest in other aspects of religion or upon formal catechisms, it is customary to receive them into membership in early puberty. At that time the impulse is less conscious of itself and less critical, but it may serve as the means of genuine attachment to the social group or religious body. Starbuck found the curve representing conversions contained three pronounced peaks indicating the points at which the greatest number of conversions occurred. These were at the ages for males of twelve, sixteen, and nineteen, the highest being at sixteen. He also found that these years represented well marked stages in the physical and mental development of adolescence. At twelve, with the beginnings of puberty, there is great im-

[1] G. A. Coe, *Education in Religion and Morals*, p. 255.

RELIGION AND ADOLESCENCE

pressionability and responsiveness to social suggestion. At sixteen the physical and psychical ferment of adolescence is at its height, and at nineteen, mental maturity and more reasoned decisions are characteristic.[1]

In liturgical churches practical wisdom through long experience has fixed upon this period of adolescence as the best time for confirmation. Greater importance belongs to this fact than is generally recognized, since such a practice involves a recognition of the fitness and readiness of children to enter into these relations. Among the orthodox Jews the oldest form of confirmation takes place at thirteen. The child now becomes responsible for his own acts. The father's responsibility ceases. The boy becomes a member of the congregation, and has the right to participate in the service of worship. In Roman Catholic countries, the age of confirmation varies. In Italy confirmation may be received as early as seven. In France and Belgium the earliest age for the rite is ten, while in America it is eleven or twelve. In the Greek Russian Church confession, which takes the place of confirmation, occurs about eight. There is reason to believe, however, that there has been a tendency here to remove back to an earlier age the rites which were once observed at puberty, just as circumcision among the Jews seems to have been moved back from early adolescence to infancy. In the Episcopal Church in England and America girls are seldom confirmed earlier than twelve, or boys earlier than fourteen. In the Lutheran Church confirmation occurs at fourteen or fifteen.

[1] E. D. Starbuck, *Psychology of Religion*, pp. 30, 206.

These ceremonies of confirmation in the religion of modern society correspond to the initiatory rites of primitive peoples. Such rites are universal. They indicate in an impressive way the radical change which transforms the individual during puberty and adolescence. "The universality of these rites and their solemn character testify impressively to a sense of the critical importance of this age almost as wide as the race." [1]

The external evidence could scarcely be more conclusive that the period of adolescence is the time in which the individual enters naturally upon religious and other social relations. At this time his social nature blooms into full power, so that the inner capacities and energies respond for the first time with spontaneity and depth of interest to the established customs and institutions of the race. The limited and external attitudes of the child give way before a sense of the importance of the group and of the ideal values of the social world.

This new social attitude, of which religion is the deepest and most intimate phase, is capable of still further explanation. The period of adolescence is marked by rapid and thorough-going changes in the whole physical and psychical nature. The entire body increases in size and weight. From fourteen to sixteen American boys average an increase in height of four and one-half inches. Girls from eleven to thirteen become five inches taller. The heart, lungs, and repro-

[1] G. S. Hall, *Adolescence*, vol. ii, p. 232. The chapter gives a survey of initiation ceremonies among savages, in classical antiquity, during the Middle Ages and throughout Christendom.

ductive organs undergo remarkable development in this period. The muscles increase in length and thickness, and according to some investigators the muscular tissue grows faster during puberty than any other tissue. There is relatively great resistance to disease. Before puberty the heart is small relative to the arteries, but in maturity the heart is large and the arteries relatively small. The blood-pressure is consequently greatly and even suddenly increased during puberty. At birth the relation of the heart to the arteries is as 25 to 20; at the beginning of puberty it is as 140 to 50; and in maturity it is as 290 to 61. These and other changes have been investigated in great detail. G. Stanley Hall, in his encyclopedic work on Adolescence, has brought together a surprising fund of information concerning the changes incident to adolescent development. Nearly all of these changes are those of enlargement, increased vitality, emotional sensitivity, and intellectual power.

The central and determining factor in this whole period is the appearance and maturing of the sexual instinct. No other feature of the complex change compares in importance with this. It is the organizing and controlling factor. Adolescence may be characterized "as primarily the time when youth comes to consciousness of the sexual functions, and when the chief problem of coördination is that of adjustment to the values of the social organism in which he lives." [1] At puberty the seat of authority shifts from the outer to the inner world. The instinct which hitherto moved parents and teachers to protect and further the wel-

[1] Irving King, *Psychology of Child Development*, p. 223.

fare of the individual now lives within his own nature, urging him forward to act for himself in the companionship and social life which love creates. This instinct radiates into many forms of expression both direct and indirect. Religion embodies many of these complex, ideal manifestations of the sexual impulse in varying degrees of elaboration in institutional agencies and in theoretical conceptions, according to the different levels of social evolution. This relation of sex and religion has sometimes received such partial and inadequate expression as to make the claim of such connection seem absurd and repulsive. This is true of those accounts of religion which emphasize vulgar, sensual cults as particularly typical of the nature of religion. Both the synchronous appearance of the sexual instinct and religious awakening, and the common social character of the two, point to their fundamental connection. "Nor is religion degraded by the recognition of this intimate relationship, save to those who either think vilely about sex or who lack insight into its real psychic nature, and so fail to realize how indissoluble is the bond that God and nature have wrought between religion and love." [1] Starbuck says, "The fact that spiritual upheavals centre mostly in the early years of adolescence rests ultimately upon the new developments then taking place in connection with the reproductive system. The physiological birth brings with it the dawning of all those spiritual accompaniments which are necessary to the fullest social activities. . . . This is the time biologically when one enters into deep relation with racial life. In a certain

[1] G. Stanley Hall, *Adolescence*, vol. ii, p. 293.

sense the religious life is an irradiation of the reproductive instinct."[1]

Those who regard religion as a perversion of the sexual instinct, and those who consider religion as antagonistic to this instinct, may be answered with facts. Phallic worship is often cited as evidence of the perversion of the sexual instinct. Crawley replies that, "Phallic worship proper is, however, extremely rare, if, indeed, it ever occurs; veneration, it is true, is frequently found, but this like many a so-called cult, is simply an affirmation of the sacredness of life. No student of anthropology now regards as serious the many attempts which have been made to raise such cases to the rank of organized 'phallic religions.'"[2] In the cruder religions where practices revolting to the modern sense are found, it is yet true that there is a love of life which affords a certain idealization of the life-giving processes upon which attention has been fixed. Among primitive peoples the gods were the givers of life and of material blessings, including the young of the flocks and the children of the family. The gods were the gods of fertility, of reproduction. All agencies and processes of this reproductive life were sacred. The sexual organs and the sexual acts were sacred, and they were accordingly consecrated by religious ceremonies. The very antagonism which some claim to discover between developed religion and the sexual instinct is due to the fact that religious customs

[1] E. D. Starbuck, *Psychology of Religion*, p. 401. The fact that Starbuck does not grasp clearly the full implications of this view does not weaken the force of the above statement of fact.

[2] Ernest Crawley, *The Tree of Life*, p. 272.

tend to regulate and thereby preserve and idealize this instinct. Any ascetic tendencies in developed religions are more than offset by the scrupulous, sympathetic regard for the reproductive life, which is expressed by making marriage a sacrament, circumcising or christening the infant, conceiving the deity as father, and exalting motherhood in worship and in art.

It is important to follow in some detail the workings of this instinct in the period of adolescence in order to make clear in what sense religion is regarded as an "irradiation of the reproductive instinct." It is the social character of the sexual nature which makes it so important in religion. This may be shown in terms of the socializing process which accompanies the rise of the sexual instinct in the individual. With the beginning of adolescence the social impulses manifest themselves in ways and with an intensity which cannot be accounted for in terms of imitation, of intellectual development, or of social pressure. There is something so spontaneous and irresistible about the social interests of youth as obviously to indicate that they have some other source than the will of teachers or other leaders. The social feeling of adolescence is original, inner, and urgent. The young man in his teens displays a sensitiveness to the praise and blame of his companions and others which is too strong to be ascribed to reason or custom. He is influenced in various ways by his new, strange interest in the opposite sex. His bluff, self-centered impulses are now softened and restrained by desire to win affection and admiration, and by anxious care for the comfort and happiness of the one he loves. No other influence is comparable to this maturing instinctive disposition for the development of attitudes of sympathy, coöperation, and sociability. For the first time in his experience there is a powerful and compelling inner motive urging regard for another to the point of complete self devotion. No labor, danger, or sacrifice is too great to win the fair one. This phenomenon affords endless material for poetry, fiction, and art. On the side of the difficulties encountered, jealousies engendered, and disappointments suffered, it is the theme of the drama and tragedy. In the common experience of average individuals, no other interest surpasses that which lovers feel in each other; and all people instinctively share this feeling with an intensity which permits no doubt that here is reënacted the most important event in the history of the individual and the race. It is through this affection and respect for the opposite sex that the whole complex system of social ends and institutions establishes its strongest hold upon the individual. Through it the individual is identified with the welfare of others by his own inmost desire: in this way through the home, the school, the shop, and the state he is placed in the midst of the vast social order of the material and ideal activities of mankind. His life is thereby disciplined, moralized, and spiritualized.

The strength of the sexual instinct on the social side appears in the extreme sensitiveness to the opinion of others, both in the craving for favorable attention and in the anguish inflicted by adverse criticism. The power and range of this sensitiveness in human life are better understood when viewed as an inheritance from man's animal ancestry. The male bird carefully grooms himself, spreads his plumage in sight of the female, calls her with wooing notes, fights his rivals with her favor as the stake, and by every means struggles to secure respect from his own and approval from the other sex. The long, exacting process of natural selection has perpetuated those types which succeeded best in securing these good opinions. The animal world is perpetuated by the individuals strongest, most clever, and most resourceful in gaining favorable attention and in avoiding neglect and disdain. The male is not alone in bidding for notice, though the female employs quite different means. She strives for effect by modesty, coyness, coquetry, pretended flight and other arts which induce excitement in the male. Her welfare also depends upon making an impression: therefore her happy song when successful, and her plaintive note or silence in defeat.

Among savages the most powerful means of enforcing social customs is the ridicule and contempt visited upon those who depart from the fashions. The boy or man who shows himself effeminate is called a woman, and often is consigned to the women's quarters for menial service. It is the brave, hardy, masterful man who wins applause from men and favors from women. The ambition of the savage youth is to kill his enemy in battle, to be successful in the hunt, and by strategy or skill to render notable aid to his tribe: and the moving desire of his heart in these things is for social recognition. "The Kite Indians have a society of young men so brave and so ostentatious of their bravery that they will not fight from cover nor turn aside to avoid running into an ambuscade or a hole in the ice. The African has the privilege of cutting a gash six inches long in his thigh for every man he has killed. The Melanesian who is planning revenge sets up a stick or stone where it can be seen; he refuses to eat, and stays away from the dance; he sits silent in the council and answers questions by whistling, and by other signs draws attention to himself, and has it understood that he is a brave and dangerous man, and that he is biding his time."

G. Stanley Hall has shown in detail the development of self-consciousness, vanity, affectation, and the inclination to show off among the youth of civilized society. Dress gains new interest. "The boy suddenly realizes that his shoes are not blacked, or his coat is worn and dirty, his hair unbrushed, his collar, necktie, or cap not of the latest pattern, while girls love to flaunt new fashions and color combinations, and have a new sense for the toilet." Manners also afford opportunity for expression of the new self-consciousness and means of bidding for good opinion. There is pleasure in playing rôles, assuming poses, cultivating moods, modifying one's speech in pronunciation, choice of words, and often in imitation of the vocabulary of favorite companions or teachers. Athletic feats, pride in physical development, trials of strength and absorbing interest in their "records" characterize boys in this epoch. The emotions of anger, fear, and pity are intensified, and relate to a much wider range of situations, particularly to those of personal relations.

PSYCHOLOGY OF RELIGIOUS EXPERIENCE

So deep and pervasive is this instinctive regard for the opinion of others that it remains vivid and excessive in after life. Fear of what the neighbors will say, the desire to see one's name in print, the constant and unflagging care of personal appearance, feeling for one's social standing, and awareness of all the little nothings by which the social self is seen to wax or wane, the nervousness which precedes and follows social functions, are evidences of the domination of non-rational, instinctive forces. "We are unduly interested when we hear that others have been talking about us; we are annoyed, even furious, at a slight criticism, and are childishly delighted by a compliment (without regard to our deserts); and children and adults alike understand how to put themselves forward and get notice, and equally well how to get notice by withdrawing themselves and staying away or out of a game. . . . All of this seems to indicate that there is an element in sensibility not accounted for on the exploit or food side, and this element is, I believe, genetically connected with sexual life. Unlike the struggle for existence in the ordinary sense of the phrase, the courtship of the sexes presents a situation in which an appeal is made for the favor of another personality, and the success of this appeal has a survival value — not for the individual but for the species through the individual." Professor Thomas expresses the conviction, therefore, "that we are justified in concluding that our vanity and susceptibility have their origin largely in sexual life, and that, in particular, our susceptibility to the opinion of others and our dependence on their good will are genetically referable to sexual life." [1]

It should be possible to make clear, in the light of the foregoing, just what is meant by the relation of the religious consciousness to the sexual instinct. It is held that sensitiveness to the opinion of others springs directly from the impulse underlying courtship between the sexes, and that this sensitivity is the basis and safeguard of social relations. It is this regard for the opinion of others which makes one amenable to the customs of society, and brings one into relation and coöperation with the conventions, fashions, duties, and ideals of society. Without this susceptibility to the opinion and example of others one is lacking in the essential quality of sociability. He is unresponsive to class restraints or stimuli, and shares to a degree the irresponsible and anti-social attitude of the criminal. The sexual instinct radiates this sympathetic, unifying disposition which produces groups for intimate association and mutual support. It is the source of the notable gregariousness of mankind. As it gives rise to larger groups, it becomes idealized in the relations of blood brotherhood among savages and in the societies of fraternity and practical endeavor among civilized peoples.

These groups continue to employ the technique of the sexual life. They appeal to the individual for his favor much after the method of courtship, and the individual is moved to respond by similar reactions. When the nation seeks volunteer recruits for its army and navy, it displays before the youth attractive pic-

[1] W. I. Thomas, *Sex and Society*, p. 113.

tures of military life, of uniforms, brilliant regiments, exploits of adventure and travel. The appeal is made through parades of picked soldiers, marching to stirring music, applauded by admiring spectators. Even the suggestion of danger on the battlefield is a claim upon the valor and gallantry which the republic, symbolized by a female figure, demands of her lovers among brave youth. The same technique of display, invitation, coyness, and modesty appears upon a vast scale when one nation visits another with a fleet of ships or entertains her visitors at a magnificent "world's exposition." The etiquette of nations is built upon the manners of my lady's drawing room, even more than upon the caution and suspicion with which strangers and enemies approach each other.

The type of social adjustment characteristic of the sexes is still more obvious in religious groups, and in the means used by such groups to win the devotion of individuals. Among the members of a religious body there exist ties of spiritual kinship supported by the strongest sentiments. The phraseology in Christian Churches is that of the family. The Church is the bride of Christ. The members are children of God; brothers and sisters to each other. They are born into this spiritual family, having been conceived by the Holy Spirit. Love is the pervading bond in all these relations. The virtues of Christian character are those which spring from love: sympathy, patience, forgiveness, fidelity, self-sacrifice, charity. The emotional attitudes aroused by the services of the churches are the tender, melting moods in which the will acquiesces in the appeal for love and comradeship.

RELIGION AND ADOLESCENCE

The derived character of the technique by which religion makes its appeal to the individual is in keeping with the organizing principle of religious groups. Professor Thomas has aptly described this process. "The appeal made during a religious revival to an unconverted person has psychologically some resemblance to the attempt of the male to overcome the hesitancy of the female. In each case the will has to be set aside, and strong suggestive means are used; and in both cases the appeal is not of the conflict type, but of an intimate, sympathetic and pleading kind. In the effort to make a moral adjustment, it consequently turns out that a technique is used which was derived originally from sexual life, and the use, so to speak, of the sexual machinery for a moral adjustment involves, in some cases, the carrying over into the general process of some sexual manifestations. The emotional forms used and the emotional states aroused are not entirely stripped of their sexual content." [1]

This controlling, organizing instinct which emerges with full power in adolescence is accompanied by an awakening of mental life on every side. The senses become more acute; the imagination is developed in new directions, with a scope and energy which often overwhelm the youth in a confusion of aspirations and longings; the will, in the form of urgent ambitions, is roused to resolve upon great enterprises such as patriotic service and social reforms; the intellect is stimulated to great activity, to criticism, analysis, careful reasoning and often to constructive production. It is

[1] W. I. Thomas, *Sex and Society*, pp. 115 f.

therefore the period of idealism, the age in which the ends set up for attainment are remote and vast. These ends are also ideal in the sense of being altruistic and disinterested. The same disregard of mere personal comfort or success which leads the youth to give himself with such abandon to win a lady's hand, is shown in devotion to other interests in which his will is once enlisted. The statistics concerning the aspirations of youth show that the tendency to go outside personal knowledge and choose historical and public characters as ideals is greatly augmented at puberty, when also the heroes of philanthropy show marked gain in prominence.[1] Earl Barnes remarks significantly, "No one can consider the regularity with which local ideals die out and are replaced by world ideals without feeling that he is in the presence of law-abiding forces." Dr. Thurber's replies from thousands of children in New York with reference to what they wanted to do when grown showed that "the desire for character increased throughout, but rapidly after twelve, and the impulse to do good to the world, which had risen slowly from nine, mounted sharply after thirteen." From his survey of many investigations, G. Stanley Hall concludes that with reference to the choice of ideals during childhood and youth, "Civic virtues certainly rise; material and utilitarian considerations do not seem to rise much, if at all, at adolescence, and in some data decline. Position, fame, honor, and general greatness increase rapidly, but moral qualities rise highest and also fastest just before and near

[1] G. S. Hall, *Adolescence*, vol. ii, p. 387, summarizes studies by Thurber, Earl Barnes, Kline.

puberty, and continue to increase later yet. By these choices both sexes, but girls far most, show increasing admiration of ethical and social qualities."[1]

By reason of instinctive awakening to the larger social interests, and by virtue of greater mental power for forming and following comprehensive ideals, youth is the period for the choice of life-occupations, for the development of patriotism, zeal for social reforms, and religious enthusiasms. At this age the whole nature is full of energy which creates boundless faith in the possibility of wonderful achievements. Idealism, in the strict psychological sense, that is, vital interest in distant and difficult, even utopian humanitarian enterprises, is natural to this age. There is, therefore, great enthusiasm for heroes, patriots, and religious leaders. It is the time when youth enlist in the army, when they devote themselves to social service, to foreign missions, and to philanthropy and charity. There are important variations from this general tendency of adolescent development which need to be kept in view. For one thing it should be said that the natural impulses of adolescence eventuate in ideal, social interests where the environment and training are such as to encourage that development. But not every youth is afforded the larger outlook upon life. Many do not get acquainted with the great characters of the race, and with the social ideals of their time. They may be children of illiterate parents whose world is small and barren; or they may be the children of well-to-do but uncultivated families lacking in seriousness of purpose and a sense of social obligations.

[1] G. Stanley Hall, *Adolescence*, vol. ii, p. 392.

PSYCHOLOGY OF RELIGIOUS EXPERIENCE

Within the middle class there is often an excess of worldly prudence which fills youth with desire for wealth and power for selfish ends. When these facts are considered it is evident that the naturally altruistic and social impulses of adolescents must be inherently powerful to be as prevalent and fruitful as they are. It is also true that much social enthusiasm spends itself in sentimentality and in other fruitless ways because it lacks wise guidance and the objectifying aids of social institutions. Many productive efforts are being made through public schools, social settlements, and other agencies to furnish all classes of youth contact with the social institutions about them. It cannot, therefore, be considered a refutation of the claim that youth is naturally susceptible to the appeal of religion considered as the inmost phase of the social consciousness, to say that the majority of youth do not become identified with the churches in protestant countries where attachment is voluntary. This may mean that religion does not secure an opportunity to present its claims fairly, that it does not have the adequate cooperation of the home and the school. Or it may mean that religion has become conventionalized and formalized upon the basis of archaic or partial views of life in a way which does not relate it to the activities and ideals which constitute for the youth of the times the essential social consciousness. Psychology does not posit an innate religious consciousness whose manifestation is inevitable any more than it posits an art consciousness which produces artists regardless of environment or training. But psychology does permit the statement that man is disposed to social relation-

RELIGION AND ADOLESCENCE

ships, especially in the period of adolescence, and that with opportunities to do so, he naturally participates in communal activities, including those of religion. If normal persons do not respond to religion during adolescence it must be due either to defects in existing religious institutions or to failure to estimate them properly. The very general current criticisms of the religion which is popularly taught, and particularly of the methods employed in religious instruction, may therefore be taken as explanations of the fact that many persons do not appear to be religious according to conventional standards. But there is reason also to believe that religion is far more vital in human experience than present statistics indicate.

Another set of facts which makes the expression of religion less simple and uniform than might be expected is the hesitancy, struggle, and confusion which the young person frequently experiences in reference to the whole subject. Adolescence is an epoch of rapid development. The individual becomes conscious of complex, established social interests which confront him with more or less strangeness and peremptoriness. His mental powers are alert. He has begun to analyze and question for himself. He labors to maintain his personality in relation to the life about him. He is not disposed to surrender his judgment or his will. He seeks to find relations in which he can realize himself in company with others, and do so with intellectual wholeness and self-respect. He is impelled to an altruism which is also self-realization. He is likely on this account to have many doubts and to question the whole system of ideas and practices of the social order, particularly if these are not readily and enthusiastically accepted by his companions or by those from whom he takes his cues for action. Social groups, religious and secular, are usually controlled by custom and authority. They make their appeal in terms of their age or prestige or of their special possession of revelation and "truth." They solicit a personal attitude of companionship, loyalty, and uncritical acceptance. But wherever there is richness and largeness of environment, the individual is summoned by many such groups, and is therefore likely to become hesitant and confused, and to question and inquire. But the social group has sprung from the instinct of gregariousness, and has been continued by imitation and social compulsion. The doubter, who demands reasons for his alliances, therefore challenges the group to an unnatural and unaccustomed defense. From the standpoint of the group, he appears unsympathetic. If he had the spirit, the sacred or holy spirit, which pervades the group, he would not question its right and its claim, but would sympathetically submit to it. Religious groups have usually shown this intolerance of dissenters and doubters, and have demanded complete submission and surrender. In modern society, where education and science train the youth in observation and in methods of independent judgment, there is an increased tendency to react against social groups which represent themselves as necessary to the individual and yet refuse to justify such claims in a rational way. The individual is none the less social, none the less impelled to respond to the supreme values which society affords. He is only seeking social and religious expression in ways which enlist his fullest loyalty, loyalty of mind as well as heart. Such persons sometimes find their way, suddenly, through an emotional experience, or gradually, through reflection and suggestion, into a religious society. But often they continue outside the conventional organizations, perhaps with conscious companionship among other types of persons and ideals, or, it may be, with waning interest in any such ideal associations. These various types of persons and their experiences in effecting social adjustments or failing to do so will be considered in the following chapters.

The study of adolescence has yielded the assurance that it is the normal period for the rise of religion in the individual. This is directly associated with the fact that the most fundamental characteristic of adolescence is the maturing of the sexual instinct. Out of this instinct spring the sympathetic social ties which are so essential to religion. The same impulse which impels to the union of individuals in courtship is carried over into the comradeship and brotherhood of families, clans, nations, and races. The same technique which characterizes the individual adjustments marks the union of groups, and is employed by society in winning the individual to its support. Religion as a social phenomenon is therefore not a perversion of the sexual instinct, but involves a complex and ideal development of that instinct. Whether specific normal individuals become truly social and religious depends upon the way in which their instinctive adolescent impulses are mediated by their environment and education.

CHAPTER XIII

NORMAL RELIGIOUS DEVELOPMENT

ALL authorities agree that the normal religious development of adolescence is one of gradual growth, including also what has been discussed by some as spontaneous awakening. In contrast to this, those experiences comprehended under the term conversion, such as intense, sudden emotional changes induced by manipulation, are regarded as abnormal. The word conversion is used by many authors in two senses. In the broader meaning it designates the transition from the world and attitude of childhood to the religious interests of maturity. In the other, it signifies the sudden, emotional and forced transformations which often occur in "revivals." G. Stanley Hall has the former in mind when he says: "In its most fundamental sense, conversion is a natural, normal, universal, and necessary process at the stage when life pivots over from an autocentric to an heterocentric basis." He further remarks that as civilization advances its revolutions cease to be sudden and violent, and become gradual without abrupt change. "The same is true of that individual crisis which physiology describes as adolescence, and of which theology formulates a spiritual aspect or potency called regeneration or conversion. True religion is normally the slowest because the most comprehensive kind of growth, and the entire ephebic decade is not too long and is well spent if altruism or love of all that is divine and human comes to assured supremacy over self before it is ended." "Conversion," writes Starbuck, "in its most characteristic aspect is identical with such spontaneous awakening as we have found in the so-called 'gradual growth' type." He also recognizes upon the basis of the results of his investigation that "it is doubtless the ideal to be striven after that the development during adolescence should be so even and symmetrical that no crisis would be reached, that the capacity for spiritual assimilation should be constantly equal to the demands that are made on consciousness."

The experience of Edward Everett Hale is frequently quoted as an illustration of the normal gradual development of religion. He says: "I observe, with profound regret, the religious struggles which come into many biographies, as if almost essential to the formation of the hero. I ought to speak of these, to say that any man has an advantage, not to be estimated, who is born, as I was, into a family where the religion is simple and rational; who is trained in the theory of such a religion, so that he never knows, for an hour, what these religious or irreligious struggles are. I always knew God loved me, and I was always grateful to Him for the world He placed me in. I always liked to tell Him so, and was always glad to receive His suggestions to me. To grow up in this way saves boy or youth from those battles which men try to describe and cannot describe, which seem to use up a great deal of young life. I can remember perfectly that, when I was coming to manhood, the half-

PSYCHOLOGY OF RELIGIOUS EXPERIENCE

philosophical novels of the time had a deal to say about the young men and maidens who were facing the 'problem of life.' I had no idea whatever what the problem of life was. To live with all my might seemed to me easy; to learn where there was so much to learn seemed pleasant and almost of course; to lend a hand, if one had a chance, natural; and if one did this, why, he enjoyed life because he could not help it, and without proving to himself that he ought to enjoy it. I suppose that a skillful professor of the business could have prodded up my conscience, which is, I think, as sensitive as another's. I suppose I could have been made very wretched, and that I could have made others very wretched. But I was in the hands of no such professor, and my relations with the God whose child I am were permitted to develop themselves in the natural way."

Professor James quotes similar experiences in his chapter on the religion of healthy-mindedness to show that many persons seem temperamentally weighted on the side of cheerfulness and optimism. They succeed, like Walt Whitman, in deriving great pleasure from ordinary people and things, and in avoiding fretfulness, antipathy, complaint, and remonstrance. In fact, the latter states of mind are not simply controlled or suppressed, but seem to be entirely absent. Where the habit of emphasizing the good and ignoring the painful factors of experience is once begun, it tends to extend itself and to radiate in all directions through one's life. This natural tendency of the habit of cheerfulness and evenness of temperament is also reinforced by the biological law through which the organism

NORMAL RELIGIOUS DEVELOPMENT

seeks to develop all pleasurable experiences and to escape or minimize all painful ones.

In the responses to my questionnaire relating to the religious experiences of childhood, adolescence, and maturity, there are many indicating a steady, quiet development. A minister writes, "Home influence was religious, with definite religious instruction. Sense of sin was not very strong at that early age. Later, say from eighteen years of age on, a sense of sin led to resolutions to be more moral. Lived a rather isolated life on a farm, was a nature lover. The question of joining the church arose upon reflection at twenty-three years of age. After due reflection, while living on the farm, went voluntarily and united with the —— Church on Sunday at regular services. Desiring, after some years, to preach, and being unable to reconcile my conscience with some things in the —— Church, united with the ——, among whom I have preached regularly ever since. Religious development has been continuous since then. In choosing occupation, etc., always acted after mature reflection."

One woman replied: "No, I have had no great struggle over decisions at any time — save once, when I tried to force myself to do a very foolish thing. The really great decisions of my life have been very easy to make." Another woman answered: "I joined the —— church very early in life because I was made to feel that I must, in order to please my parents, and to save my soul. It arose through the influence of my pastor, teacher, and mother. I was never satisfied with myself, because the problem was not as intense as I constantly saw that it was with others. I do not know that I had much religious development until I was twenty-four years of age. I accidentally became interested in the —— church. After uniting with this church I had a different feeling in regard to everything religious. Have been active since, and have enjoyed a gradual growth."

Another says: "I joined the church at twelve; it was hardly a question, certainly not a problem. I had always considered myself a child of God, and, when mother decided I was old enough, I entered the church without any struggle. It meant most to me in that the ceremony showed publicly that I was a Christian, a fact of which I did not want others, particularly children of my own age, to think that I was ashamed. My religious development has been continuous since then; that is, it has been definite growth, without intense struggles."

Probably one reason such cases have not been more frequently reported is that they appear uneventful and perhaps not so deeply religious. But it is necessary to include within the normal cases also those which are not quite so smooth and painless. The methods and atmosphere of the liturgical churches tend to gradual growth, but there often occur within them very pronounced emotional experiences. A Catholic child upon partaking of his first communion may experience as intense emotion as is found in the converts of evangelical churches.[1] The same tension is also found among those initiated into savage tribes.

In the records I have gathered there are many which

---

[1] Geo. A. Coe, *The Spiritual Life*, p. 48.

NORMAL RELIGIOUS DEVELOPMENT

confirm the results of other inquiries relative to the unevenness of the natural development. One respondent says: "As far back as I can remember I was interested in the church and its prosperity, never thought of myself as a spectator but as one engaged in and partly responsible for the work. This was the family attitude. Joined the church at about the age of eleven. Development not continuous. Occasional periods of conscious dereliction and of indifference, though chiefly the former. After entering college, I was pretty continuously engaged in some more or less public religious work, and the feeling of responsibility for this, as well as the sense of the need of consistency, usually carried me along. Had many times of inspiration and high resolve, usually coming through some speaker or some book."

An interesting illustration of recurring impulses toward larger development, continuing through several years, appears in the following: "My life can hardly be said to have had any sudden changes or radical awakenings, though there are in it a number of places where a new point of view or new interest has come with epoch-making effect. These old revivals of Methodists and Baptists undoubtedly exerted great influence, set up new ideals, and changed me. A great Presbyterian revival after I had joined the church left a lasting impression. A sermon by Stalker gave me guidance for a year or more; lectures on Dante at Johns Hopkins University, a stirring week with F. B. Meyer, Northfield, 1892; beginning critical work in the Old Testament under Paul Haupt, each of these brought such an awakening, though not in the nature of the sudden conversion which breaks utterly with the past."

The following extract is from the record of a woman highly trained in introspection. She joined the church at nine on her mother's suggestion. "Between the ages of sixteen and seventeen, I had an awakening which almost amounted to a conversion. That was my first year in college. I could not state the precise day or even month, but it was due to the religious life of Oberlin, and particularly to President King's training class. Religion became a much more personal matter; it suddenly occurred to me that instead of 'trying to be good' in the rather hopeless way I had always done, all I needed was to love God and 'people' so intensely that I would naturally want to do good, and would n't have to worry about particular actions. I do not think any change was visible outwardly. But inwardly, everything seemed to have a new meaning. I used to sit by the open window, night after night, after my room-mate had gone to sleep, praying. God seemed very real. A new love of people took possession of me; I don't think I had ever before cared deeply for any one. Now, even the meanest person seemed wonderfully significant, simply as a human being." Two years later there was another "distinct emotional awakening" which turned upon an intense affection for an older woman. The two finally became close friends. "In many respects it was like a religious awakening, especially in its sense of unworthiness."

The naturalness and normal character of sudden awakenings in adolescence is accounted for by the fact that at this time there is such a transformation of

NORMAL RELIGIOUS DEVELOPMENT

the individual through radical and rapid physical development; and so pronounced an emergence of the sexual instinct with its intense emotional and social elements. This wealth of energy and interest is not always provided by early training with models and habits which allow easy and frictionless adjustment. In many individuals the sense of novelty and wonder amount to confusion, hesitancy, and inhibition. In this state a slight outward circumstance may release the tension and precipitate into clearness and order the turbulent, chaotic inner world. In such solving moods the attention is narrowed and sometimes filled by quite incidental objects or events, which may remain vivid in memory long after. The senses acquire unusual sensitiveness. Hallucinations and illusions are frequent. Voices are heard and visions seen, sometimes in but this single instance in the lifetime. These easily become way-marks, if not commanding and guiding moments for the entire after life. Modern psychology recognizes the reality and even the normality of such experiences, but it does so simply in its effort to recognize the variety of temperaments and processes of development which different persons exhibit. It attaches no greater value to one type than to another, unless it does so by the tendency to consider those experiences most normal in which there is the fullest and best proportioned functioning of all powers of the mind. It is from this point of view that Professor Coe raises the query, "Has not the time come when we should frankly and persistently deny that the culminating type of religious experience, by which all other types are to be judged, is a state in which rational self-control lapses?" This question follows the observation that "we are obliged to face the fact that some devoted souls appear to themselves not to have experienced any such personal revelation. They have seen no visions, heard no voices, enjoyed no ecstatic communion, received no inspirations, been conscious of nothing beyond what they are able to classify under the ordinary workings of the mind." [1]

That these spontaneous awakenings are natural and not possessed of any inherent superiority over the more prosaic experiences is seen in similar phenomena in other than the religious sphere. One of my respondents writes: "I have had awakenings other than religious, that is, the historical conception of literature was almost an awakening. The study of Browning stirred me more deeply than most religious instruction given directly. The poems that interested me most were the religious and ethical poems together with those on art subjects." This person's ethical development was of the same kind. He stopped various bad habits abruptly — swearing, smoking cigarettes, and drinking. Another man could not find any specialized religious emotions in his experience. "I have never experienced any which were peculiar to any part I ever took in religious activity. The same feeling of exhilaration has been often experienced in periods of excitement over any successful outcome and in cases where I appear to advantage, such as a good run in football, a good hit at baseball, a good recitation at school. I can experience this feeling in slight degree by voluntary imagery."

[1] G. A. Coe, *Religion of a Mature Mind*, pp. 232, 233.

NORMAL RELIGIOUS DEVELOPMENT

An illuminating illustration of essentially religious interest and enthusiasm in the direct relationship of mutual human helpfulness is contained in the last sentence of the following statement: "I did much church and charity work. In the former I was greatly hampered by my lack of acquaintance with myself and other people; I had to learn to express myself in deeds and words in the terms of ordinary conventional life, and the process was full of misunderstandings. In the latter I was at home from the first, and I had an almost pagan delight in the feeling of kinship, which one has with all classes of people in those things which are real to them — usually their needs or their work." Another woman developed a somewhat similar experience through initiation into a fraternal order. She had joined the church at fifteen under the influence of her mother, but was not very enthusiastic. "My mother became president of a philanthropic society, composed of members of the Order of the Eastern Star. I began (about the age of eighteen) to see what the women of that society were doing, and saw it was a good work. Now for the first time in my life did I see the great significance of a religious society. My mother said nothing of joining and I said little. Several nights, however, I thought of the wonderful work the order was doing, and after some contemplation I decided to become a candidate for the O. E. S. I joined the Order. The initiation ceremonies could not have been more impressive; I felt most happy; I was overjoyed. I now thought I knew what true religion was."

In quite different fields this process of inquiry and

anxiety often issues in sudden insight and reshaping of interest and activity. Starbuck cites the fact that the athlete "sometimes awakens suddenly to an understanding of the fine points of the game, and to a real enjoyment of it, just as the convert awakens to an appreciation of religion." [1] William Lowe Bryan's investigation of learning telegraphy contributes valuable data on this point. He found that before facility is attained, there is a long time in which the efforts of the student register no appreciable gain. "Suddenly, within a few days, the change comes, and the senseless clatter becomes intelligible speech." [2] Other instances, analogous to spontaneous religious awakening, are those in which the illumination occurs in moments of mental leisure, when there is no effort or anxiety to get the result. The cases of Sir William Hamilton's conception of quaternions and Mozart's composition of the aria of the quintette in the Magic Flute are well known.[3]

The process of gradual growth is to be regarded, therefore, as inclusive of various types. These depend upon differences of temperament. Persons of phlegmatic and persons of mercurial temperament naturally react differently to the same situations and problems. It is also true that the same person, in different stages of development, in different states of physical energy, and in varying moods will not be uniform in intensity and quality of experience. Grad-

[1] E. D. Starbuck, *Psychology of Religion*, p. 385.
[2] "Studies in the Physiology and Psychology of the Telegraphic Language," *Psychological Review*, January, 1897.
[3] Joseph Jastrow, *The Subconscious*, p. 95.

NORMAL RELIGIOUS DEVELOPMENT

ual growth is not to be conceived as an absolutely regular movement, advancing always with the same measured increment. None of the processes of nature conform strictly to that conception. On the contrary there are in all biological growth rhythm, periodicity, epochal moments and level planes. Even shocks and crises occur. This is true of the highest forms of human development. The intellectual and the esthetic life, the attainment of skill in any technique of a spiritual as of a practical character involve some vibration of interest, some pulsation of attention and emotion. All such phenomena have a legitimate place within the natural development of religious life, but they do not justify accentuation of the crises as though they possessed extraordinary value. The ideal growth in any organism is that which maintains proportion, fosters adaptability, and affords energy. The ideal religious development is that in which the individual progressively participates in the practical activities and ethical consciousness of the best of the race.

The psychology of growth implies the operation of the educational process. It is the very nature of the educational method to mediate to the individual the experience and enthusiasm of society in such a way that he lives the fullest possible life of which he is capable at each stage of development. The educational process is in principle simply the furnishing of the natural impulses and instincts with such materials and direction as are suited to them at any given time. In religion, even more than in other subjects, it is necessary to emphasize the protest of modern educational psychology that education is not a preparation for life, but that it is rather a means of larger life at each stage as it unfolds. Religious education not only has been viewed as a means of preparing for the future, but has often assumed the inadequacy of its method in two other respects. Where conversion is regarded as the great point in individual experience, it is usually conceived as a crisis in which other than the normal processes of educational development are at work. The most that education can do, then, is to lead one up to a point where one becomes the subject of non-natural influences. It follows in the popular mind, and is not without academic endorsement, that the religious experience may be attained without the educational process. Nor is the religious experience discounted by seeming to occur apart from such preliminary training. The result is that in many evangelical churches the work of the church school is interrupted, if not annulled, by "revivals" and "decision days," in which other than normal educational influences are sought. Membership in the church and the democracy of its personal relationships are then based upon this emotional event, rather than upon participation in the practical ideals and objective activities of the organization. It is important, therefore, to consider the psychology of the educational process to determine whether it is capable of fostering genuine religious experience without resorting to some additional extraneous agency.

Another consequence of this widely prevalent notion of religion is the view that if the educational method is employed for the advancement of religion,

NORMAL RELIGIOUS DEVELOPMENT

yet only a certain subject matter, such as biblical history and later religious biography, should be used. Here again the educational process is in theory abstracted from the actual religious experience. Education thus becomes a vehicle, indifferent in itself, by which the quality of religion is somehow transferred to the inquirer. Because of such supposed uniqueness of religion, both in the manner by which it is limited to a given historical tradition and in the strange method of being imparted to the individual, there is distrust and inefficiency in the use of religious education. So long as this fallacy persists the educational process cannot be fully accepted as the instrument of religious development. It is the task of the psychology of religion to discover the nature, genesis, and development of the religious consciousness, in terms of the mental life of the race and the individual. In the light of its results it may determine whether the educational process is the natural and necessary method of cultivating religion in the individual.

The results of our study have indicated that religion arises naturally, being an inherent and intimate phase of the social consciousness. It is not within the intent of this investigation to estimate the differences in value between the religions of various races, but it is legitimate to note the fact that anthropology and historical science do not show any fundamentally different psychical factors in different religions. Rather does it become apparent that there is a striking similarity in their underlying patterns and in their development. The differences are those of degree of morality, ideality, and method. The religion of a

PSYCHOLOGY OF RELIGIOUS EXPERIENCE

people is a reflex, the most inward and revealing reflex, of the civilization and spirit of that people. The process by which the individual comes to share in the religion of his people — or of another people — is just the process by which he enters into and becomes dominated by the civilization, the art, the science, the social ideals of that people. This process is that of education. It is a gradual attainment, rising in adolescence to its first full inwardness in accordance with deep grounded laws both of the individual organism and of the social body. It is a psychological fallacy, which has borne bitter fruit, to allow the point where this tidal movement expands and registers itself with vivid consciousness for some individuals to obscure the far more important and permanent processes. These underlying processes occur for many persons in whom they never create acute and revolutionary states of consciousness, and it is psychologically untrue and unjust to exclude such persons in theory from the ranks of the religious.

The psychology of the religious consciousness is furnishing religious education with certain general principles. These are not essentially different from the principles which general psychology contributes to pedagogy, but they may be stated in terms of religious experience. First, the psychology of religion does not find child nature irreligious. It condemns the old theories of natural depravity and perversity. It recognizes the spontaneous, instinctively selective activity of the child. This activity is the important thing and is the determining factor with reference to the materials needed to satisfy it and the influ-

NORMAL RELIGIOUS DEVELOPMENT

ences valuable for directing it to fuller self-realization. This insight into child nature emphasizes differences of temperament and energy. One sees in groups of kindergarten children, and even in the nursery at an earlier age, variations of disposition. Some are quicker in reaction to suggestion; some reflect longer and more aptly upon their experiences; some are more sensitive to companionship, music, rhythm, or pictures. A set of little children displays as much variation as the same number of adults from the same social stratum, and the children are less habituated to limited types. Religious education is therefore under obligation to respect the nature of the child and to have regard for the individuality which it possesses. The latter requires individual training in small groups.

Second, the education of the child must be more than intellectual. Perhaps religious training is not in danger of exaggerating the intellectual side, but it is remarkable how much attention has been given to imparting knowledge of religious books, facts of history and doctrine, involving memory training chiefly. The child is open to indirect influences such as those of example and surroundings. By these, as well as by music, pictures, games, plays, manual work, caring for pets and aiding others in real tasks in the home and school, he gains valuable habits, sympathies, and a sense of usefulness which are real factors in education. In these ways his emotions are more likely to grow out of real interests, rather than to arise as detached experiences. The latter occurs where the training has been bookish and abstract. This formal and lifeless mental work has been partly responsible for the common opinion that emotional experiences, with which religion is too often identified, must be cultivated apart from educational processes and by some other method. The difficulty arises from a narrow and partial conception of education. Where this term is properly used, to designate the enrichment and enlargement of the whole nature, it is understood to involve the proper exercise of the will and emotions as well as of the intellect. Considering education in the truest sense, the individual probably derives as much of it from the informal experiences "out of hours" as he does in class exercises or other formal occasions.

Third, the child's interest is primarily in activities and in concrete things close at hand. Much of the material for religious training must therefore be found in the duties and companionships of the home and neighborhood; in the movements of community life affecting its health, beauty, and safety; in the festival occasions connected with private and public interests; and in the services of public leaders whose work takes on great social importance. With these natural interests, the records of peoples remote in time and custom may be easily related, but psychologically these records are only means and instruments. Their value consists in the degree to which they suggest and cultivate attitudes and tendencies which are available in the present concerns of life. If they serve to show in simple form social processes and qualities which have now grown complex; if they intensify with color and ruggedness the story of moral endeavor and achievement in ways which appeal to the child's imagi-

NORMAL RELIGIOUS DEVELOPMENT

nation, then, they are valuable educational servants. The phenomena of nature also become aids in religious training by their relation to human needs and welfare. Man lives close to the soil and to what it produces. His social activities are largely those concerned with these products, and these processes of nature relate to past ages and to distant suns in such a way that the profoundest interests of the race are bound up with them. There is consequently the sense of great reality, power, law, and vast proportions in the natural environment. From the earliest myths to the highest reflections of the mind this realm of nature has been conspicuous in religion, and it is not difficult to utilize it for the religious development of the child.

Fourth, psychology has discovered the epochal, yet continuous, character of the child's development. While the period of adolescence is without question the time at which the religious development is rapid, full, and vivid, yet it is not lacking in earlier years. The presence of the social attitudes of sympathy, trustfulness, and coöperation, though in slight degree and with striking unsteadiness, proves the continuity of religious experience. Genetic psychology here, as in other interests, teaches respect for each stage of experience as possessing its own level of achievement and the standards by which it should be cultivated. Thus early childhood is one of great activity and imitativeness. The stories dramatized and the ritual imitated may not have any ulterior reference in the mind of the child, but they afford an immediate and legitimate satisfaction. About the age of nine there appears keen interest in picturesque biography and in thrilling events. The heroes and wars of migrations are greatly appreciated. This is the period, up to the age of twelve, of habit-forming and of maximum power of memorizing. Perhaps the religion normal to this period may be characterized as that of forming the habits of cleanliness, industry, honesty, and obedience, and of memorizing the great literature, poems, and hymns of religion. At twelve appear the pre-adolescent social impulses which make membership in social groups natural. Altruistic tendencies manifest themselves in this social interest and in the desire to turn one's activity to account, for example, in making useful objects. And here is begun that positive constructive process of moralizing and socializing the individual's experience which makes the following period the birth time of the new and larger self. Psychology therefore does not need to impart knowledge of these processes in order to enable education to produce them in individuals, but rather to make educational methods efficient in giving richness, symmetry, and freedom to adolescent life in its natural regeneration or "second birth."

Fifth, the educational process is one which psychology shows to be possible of continuance far beyond adolescence. The brain power does not begin to diminish normally until after the age of fifty-five. Many individual cases of mental alertness and development beyond that age are well known. Gladstone is an example. Continuous mental development in maturity may be said to be determined largely by the presence or absence of essentially educational influ-

NORMAL RELIGIOUS DEVELOPMENT

ences such as new stimuli, change of environment, fresh materials in tasks and thought. The attitude of the individual is also a contributing factor. If he cultivates expectancy, disciplines himself to new adjustments and keeps his powers in constant use, his development is more likely to be prolonged.

The psychological data in this period of post-adolescent religious experience are as yet entirely inadequate. The study of religious awakening shows that it does occur in some instances after sixty, and in a larger number of cases during each of the earlier decades after forty.[1] Religion in the process of gradual growth is psychologically just as capable of extension and enrichment in middle life, as are professional, business, and social interests. These may attain almost as radical and vivid a character as the adolescent experiences. Tolstoy at the age of fifty passed through three years of storm and stress. He describes the outcome in his Confession. "After this, things cleared up within me and about me better than ever, and the light has never wholly died away. I was saved from suicide. Just how or when the change took place I cannot tell. But as insensibly and gradually as the force of life had been annulled within me, and I had reached my moral death-bed, just as gradually and imperceptibly did the energy of life come back. And what was strange was that this energy that came back was nothing new. It was my ancient juvenile force of faith, the belief that the sole purpose of my life was to be *better*. I gave up the life of the conventional world, recognizing it to be no life, but a

[1] G. Stanley Hall, *Adolescence*, p. 289.

parody on life, which its superfluities simply keep us from comprehending."[1]

[1] William James, *Varieties of Religious Experience*, p. 185. The phenomena of "sanctification" are of interest in this connection. These do not seem to involve processes radically different from adolescent awakenings. Cf. E. D. Starbuck, *Psychology of Religion*, chapter xxix.

CHAPTER XIV

CONVERSION

IN contrast to the normal process of gradual growth including spontaneous awakenings are the phenomena of conversion in the narrower use of the term. Conversion designates the more sudden, intense, and extreme emotional experience. It is the result of immediate, direct control and suggestion on the part of evangelists, parents, teachers. It is common among certain evangelical protestant denominations. It occurs chiefly in those communions which have cultivated an elaborate technique to produce it. Such religious bodies are constituted largely by persons who have themselves experienced religion in that way and who therefore naturally value it highly. The liturgical cults and the more intellectual churches tend to emphasize gradual growth through education and ceremonies of confirmation. These ceremonies are designed to give recognition to the attainment of religious experience as much as to induce it. Certain temperaments experience conversion easier than others. The racial characteristics of some nations seem to be favorable soil for it. Professor James observes that "on the whole, the Latin races have leaned more to the way of looking upon evil as made up of ills and sins in the plural, removable in detail; while the Germanic races have tended rather to think of Sin in the singular and with a capital S, as of something ineradicably ingrained in our natural subjectivity, and never to be removed by any superficial piecemeal operations." The latter accordingly have prized the profound emotional experiences of the mystical type.

The stages of the process of conversion are just those found in working out any intense problem under pressure — first, a sense of perplexity and uneasiness; second, a climax and turning point; and third, a relaxation marked by rest and joy. It is not difficult to induce such experiences in adolescence because it is so much a period of new problems and adjustments. The emotional accompaniment is correspondingly marked, and greatly heightened effects are secured by suggestions which add to the tension, and which, at the same time, assure the subject of the great spiritual significance and value of such tension.

The first stage, the one in which the person feels keen dissatisfaction with himself, has been intensified in many denominations by the prevalent doctrine of the natural sinfulness of human nature. Slight misdeeds were regarded as evil not merely in their own character but especially as indications of the sinful heart from which they sprang. The childish lie or cruel act was a surface symptom of abysmal depths of iniquity which only the most searching regeneration could eradicate. It is a common characteristic of puberty to be hypersensitive with reference to its faults. Youth is liable to become finical and to set up extreme and rigid standards for puerile details. Coe cites the case of a girl about twelve who was troubled with "over nice conscientiousness about stealing." "She would not take so much as a pin without permission, or if, when visiting any of her friends, she found it necessary to take one, she inflexibly compelled herself to tell the hostess, saying, 'I took one of your pins.' This was a very painful process to her, though she did not see the absurdity of it, but thought she was merely doing her duty."[1] G. Stanley Hall observes that "in this state of nerves and moral touchiness, youth often grow irritable and have bitter and long conflicts with their tempers. Fears of having committed the unpardonable sin, in rare cases, become tragic."[2] It is of course not difficult to produce an intense "conviction of sin" in such persons. The natural division of the self is easily widened into a chasm of despair, so that the subject agonizes over his lost and helpless state. Starbuck's cases[3] show that the central fact in the consciousness of converts is the sense of sin, of having a "black heart," "a great and unaccountable wretchedness." They are marked by depression and sadness, by self-distrust and helplessness, by estrangement, by restlessness and anxiety. In many instances the strain involved loss of sleep and appetite, nervousness, affection of the sight, hearing, touch, and other bodily functions. This state may continue for weeks or months, and in not a few individuals has produced melancholia and insanity. Adolescent suicide is sometimes the outcome of this sense of misery and gloomy foreboding. This sense of sin is an experience

[1] G. A. Coe, *The Spiritual Life*, p. 77.
[2] G. Stanley Hall, *Adolescence*, vol. ii, p. 348.
[3] E. D. Starbuck, *Psychology of Religion*, chapter v.

of pain and remorse. "It pricks, stings, burns, wounds, brings restlessness and anxiety, a sense of oppression, as under a heavy load." It is not due exclusively to actual sinfulness. Those who are relatively innocent often suffer as keenly as those who have sinned deeply. The chasm created in the inner nature depends for both classes very much upon the imagination and sensitiveness of the subject, and upon suggestions as to how one should feel. The qualms felt bear no definite relation to the sins. Starbuck found that while the sense of sin follows naturally in the wake of evil, it has other causes, such as temperament and ill health. Hysteria and other nervous and circulatory disorders are common causes. He found that among those of good training two thirds of his cases experienced a sense of sin, due doubtless to the suggestion that they ought to feel it. In this way the normal sensitiveness and confusion of adolescence, the consciousness of contrast between the actual and ideal self, between the subjective, individual self and the great organized social order, is increased by various kinds of pressure to the abnormal degree common in the conviction period of conversion.

The second moment in the conversion experience is the turning point at which the tension, confusion, and strife between the old and the new are overcome. This decisive moment is the culmination of a positive struggle in some persons. In others it seems to come unexpectedly in moments of passivity and diffused attention. It is the moment at which the "hot spot" or focus shifts from one system of ideas to another, establishing a new centre of interest in the as-

CONVERSION

sociative processes of the mind. One author describes the crisis as if the present sinful life and the wished-for righteous one were pressed together in intense opposition, and were struggling for possession of consciousness. Relative to this conflict the subject himself may seem a passive observer, witnessing within his own soul the conflict between the good and evil spirits. This turmoil is resolved in a great variety of ways. In those persons who are susceptible of automatisms, and who have been taught to prize such experiences, the decisive moment may be one in which involuntary muscular reactions occur, such as clapping the hands, uncontrolled laughter, shouting, gesticulations, or a thrill through the whole body. In great revival meetings, under the contagion of suggestive examples, many strange extravagances — falling, jerking, jumping, rolling, barking — have occurred. Striking dreams and hallucinations, particularly of a visual character, are still more common. Professor Coe found in examining several persons with reference to such phenomena that those who experienced automatisms in religion usually had also experienced them in other than religious situations; and that those who did not have them outside of religion were not likely to undergo them in conversion, no matter how much they desired it. These facts point to the conclusion that the automatisms are matters of temperament, and have no religious value, and cannot be regarded as evidence of religious development in the truest sense. They are psychologically irrelevant and exceptional, and are therefore abnormal so far as religious awakening is concerned.

PSYCHOLOGY OF RELIGIOUS EXPERIENCE

It would be equally misleading to attach special religious importance to other incidental factors through which the extreme emotional sensitiveness of the convert may happen to be precipitated into the new state. The singing of the choir, the pleading of voices in prayer, the sermon, the touch of a friendly hand, a text of scripture, memory of a childhood scene, a glimpse of the sunset, the sound of a storm, the quiet of the forest, the silence of the night — any one of innumerable experiences or images may fill the moment in which the die is cast. Or there may be no such discoverable moment at all, as where the change takes place "while asleep" or while reading. Even with intense conviction of sin and with pronounced feelings of satisfaction in the new state the exact point of transition may not be localized nor identified with specific mental content.

The crucial moment of conversion presents two main types, self-surrender and active effort toward the new life. The attitude of self-surrender seems many times to result from fatigue and nervous exhaustion due to the anxiety for one's sins or to the effort to resist the conviction of sin. As Professor James expresses it, "Our emotional brain-centres strike work, and we lapse into a temporary apathy. Now there is documentary proof that this state of temporary exhaustion not infrequently forms part of the conversion crisis. So long as the egoistic worry of the sick soul guards the door, the expansive confidence of the soul of faith gains no presence. But let the former faint away, even but for a moment, and the latter can profit by the opportunity, and, having once

CONVERSION

acquired possession, may retain it." This type is more common in extremely sudden and intense conversions. That of active effort toward the new life, where one breaks through into new insight and adjustment, is often found in cases of normal development, although at times it reaches an extreme intensity.

The third stage is physically and psychically a reaction from the previous strain, and is largely determined in character and intensity by the earlier experience. It is essentially a new adjustment which is accompanied by the emotions belonging to harmony, victory, a release from tension. This harmony may consist in the sense of escape from sin and its consequences, or in the feeling of completeness and exalted personality. The emotions are largely those of joy, peace, happiness, and acceptance. There is frequently a sense of newness or purification which suffuses commonplace objects and experiences with fresh interest. One says, "I wept and laughed alternately. I was as light as if walking on air. I felt as if I had gained greater peace and happiness than I had ever expected to experience." Another says, "There followed a delightful feeling of reconciliation with God and love for Him." Where the pre-conversion state has been the conviction of sin and the desire to rid one's self of it, the post-conversion state is more passive, and its joy is more that of relief and safety. Where aspiration after a new and larger life has prevailed, the joy has an active quality, a sense of participation in new companionships and nobler tasks. But in the most typical conversion experiences all dissatisfaction with one's self, whether in reference to evil habits chaining one to a bitter past, or the sense of need and longing for greater completeness in the future, are attributed to one's sinful nature. In reference to this sinful nature sorrow and travail of soul are cultivated.

It has been found that conversions vary in the different sexes, ages, and temperaments. Among females the struggle is likely to be less prolonged and intense in public meetings. This indicates greater suggestibility, readier response to social pressure, and more extreme emotionalism. Females have more intense and longer periods of struggle where they endeavor to work out the problem alone. Males, on the contrary, resist public appeals stubbornly and persistently. Their intellectual activity is more in evidence and the conflict becomes more intense in revivals. In private the process is easier. This difference in the sexes is probably an expression of fundamental biological contrasts which show woman to be more passive and receptive, more subject to manipulation; while man is active, aggressive, given to independence and resistance. He submits less readily to authority, and prefers to have the sense of reaching his own conclusions. This individualism tends to private reflection, and is inhibited by public pressure and emotional appeals.

In regard to age, adolescence is the period of most conversions, but within this time there are three points at which the phenomena of conversion take on different aspects. Starbuck's tables [1] seem to show

[1] E. D. Starbuck, *Psychology of Religion*, p. 57.

CONVERSION

that at the age of twelve the greater number are influenced by example and social pressure; that is, imitation is most conspicuous. At about fifteen or sixteen, for both sexes, conviction of sin with fear is dominant; while at about eighteen the desire to follow out the moral ideal of completeness of character prevails.

The differences of temperament pertain largely to susceptibility to suggestion and to automatisms. It is of great importance historically that the apostle Paul and St. Augustine belonged to the type for which the extreme form of emotional, dramatic conversion is possible. Their personal experience has been regarded as of superior value because it has been assumed uncritically that their moral characters and achievements were determined by the manner of their conversion. But when it is recognized that Paul was probably a neurotic, and that Augustine was a sensualist with a highly developed nervous temperament, it becomes apparent that there were very special individual reasons for their dramatic conversions. It also appears that the forms of their conversions are accidental and not essential in spiritual development. The attempts to induce that type of experience among all classes of persons have failed, and such failures have proved not the depravity of the recalcitrant, unresponsive persons, but the one-sided and abnormal character of the cases set up as the standard.[1]

The nature of the conversion experience appears

[1] Frank Granger, *The Soul of a Christian*, p. 76; Royse, "The Psychology of Saul's Conversion," *American Journal of Religious Psychology and Education*, vol. i, 1904.

clearly in that it is induced through the manipulation of natural tendencies, and results in the strained, partial, and abortive issue of such tendencies. The fact that conversion is due to artificial control and forcing of natural processes is definitely recognized by Starbuck. "Theology takes these adolescent tendencies and builds upon them; it sees that the essential thing in adolescent growth is bringing the person out of childhood into the new life of maturity and personal insight. It accordingly brings those means to bear which will intensify the normal tendencies that work in human nature. It shortens up the period of duration of storm and stress, but they are very much more intense. The bodily accompaniments — loss of sleep and appetite, for example — are much more frequent." [1] Instead of "theology" it perhaps should be said that current religious practice in many sects is the instrument for working these results. This practice is more or less consciously related to certain theological presuppositions, but it measures itself not by its theoretical principles but by its ability to get results.

The most common methods of inducing conversion are those of the revival. Under this term may be included the evangelistic sermons of pastors, the "rally days" of Sunday Schools, and the exhortations of "personal workers." These are usually auxiliary to the revival, but are also employed independently. The process of suggestion in the work of the most expert evangelists is begun months before they reach the community where the revival is to occur. They

[1] E. D. Starbuck, *Psychology of Religion*, p. 224.

CONVERSION

send advance agents, advertising material, and directions for local workers. All these are employed to cultivate expectation and to fix attention upon the revivalist and his work. An important factor for this purpose is the recital of what has been accomplished by him in other places. The longer, more varied and better known his record, the keener is the interest in his appearance in the community. Even the difference of opinion as to the legitimacy of his work is an aid, since it provokes discussion, makes his mission known, and stimulates curiosity. When the revivalist comes he gives detailed instructions to all workers, especially with reference to creating conditions under which attention can be focused upon his mission and his appeal. As many religious persons as possible are urged to give up all other interests, and to think, pray, converse, and labor only for the "salvation of souls." The public meetings are conducted with scrupulous care to the fixation of attention and to the cultivation of the same sentiments and emotions throughout the mass of the people. An atmosphere of group consciousness through common ideas and concerted action is thus created which exerts a powerful influence. Several services may be held before a definite "invitation" is given. Those who are ready to declare themselves at once are kept from doing so until enough are ready to make a more profound impression by their joint action. It is found to be more telling, for example, to secure fifty public confessions for the end of the first week of sustained expectancy than to have them distributed in smaller groups.

The service is begun with familiar, pleading songs

and prayers, and moves suggestively on to the sermon. And the sermon is artfully constructed to produce the customary responses on the part of "seekers." The sermon is hortatory in character, and is delivered with every device which will hold attention; sensory attention being quite as important as intellectual attention. The doctrine preached is that which is current in the popular mind, and it is employed as a familiar background without argument or logical presentation. Revival sermons are therefore always theologically conservative. As theological opinion changes, the doctrine of evangelists is gradually though tardily readjusted. Jonathan Edwards employed the theology of the older Calvinism and appealed to the emotion of fear. Dwight L. Moody adopted modified Calvinism and dwelt upon the emotion of love with its radiating forms of pity, remorse, self-sacrifice, and devotion. There have been later attempts to develop revivals of ethical religion in response to the newer doctrines of moral and social philosophy, but these attempts have tended to make clear the superiority of the method of education to that of conversion for promoting such ideals. There are now, accordingly, numerous efforts to substitute educational work for revivalism. This is notably true in Mr. Moody's later work, in the Young Men's Christian Association, and in the increasing effort to supply the Sunday School with the means and methods of genuine education. The characteristic revival sermon puts the commonly accepted theological notions into vivid, stirring imagery and into appealing stories of the tragedies of the inner life as they occur among the people. It employs

CONVERSION

familiar symbolism, — the cross and crown, heaven and hell, home and mother. Reminiscent associations are employed to awaken the sense of lost virtue, of unforgiven sins, and of the pleading, persuasive influences once effective but now long forgotten or resisted. The main themes of guilt and forgiveness are thus, with all these accessories of suggestion, affirmed and repeated, affirmation and repetition being indispensable in producing the desired result. The speaker is dramatic in manner, epigrammatic and colloquial in style, rapid and impassioned in speech. Even grotesque and startling devices are effective, such as striking the pulpit or the floor with the hands, standing on chairs, walking through the audience while speaking, removing one's coat, singing, shouting, and similar various sensational feats.

Another powerful agency coöperates with the sermon, songs, and prayers: the influence of the crowd. The whole service fixes attention upon certain ideas familiar to all and actively assented to by the majority in such religious gatherings. The appeals from the pulpit are intensified and vibrated through the crowd by waves of feeling and subdued response. The process of radiation, usually quite unconscious, consists in nodding assent, smiling approval, whispering catch-words, sinking into intent silence, or shouting "Amen!" and "Hallelujah!" There is something very real and compelling about the "strained attention," "bated breath," and "ominous hush" of the crowd. Few persons can resist the social pressure thus generated. The effect upon most people is to reduce their independence and to impel them to the prevailing sentiment and proposed action. This becomes most extreme, and the suggestibility and demonstrative responsiveness greatest among those in the audience standing crowded together at the sides or in the aisles. The variety and intensity of their voluntary movements are greatly inhibited and suggestion is less resisted. "It is said that in the French theatre of the old régime the standing portion of the audience (pit) was always more emotional and violent in its demonstrations than the sitting portion (parquet), and that the providing of seats for the pit spectators greatly quieted their demeanor."[1] The mass of people dominated by an evangelist acts as a means of multiplying emotion until it radiates to those who are indifferent or antagonistic to it. Davenport cites two such instances.[2] One is that of the young man witnessing a camp-meeting. "He had had no religious experience and at that time did not wish any. The crowd was laboring under great religious excitement, and reflex phenomena were abundantly in evidence. Suddenly my friend found himself with his hands pressed against his lungs, shouting 'Hallelujah!' at the top of his voice." The other instance is still more striking: "The old tobacco planters in the rear, who had not listened to one word of the sermon, displayed tremulous emotion in every muscle of their brawny faces, while the tears coursed down their wrinkled cheeks." The whole tendency of the crowd influence is to aid greatly in fixing attention upon the narrow brightly lighted field of ideas presented by

[1] E. A. Ross, *Social Psychology*, p. 44.
[2] F. M. Davenport, *Primitive Traits in Religious Revivals*, pp. 226 f.

CONVERSION

the speaker; to magnify many fold the emotional stress; and by both of these characteristics to inhibit the intellectual processes. The finer and later developed mental processes are thrown out of gear, and the cruder, commoner, and lower levels of mind are put into unrestrained operation. Davenport shows how the more primitive traits appear in religious revivals displacing those which belong to higher and more civilized mind. He traces the identity of the revival with the ghost dance of the Indians and the "experience meeting" of the Negroes.

A further fact concerning the revival is that the reactions which are the objective of its elaborate technique are in themselves quite insignificant and capable of complete dissociation from their intended ideal significance. The effort of the evangelist is to persuade persons to commit themselves by signing cards, rising for prayers, lifting the hand, moving to the front seat, answering a single question affirmatively. Much is said in his sermons about a better life, new resolves, and unselfish service, but when the appeal is finally made it is a summons to make certain simple familiar reactions. The result is that many give the sign demanded and are counted among the converts, but do not become permanent, dependable members of religious organizations, or otherwise display genuine, lasting interest. Many persons feel chagrined and humiliated that they have been "carried away" by the excitement, and as a consequence they are henceforth repelled from conventional religious activities.

In no respect is there greater agreement among

the psychologists of religion than in this: that the methods and many conversions of revivals are essentially the methods and effects of hypnotism. The fixation of attention, the manipulation of subjects through a series of suggestions, the final mandatory exhortation to surrender and to indicate it by a simple motor response — these are the well known methods of hypnotism. The subject may feel himself held in spite of himself to the ideas and acts presented. He has the sense of being borne on by forces outside himself, and is often assured that this is the most precious and reassuring element of his "experience." He is urged to surrender his will, to trust, to have faith, and these are precisely the attitudes and moods which facilitate hypnotism. As Professor Coe says: "The striking psychic manifestations which reach their climax among us in emotional revivals, camp-meetings, and negro services have a direct relation to certain states of an essentially hypnotic and hallucinatory kind." In another connection he asserts that "the phenomenon in Methodist history known as the 'power' was induced by hypnotic processes now well understood." [1]

Psychologically, the defects of the conversion experience may be stated in terms of the limitations of hypnotic control. It does not present intelligent and rational grounds of action. Conversion is made to turn upon "a sense of sin," but it does not develop the realization of sin in a large way. It seeks for the sensi-

[1] G. A. Coe, *The Spiritual Life*, p. 141; Coe, *Religion of a Mature Mind*, ch. ix; Starbuck, *Psychology of Religion*, p. 171; Davenport, *Primitive Traits in Religious Revivals*, ch. xii, "Conversion by Suggestion."

CONVERSION

tive point in the conscience of the subject, and works upon this, without adequate reference to the reality and objectivity, moral quality, and social character of his sin. The pressure is apt to centre upon some secondary and minor matters, such as popular amusements. Participation in them is represented as a chief thing for which forgiveness is needed. There is danger, therefore, that the virtues of the new life shall be as insignificant as the sins of the old. The occasions of "joining the church" may appear slight when the stress is over, and further devotion to religious interests may be held lightly as a consequence. Such methods afford no sufficient sense of reality and depth for the religious life. They tend to produce formal and superficial, not to say hypocritical religionists. They conspire to set religion apart from one's normal, sane, and well regulated activities, making it seem unnatural and weird. Methods of this kind obscure and minimize the function of education in religion, whereas any important results which seem to follow from the conversion experience actually consist either in making vital some past discipline inoperative at the time of conversion, or in setting the individual upon the path of new educative influences. Unless conversion is preceded or followed by the effective development of habits belonging to good character, then conversion becomes a momentary emotion with no positive significance.

It is sometimes argued in defense of conversion that it is of value in those cases where the individual has become encased in injurious habits and needs a powerful force to release him and set him in a new direction.

Such cases do occur. But the effort to reach them in revivals is complicated with serious disadvantages aside from those already indicated. There is no sufficient recognition of individual problems and experiences. In order to move the hardened sinner the sensibilities of many innocent persons and highly suggestible children are wrought upon. In detailing the sins of such evil doers suggestions of crime may be lodged where they would not otherwise have entered. Many thoughtful, better controlled auditors resist all such appeals, fail to find instruction for their problems, and are led to take religion at the apparent estimate of its representatives, as something not intended for those who are incapable of conversion. The statistics show that very few persons past the adolescent period ever respond to the conversion methods, and all psychologists agree that for the adolescents gradual development by means of education is far preferable. It is further probable that individual cases of sinfulness, like those of disease, can be most effectively treated by specific remedies, among which even hypnotic suggestion, privately instead of publicly administered, might find a place. But in religion, as in medicine, it becomes increasingly apparent that the great need is prevention through normal activity and development, and, therefore, "salvation by education" rather than by conversion.

The defects of conversion appear even more clearly in its secondary results. It creates a desire for the repetition of the excitement and emotion of the revival. Many churches fall into a rhythm of interest and indifference accompanying the periods of revival

CONVERSION

and of the regular work, which latter comes to be felt as routine and drudgery. The illusion develops under which things done in the excitement of a "great meeting" appear more important than the same things done quietly. Churches seem to themselves to have accomplished more when they make a hundred converts in the annual revival than if they receive the same number in the year's regular services. In some local churches the annual "protracted meeting" is felt to be necessary although the work of training and enlisting new recruits is already practically effected by class work and other educational agencies. An interesting illustration of the type created by conversion is seen in those persons who remove into new localities and do not become identified with a religious organization until appealed to by revival services. In effect they are dependent upon the revival stimulus for so simple a matter as the transfer of their church letters. In a similar way the radiation of the revival method appears in the administration of practical interests such as finances and social reforms. In order to secure funds for missions, for buildings, and for ordinary expenses it is quite customary to hold "rallies" and various special meetings. Actual experience proves, however, that more can be accomplished in such matters, and more general cooperation secured by individual, systematic solicitation. Again, when social reforms are undertaken by religious people they are likely to organize mass meetings and employ oratory. They have a predilection to rely upon public demonstrations and skillful speech-making. It is well understood that such meetings are seldom the source of sustained, organized effort. Church people are generally better able to agitate a reform than to administer it permanently. Davenport has suggested that in some sections of the country, notably in certain counties of Kentucky, the religious emotionalism generated by revivals may be causally connected with social disorder in the form of feuds and lynchings. He took the period from 1882 to 1903, and found that where the great Kentucky revivals of 1800 occurred, the lynchings were most numerous. "In a region containing only one-fortieth of the population of the state and not much more than one-fortieth of the area, one-sixth of all the cases of lynching are to be found."[1] In his recent work on social psychology Professor Ross characterizes the crowd, including the religious crowd of revivals, as ephemeral, irrational, and immoral. "The crowd may generate moral fervor, but it never sheds light. If at times it has furthered progress, it is because the mob serves as a battering ram to raze some mouldering, bat-infested institution and clean the ground for something better. This better will be the creation of gifted individuals or of deliberative bodies, never of anonymous crowds. It is easier for masses to agree on a Nay than a Yea. Hence crowds destroy despotisms, but never build free states; abolish evils, but never found works of beneficence. Essentially atavistic and sterile, the crowd ranks as the lowest of the forms of human association."[2]

[1] F. M. Davenport, *Primitive Traits in Religious Revivals*, p. 303.
[2] E. A. Ross, *Social Psychology*, p. 56.

PART IV

THE PLACE OF RELIGION IN THE EXPERIENCE
OF THE INDIVIDUAL AND SOCIETY

CHAPTER XV

RELIGION AS INVOLVING THE ENTIRE PSYCHICAL LIFE

As human life becomes complex it is specialized into many social organizations and activities. The homogeneity of simple primitive society differentiates into numberless classes, parties, associations, and alliances. Law, art, science, and religion in the early stages of society are scarcely distinguishable from each other. In advanced civilizations they often appear separate and sometimes antagonistic. Not only do they seem to diverge from each other, but they tend to lose connection with the stream of concrete activity which produced them. Each specialized interest in turn develops parties and schools of thought within itself which threaten its unity. Obviously this is true of religion, and the case is not greatly different in law, art, and science. Such parties with their doctrines develop around partial, special interests, and finally become remote, abstract, and rent by internal conflict. Some protestant sects have as their distinguishing mark a doctrine of the ordinances or the observance of a certain day of worship! But it is possible to put these varying developments within their proper genetic perspective where their divergence may be understood and their ultimate source in vital processes be made clear. Religion, with its changing forms, may thus be seen in its natural, concrete character as a phase of all socialized human experience. None of its manifestations remains the unmodified embodiment of all the spiritual values of this growing experience. Both apologists and critics of religion have neglected this fact. They have been misled by the persistent and pernicious fallacy which identifies a part with the whole, or a stage of development with the whole process. If one starts with the assumption that religion is synonymous with animism, then in a scientific age religion becomes remote from life and is destined to perish. Or if by religion is meant the development of the Hebrew tradition, it is a foregone conclusion that there is no religion among native Africans and Australians.

The results of genetic social psychology make it possible to overcome the various partial and limited conceptions of the relation of religion and life. Since the religious consciousness, according to these results, is just the consciousness of the great interests and purposes of life in their most idealized and intensified forms, it is evident that in its generic nature religion is a most intimate aspect of human life. This has been shown in detail with reference to ceremonies, mythology, sacrifice, and prayer. Everywhere the sacred objects and functions are those in which the life of society is felt to centre. But different stages in social development estimate these things differently and express social valuations in different ways. When all phases of life are permeated with superstition and magic, religion shares in this confused, childish attitude. But when custom has been criticised and given moral character through reflection and self-

RELIGION AS INVOLVING THE PSYCHICAL LIFE

direction, religion centres in moral ideals and in rational methods of control. In early society religion is more likely to remain identified with older customs, but even there the different phases of social life interact. Economic conditions compel reconstruction in traditional customs, and often produce an advance in morals which finally registers itself in religious symbols. Or again a prophetic religion may gain moral insight through its leaders in advance of the masses and thereby become an effective moralizing agency. In some instances the religion of one people has been taken to other races and has presented sharp contrasts to the existing cults. Religion in such a case may become the occasion of social reconstruction and moral progress; but such an aggressive religion always requires an interpretation in terms of the historic social life of its origin. It is necessary to achieve an imaginative reproduction of the actual life of the society in which a religion arose in order to make it effective in a new environment. Christianity undoubtedly presented high moral ideals and great ethical energy to the perishing civilizations of Greece and Rome. But it was not Christianity alone. The whole idealized social history of the Hebrew people, through their own literature, was carried over to the Gentiles. The task of orienting the history and concrete life of this people with warmth and color for the nations of Europe has been the gigantic task of generations of Christian scholars, orators, and artists. At the same time the growing life of the peoples which accepted Christianity has necessitated modifications in that religion. The culture of the Renaissance demanded, and the democracy and science of the present time demand great readjustments in the prevailing religious institutions.

The moralization of religion moves forward with the practical and ethical development of the race. This is becoming clearer as the processes of social evolution are better understood. New ethical problems constantly arise in modern life with the emergence of new commercial and industrial activities. For example, the new methods and forms of organization in industry represented by the corporation and the labor union, necessitate a new meaning for the term justice. This sense of new social relations is demanding recognition in new developments of religious activity and doctrine. Along with these claims for specific modifications there is also a growing insistence upon the underlying principle of evolution. The age of invention and discovery has destroyed the old static life. With the wider knowledge of nature which science affords the doctrine of development is passing into practical terms and taking the form of an ideal of individual and social progress. A consequent readjustment of religion is recognized as necessary in order to enable it to embody the spirit of the new life which society is attaining.[1] This readjustment is demanded not in this or that particular, but as a continuous, thoroughgoing process to be conscientiously facilitated and maintained. The age begins to regard experimentation and progress as moral demands in every

[1] The tendency is expressed in many recent works, such as Rauschenbusch's *Christianity and the Social Crisis*; Francis G. Peabody's *Jesus Christ and the Social Question*.

RELIGION AS INVOLVING THE PSYCHICAL LIFE

sphere of activity, and therefore is attaching religious significance to them. The movement is under way which is destined to exalt the very process of development to the place of a religious obligation. It may even add the attribute of evolution to the character of the Deity, and embody the quality of dynamic, purposeful activity among the cardinal virtues. If the organized, institutionalized forms of religion appear barren and powerless it is likely that a more real and vital religious consciousness will be found in other social movements which are not yet designated as religious and may not regard themselves as such.

These conventionalized, lifeless forms arrogate to themselves the name of religion, and thereby succeed in creating the illusion that religion itself is inert and decadent. It is this fact which lends the color of truth to the statement that religion is characteristically conservative and naturally follows rather than leads civilization's pioneers. This has come to be a common view among a certain school of social theorists.[1] An almost equally extreme view on the opposite side is that which attributes social progress too largely to religious initiative, ignoring the complex economic, social influences which are operative. A truer view is that the ideal values of each age and of each type of social development tend to reach an intensity, a volume, and a symbolic expression which are religious.

There is accordingly a conflict among religious as among all other types of social experience. If the re-

[1] T. Veblen, *Theory of the Leisure Class*, chapter xii.

ligious struggles are the most tragic it is because all parties are here contending for what seem to them the most profoundly important interests of life. Such struggles are finally settled, not by argument or war, but by the onward movement of the whole social development of mankind. Professor Ross has contrasted the religious aspects of this movement in terms of "legal religion" and "social religion." The former belongs in his view to the patriarchal type of society, the latter to that type of society in which sympathy and brotherhood prevail. He recognizes that religion persists in new forms with changing intellectual and social interests. "Geology, or higher criticism, or comparative mythology, may undermine particular beliefs with which ethical-religious feeling has associated itself. But the soul of religion has a marvelous and little-suspected power of escaping into new forms of belief." "In western society, the beliefs that create legal religion are perishing before our eyes. They stand in flat contradiction to our knowledge, and as the state becomes more able to secure civil order, the social ego takes less pains to keep them alive for the sake of their usefulness. The idealism that creates social religion, however, is not suffering so much. . . . Social religion then has a long and possibly great career awaiting it. As it disengages itself from that which is transient and perishable, as the dross is purged away from its beliefs and the element of social compulsion entirely disappears from it, social religion will become purer and nobler. No longer a paid ally of the policeman, no longer a pillar of social order, it will take its unquestioned place with art and science and

RELIGION AS INVOLVING THE PSYCHICAL LIFE

wisdom, as one of the free manifestations of the higher human spirit."[1]

This concrete essential relation of religion and life is evidenced also in a psychological analysis of ideals. Psychologically ideals are more or less remote ends of action whose realization is sought through the mediation of reflection and effort. The term moral has been used to designate those ideals which pertain particularly to human social welfare, in distinction from the claims of religion which seeks authority and action for conduct in the will of a Deity. The contrast between moral and religious conduct belongs to that conception of the world which makes a rigid distinction between the natural and supernatural, between the human and divine. But if religion is identified with the most intimate and vital phases of the social consciousness, then the distinction between morality and religion is not real. That which makes an end or ideal of action moral is the fact that it is accepted with awareness; that it is compared with other ends; that it is analyzed; and that it is voluntarily chosen as good. This means that the social significance of the end desired is taken into account. All truly human conduct is necessarily social because its means and ends, its source and its consequences are socially conditioned. Just because man's mind is a social reality, his moral or reflective ideals are also social. It is true that many social ends both among primitive and civilized people are not moral because they have not been reflectively selected. But all moral conduct is by necessity social. It follows that some

[1] E. A. Ross, *Social Control*, pp. 213, 216.

forms of early religious consciousness may be lacking in moral quality, but that no genuinely moral consciousness can be without religious quality. In so far as religion is non-moral it is primitive and controlled by custom. On the other hand all moral ideals are religious in the degree to which they are the expression of great, vital interests of society. Religion, in the minds of its best representatives at the present time, consciously and frankly accepts as its highest conception the ideal of a kingdom or brotherhood of moral agents coöperating for the attainment of further moral ends. A representative theologian gives the following statement as the central doctrine of Christianity: "Jesus was wholly concerned with ethics, with begetting and fostering in men the Godlike life. The word 'character' summarizes the great interest and life-purpose of Jesus Christ." [1] Professor Coe, after giving a psychological statement of the nature of ideals, says: "It should be noted also that there is no break between morals and religion as we here conceive them. Both move within the sphere of the good. The race becomes religious just where it becomes moral, namely, wherever our uncouth ancestors took a step beyond instinct by defining some object as their good and forming corresponding ideals." [2] The attempt to delimit the field of natural morality from religion presupposes in the older writers a dualism between human and divine, natural and "regenerated" natures. Without the definite assumption of

[1] G. B. Stevens, *The Christian Doctrine of Salvation*, p. 475.
[2] G. A. Coe, "Moral and Religious Education from the Psychological Point of View," *Journal of Religious Education*, vol. iii, December, 1908.

RELIGION AS INVOLVING THE PSYCHICAL LIFE

this dualism the line between morality and religion becomes obscure and tends to vanish completely.[1]

When one turns from the theologians and theorists to the concrete experience of religious people, the presence and importance of the moral ideal as the core of religion is still more evident. One result of Starbuck's investigation gives striking confirmation to this point. His subjects were representative of average orthodox evangelical church members. They insisted that the most constant and persistent element in their religious consciousness was the moral ideal. "In adolescence," writes Starbuck, "when the new life bursts forth, its most important content was ethical. During storm and stress and doubt that which remained firmest when life was least organized was this same instinct. And now we find, in describing their fundamental attitudes toward life, that the respondents already in the late teens and twenties mention conduct almost as frequently as at any later time in life. . . . It should be recalled that among the things which are given as absolutely essential, the *sine qua non* of religion, conduct was most frequently mentioned."[2] The respondents say: "The test of religion is conduct towards my fellow-beings." "Religion is more a *life*, a living, than a system. It is a series of daily actions which determines conduct. Its essence is daily doing of good to one's fellow men."

[1] G. H. Palmer, *The Field of Ethics*, chapter iv. The attempt in this chapter to show what religion adds to morality issues in the claim that it adds "horizon, stability, and hope"! But are not these qualities afforded to some degree by every ideal?

[2] E. D. Starbuck, *Psychology of Religion*, p. 321.

PSYCHOLOGY OF RELIGIOUS EXPERIENCE

This conscious recognition of moral conduct as the deepest thing in their religious experience is all the more impressive when it is taken in connection with the fact that much of their training in religion must have emphasized the customary doctrine that mere morality has nothing in common with religion. Theoretically the popular presentation of religion moves largely within sacramental conceptions. The saving power of ordinances survives in practice even when the doctrine has been silenced. It is the usual keynote of evangelistic appeals that the good works one does in his natural state are of themselves of no avail. It is necessary to "surrender," "obey," "confess" and receive a "spirit" in order to become genuinely religious. Of course all such expressions may be given a justifiable and reasonable moral content, but in religious usage they ordinarily mean that in some unaccountable way a new life, which was foreign before, comes into one's experience. Thenceforth it gives efficacy to good resolutions and good deeds. But in spite of the prevalence of such teaching the investigation referred to above shows that during storm and stress and doubt that which remained firmest was the natural ethical character; and it was this moral life which afterwards constituted the substance of religion.

The comparison of this moral and social religious ideal with the mediæval notion of saintliness is thus described by Professor James: "The Catholicism of the sixteenth century paid little heed to social righteousness; and to leave the world to the devil whilst saving one's own soul was then accounted no dis-

RELIGION AS INVOLVING THE PSYCHICAL LIFE

creditable scheme. To-day, rightly or wrongly, helpfulness in general human affairs is, in consequence of one of those secular mutations in moral sentiment of which I spoke, deemed an essential element of worth in character; and to be of some public or private use is also reckoned as a species of divine service.[1]

The clear apprehension of the concrete relation of religion to the total life process furnishes a corrective for the erroneous view that within the individual religion is due to some unique faculty or instinct. The extreme form of the faculty theory of psychology arose historically with individualism, while individualism in turn accompanied the differentiation of the old social unity into various activities. "This extreme individualistic tendency was contemporaneous with a transfer of interest from the supernatural church-state over to commercial, social, and political bodies with which the modern man found himself identified. . . . The individualistic tendency found a convenient intellectual tool in a psychology which resolved the individual into an association or series of particular states of feeling and sensations; and the good into a like collection of pleasures also regarded as particular mental states."[2] The psychologists of that period, whether of the associationist or intuitionist type, viewed the mental life as separated into discrete elements and processes. Reason, feeling, and volition were distinct from each other. The rational nature, the moral nature, the religious nature were taken as having their own psychological mechanisms. The ac-

[1] William James, *Varieties of Religious Experience*, p. 354.
[2] Dewey and Tufts, *Ethics*, pp. 220, 221.

tivity and development of these endowments identified the individual with the corresponding human interests. The operations of reason made him rational, those of the moral nature made him moral, and those of the religious nature made him religious. But modern life is revealing not merely the harmony of its various departments in a working alliance, but their vital and organic relations with each other in purposive life history. In the same way the various phases of human nature are found to be more than attributes or qualities inhering in man's metaphysical being. They are different aspects, stages, or abstracted processes of the total, pulsating life of the organism. The normal mental life is a complex, functionally organized activity. Like other high biological organisms, man is capable of doing a variety of things and of gaining a wealth of experience in the process, but there is only one mental life involved. The various interests which he pursues — business, art, science, politics, religion — employ his whole nature. Their differences are those of direction, of emphasis, of methods. This functional specialization of activity creates appropriate systems of habits and attitudes, and these systems may be called different "selves," but the differences between such selves are only relative and provisional. Religion in this view, like all other interests, is a matter of habits and attitudes. The religious nature is not something distinguishable and separable in any mechanical and exclusive way. Such a "nature" is just one of the "selves" in a functional and relative sense. It has no more independence or uniqueness than one's artistic nature or one's scientific nature. But it has

RELIGION AS INVOLVING THE PSYCHICAL LIFE

just as much. Religion, like every other specialized interest of man, involves the reaction of his entire nature. It is not the product of any one agency within him. In its most natural, normal development it is just the expression and appreciation of those ideal relationships and values which are inherent in all earnest moral efforts.

Those who tend to identify religious experience with the activity of some peculiar organ or element of the mental life have recently made much use of the subconscious. Here there seemed to be a safe retreat for the hard-pressed advocates of the uniqueness of religious experience. But as the phenomena of the subconscious are more carefully examined and compared with the conscious processes the more do they disclose relations and resemblances to these better understood experiences. The importance of the subconscious in recent psychology is expressed by Professor James in these words: "I cannot but think that the most important step forward that has occurred in psychology since I have been a student of that science is the discovery first made in 1886, that, in certain subjects at least, there is not only the consciousness of the ordinary field with its usual centre and margin, but an addition thereto in the shape of a set of memories, thoughts and feelings which are extra-marginal and outside of the primary consciousness altogether, but yet must be classed as conscious facts of some sort, able to reveal their presence by unmistakable signs. I call this the most important step forward because, unlike the other advances which psychology has made, this discovery has revealed to us an entirely unsuspected peculiarity in the constitution of human nature. No other step forward which psychology has made can proffer any such claim as this." [1]

The nature of this subconscious or subliminal reality is perhaps best described as a marginal field extending out from the focus of attention and full consciousness. Just as in the visual field, brightness and sharpness of definition fail at the margin, so in other types of consciousness the illuminated centre shades off into an irregular, vanishing fringe. The same relation may be suggested by the figure of a pyramid at whose top a small section is in the clear light of consciousness, while below, all is vague and opaque. The boundary between the two is not a fixed line, but an indeterminate plane moving slightly upward or downward under the varying influence of attention and general mental activity. But no such figures of speech are entirely satisfactory, and they must be held lightly to avoid abuse.

Certain familiar phenomena of attention and habit may be cited to aid in defining the present use of the term subconscious and also to show the relation in which it stands to full consciousness. If we listen to a just discernible sound, such as the ticking of a watch, the watch may be moved a slight distance farther from the ear, where undiscriminated stimulation seems still to continue. For if the watch is now stopped a relief is felt, though the sound stimulus had already ceased for consciousness. Still more remarkable evidence has been furnished by experiments in which it was shown that shadow lines imperceptible by them-

[1] William James, *Varieties of Religious Experience*, p. 233.

RELIGION AS INVOLVING THE PSYCHICAL LIFE

selves influenced the judgment as to the length of visible lines when the visible and shadow lines were employed together.[1] Again, in many instances of "summation of stimuli" the mind is at last brought to conscious reaction though it is unaware of the separate impressions whose cumulative influence produces the result. When absorbed in study one sometimes becomes aware that the telephone bell has been ringing or that the clock is furnishing the long series of strokes for a late hour.

In the phenomena of habit it may almost be said that one sees the subconscious in the process of formation. A complicated set of reactions, which at first are laboriously and slowly acquired under the control of attention, comes to be accomplished with such facility and precision that attention may be engaged with other interests during the performance. This is illustrated in any activity requiring great technical skill, as operating complex delicate machinery, playing musical instruments, or acquiring foreign languages. The more striking phenomena of habit, on their unconscious side, appear when the habitual reaction is occasioned as well as completed without the knowledge of the subject. This is illustrated by the familiar example of winding one's watch when changing the waistcoat for dinner. The removal of the waistcoat upon retiring having been the customary cue and occasion for winding the watch, the act is accomplished at an unusual time without attracting attention to itself. The habitual action maintains itself by the

[1] Dunlap, "The Effect of Imperceptible Shadows on the Judgment of Distance," *Psychological Review*, vol. vii, p. 435.

PSYCHOLOGY OF RELIGIOUS EXPERIENCE

stimulus generated in each adjustment. Each step in walking produces sensations which, unless inhibited by other stimuli, occasion the next step. If this theory is correct the sensations as well as the motor reactions in the above instance of winding the watch occur outside of consciousness. The seeming independence of consciousness in acquired habits is seen in the fact that attending to an act often interrupts it. To be suddenly called upon to spell a familiar word may throw one into complete uncertainty about it.

The investigations of the more extreme phenomena of subconsciousness — dreams, somnambulism, hypnotism, lapses of personality, and the like — have revealed fundamental similarities with the commoner phenomena, such as the variations of attention, habit-formation, absent-mindedness, and association of ideas. In general the doctrine of different selves and of the centre and fringe of consciousness so brilliantly set forth by Professor James affords a key from normal, familiar experience with which the abnormal occurrences may be opened to almost as clear explanation as any other features of the mental life. The result is a bridge of considerable scientific stability over the chasm which for many writers seems to separate the waking self of conscious life and the mysterious subconscious self.

In any case no scientific inquiries into this marginal field of our experience support the claim that the subconscious self is in any way the peculiar organ of religion. It is the massive encircling *milieu* of custom, tradition, sympathies and tastes within which any

RELIGION AS INVOLVING THE PSYCHICAL LIFE

kind of clear consciousness exists. It is the depth and range of these influences, whether consciously acquired or assimilated in subtle ways from one's social environment, which give expertness and sensitivity to the artist and mechanic as well as to the saint. It is in the environment moulded by tradition that our present selves find a potent condition of their own development. It was these influences, likewise, that "imparted unity and continuity to the great civilizing movements of mankind in art, in architecture, in music, in poetry, in literature, in science, in philosophy, in invention." [1] In a similar way and in no different way religion draws its sustenance from the deep soil of accumulated social experience and from the wide spreading roots of individual inheritance and impressionability. The subtle, powerful influences of imitation, suggestion, and subconscious habits operate in religion, giving it stability and intensity. It is by this means that the racial ideas possess such urgency, objectivity, and formative power. They are the result of the long arduous life struggles of mankind. It is no wonder they have been proclaimed with prophetic zeal and obeyed with tragic devotion. But every interest of society moves forward by the aid of similar forces. In respect, then, to the operation of subconscious elements, religion is not unique. It stands in the normal relations characteristic of all other genuine social interests.

These general considerations concerning the naturalness of religion have suggestive application to particular phases of religious experience. Recent

[1] Joseph Jastrow, *The Subconscious*, pp. 157 f.

studies have undertaken to describe and classify various phenomena, such as faith, prayer, worship, and mysticism.[1] There is usually a tendency to limit these terms in a way which betrays a failure to relate them with sufficient concreteness and complexity to the total activity of the religious consciousness. The fallacies of taking religion apart from life and of mistaking some partial factor for the whole, reappear in the treatment of special topics.

Faith is very commonly viewed in this way. It is regarded as peculiar to religion and as due to some special endowment or experience. Faith is called the instrument of religion, and knowledge the instrument of science. But in reality religion and science both involve the whole mental life, — emotion, imagination, reason, and action. They are differentiated by their centre of interest within the total life history of human action. Science, religion, art, and other interests are distinguished simply by emphasis upon different aspects of human purposive action. They therefore harmonize with each other while maintaining relatively definite characters of their own. The phenomena of faith at once appear simple and clear when viewed with reference to the moving circuit characteristic of all purposive activity. It is the piecemeal and unarticulated view which makes faith the occasion of so many problems and mysteries. It is not to be supposed that all difficulties of interpretation disappear when these phenomena are approached with the methods and presuppositions of functional psy-

[1] *The American Journal of Religious Psychology and Education*, Clark University Press.

RELIGION AS INVOLVING THE PSYCHICAL LIFE

chology. But it is nevertheless true that many difficulties are at once resolved or eliminated.

When faith is examined psychologically and compared with similar phenomena in other than religious experiences, it is found to correspond with the purposive factor in activity. It may be said that wherever there is an ideal of any kind, there is faith. This is clear and obvious in so far as ideals are conceived dynamically. An ideal as an end of action — that is, as something desired, something for whose realization means are intelligently sought, and something toward whose attainment effort is confidently put forth — involves faith. For faith is just that interest, confidence, and vivid envisagement which makes the ends sought so vital and appealing. Faith is a vital working interest in anything. It is the attitude which belongs to a *live* proposition accepted as a practical plan of action. Religious faith is differentiated from other types of faith simply by the ends or ideals which it seeks. Faith in ideals which are felt to be the highest, the most valuable, and the most essential, is religious faith. Religious faith is therefore only another term for the religious consciousness itself, since that consciousness is purposive and dynamic and centres in supreme ideal values.

From this point of view several specific problems concerning faith may be settled. The beginning of religious faith is the point at which religious ideals become warm and attractive. The psychological process by which they attain this warmth and attractiveness is that of the association of ideas. The ideas are brought to attention by suggestion, inquiry, education, or in some chance way. By recurring to the attention, by gathering associations, sometimes unconsciously, these ideals finally move over into the focus of attention and interest. There they become the object of effort and influence conduct. This beginning of interest, of enthusiastic devotion to ideals, is described in religious biographies as the attainment of faith. It is often attended by keenest satisfaction and by a sense of calm and peace together with the active attitude. This process has already been dealt with in the descriptions of conversion. There is evidently a very pronounced emotional quality in such an experience. This has led some writers to consider faith as peculiarly an emotion. Professor Leuba takes this view: "The core of the Faith-state is a particular attitude and an increased efficiency of the will in consequence of which an ideal of life becomes realizable. It is a constructive response to a need, a specific emotion of the sthenic type, subserving, as emotions do, a particular end."[1] But if faith is rightly held to be equivalent to confident purposive activity, then it may include also the intermediate stage of reflective analysis, reasoning, and scientific experiment within which the best means of attaining the ideal are selected. During this process the faith attitude is not absent. It gives zest, support, and even patience in the quest for knowledge, for although the scientific inquiry might at first seem to arrest and thwart the attainment of the ideal end, experience shows that science facilitates the realization of practical ideals.

[1] James H. Leuba, "Faith," *The American Journal of Religious Psychology and Education*, vol. i, 1904, p. 73.

RELIGION AS INVOLVING THE PSYCHICAL LIFE

Professor Leuba refers to "faith-beliefs" as propositions which are often accepted by the religious convert without rational examination, and held by him in a quite non-rational way. That is undoubtedly true in many cases, especially where religion has become conventionalized into dogma. But if religious faith attaches, as it may, to propositions which are socially significant and scientifically verifiable, it is possible for that faith to become the incentive and support of the most elaborate scientific investigations and rational control. That is, a rational procedure is normal and, in modern society, increasingly necessary to purposeful or ideal activity. It is as natural and necessary in the ventures of faith, in the sphere of religion, as in the realms of business or statecraft.

There is also at hand, in this functional view, a reconciliation of faith and works. It is because faith has been used erroneously to designate the more intellectual, passive assent to creedal statements that it has seemed possible to divorce it from works. In the proper sense faith is a vital interest and, therefore, one which moves on to complete itself in action. There are many difficulties and dangers, however, in the process. Religious education has often emphasized the memorizing and repetition of sentiments without relating them to practice. It has often left its protégés stranded in a sea of contemplation. But these phenomena are just as deplorable in religion as in language and literature. Did no one ever learn the forms of a foreign or a "dead" language without relating them to useful objects? Did any one ever become a dreamer and sentimentalist in the realms of literature? Faith is normally dynamic and practical whether in religion or elsewhere. It is just a convenient term for the propulsive, forward striving effort of human nature. It is at its best when, under the control of the highest intelligence, it fulfills in practical ways with energy and power the noblest ideals of the race.

Prayer, even more than faith, has been regarded as psychologically peculiar to religion. But it is not. It is in reality a fundamental characteristic of all consciousness, especially of that in which there is a keen sense of personal needs. Prayer, as was shown in the case of primitive religion, is a natural expression of the social character of all consciousness. All thought, unless it be in the case of exceedingly refined and abstract mental processes, is personal and interlocutory. The conscious life of the individual is largely an interplay between the different selves of his different attitudes and habits. These argue, confer, advise, and contend with each other quite as actual people do. These selves may be exalted moral beings with which the lesser selves of one's actual temper and deeds seek communion and from which they petition aid of every kind. One particular type of self often becomes the standard for the individual, and this self is largely or solely formed upon the model of some definite historical or imaginary character. Where this is true, prayer may attain all the vividness of personal communion, even including hallucinations and visions in which the ideal personality speaks to one or intervenes in one's behalf. It is noticeable that with the increasing rationalization and organization of experi-

RELIGION AS INVOLVING THE PSYCHICAL LIFE

ence prayer tends to lose this character of literal, direct appeal to a definitely imaged Being. It becomes more and more an aspiration to understand the laws and nature of reality whether in the large or in detail, and to work in harmony with the forces and tendencies of such reality. On the contemplative, esthetic side, adoration and reverence are directed to the magnitude, power, progress, and beauty of nature and of society. The two chief factors in prayer are craving and contemplation. Just what expression these shall have depends upon many factors. The expression changes with the growth of intelligence and with the development of new symbols, but the aspiration and reverence continue to characterize all human consciousness which is sensitive to the ideal values of life.

What is true of prayer is true of other forms of worship. All take their place within the circuit of teleological activity. All express attitudes toward the processes of life, toward individual and social achievements. They express all moods and represent all phases of failure and success, of despair and hope within the experience of mankind. The symbolic forms of worship are originally the free and natural expression of concrete social experience. They are the art forms in which mankind have registered their spiritual values. Religion, in its creative periods, has ever employed the drama, music, and painting, and in its higher stages, poetry, sculpture, and architecture. No religion has ever been devoid of all these arts, and no religion of civilization has ever been permanently lacking in any of them. These esthetic forms are also the natural means employed to symbolize the ideals of patriotism, of war, of industry, and of science. In this esthetic element, then, the religious consciousness is normally at one with other human interests; and here, as in other respects, religion is differentiated by the inclusiveness and ideality of the ends which belong to it.

CHAPTER XVI

IDEAS AND RELIGIOUS EXPERIENCE

THERE is at present a decided reaction against the extreme intellectualism of the older rational psychology. This has been one phase of a very general tendency in modern social history. Schopenhauer's presentation of the will to live as against the intellectualism of Hegel; the utilitarianism of Mill in preference to the rationalism of Kant; Rousseau's education according to nature in contrast to the doctrinaire discipline of the Schoolmen; and the pietistic impressionism of Ritschl in protest against the authority of dogma and science are expressions of the same movement. Within the domain of psychology the new development has come through genetic, social, and experimental investigations. These in turn have been profoundly influenced by the remarkable progress of the biological sciences. Psychology has discovered the great extent and dominance in all conscious life of instinct, desire, habit, and emotion. It has been found that man's life is controlled much more by these factors than by explicit ideas and exact methods of reasoning. The non-rational phenomena of suggestion and imitation, of custom and the "mob mind" have attained increasing importance. They not only represent an astonishing variety and organization of activities within the subconscious life, but they dominate the conscious processes far more than is commonly realized.

The discovery of the genesis of ideas from instinctive and habitual types of activity is one of the most fruitful and revolutionary achievements of modern psychology. For example, it was formerly customary to say that animals are guided by instinct and man by reason, with the implication that the terms instinct and reason are mutually exclusive. But modern psychologists do not insist upon such a radical difference between animal and human intelligence. In fact their investigations issue in this paradox for the older psychology: Man's higher intelligence is directly related to his possession of more instincts than any other animal possesses. Not only is it found to be true that man has actually a greater number and variety of instincts, but also that it is in their conflict and tendency to inhibit each other that reflective, cognitive consciousness is called forth. Man's finer and larger nervous system enables him to have better memory of his experiences, and therefore in case of conflict of impulses he has a basis for comparing their outcome or meaning. It is in this way that different lines of action are suggested by a given situation, and a reasoned course of conduct made possible. "These higher forms of behavior grow out of the fact that at any given moment there may be a conflict between the various tendencies toward impulsive behavior. . . . If such a conflict as this arises in the experience of an individual who is capable of the higher forms of ideational activity he takes the various tendencies of behavior up into a more elaborate sphere of comparison

IDEAS AND RELIGIOUS EXPERIENCE

and deliberation. Without acting immediately upon one impulse or the other, he is likely to follow out in a train of ideational processes a consideration of the consequences to which one or the other impulse might lead him." [1]

That the ideational processes presuppose and involve impulsive and involuntary activities is shown in Professor James's analysis of voluntary action. He emphasizes the important fact that one gets the idea of an act from the act, and that consequently the first step in the initiation of a movement by means of an idea is the production of the idea itself by the impulsive or random occurrence of the movement. When attention is directed to the act as it occurs, then an image or memory of it may be obtained. After that the presence of the idea, or image of the act in consciousness, is sufficient to reproduce the act, if there is no inhibiting idea present. In other words, the impulsive or instinctive acts which constantly occur in the human organism may get registered in consciousness through the agreeable or disagreeable feelings they induce. In a conflict of such impulses each is brought into still greater vividness, and the sensations, images, and emotional quality which constitute the idea attain elaboration and distinctness. Voluntary acts, that is acts accompanied by the idea or consciousness of the end, are therefore by necessity secondary. They are always reproductions, not originals, and the process of reproduction is through the memory of how they felt originally.

[1] C. H. Judd, *Psychology*, pp. 326, 327; cf. William James, *Psychology*, vol. ii, p. 390.

This derived and dependent character of ideas is further emphasized by their inherent dynamic character. It has been the common notion that an idea is generically different from an act, and could precede the act in time, and might or might not be followed by movement. If, however, as many writers insist, the basic type of conscious control is seen in ideo-motor activity, then the idea is not radically different from the act. It is rather the incipient stage or the preliminary but real rehearsal of the act. In this lies the significance of the doctrine that there is no impression without expression, that every state of consciousness tends to issue in motor adjustment. "The idea of movement is, neurally considered, the beginning of that movement." [1] In ideo-motor activity the ideational process attains its normal and full development in movement immediately. The idea and the muscular adjustment are continuous. There is no complication, hesitation, or indirection. The circuit is completed at once, and the fruit may be seen to mature directly from the bloom. It is difficult to maintain this sense of the organic relation of ideational activity and motor adjustment where the circuit is indefinitely extended, and it is of course true that many mental states never reach their full motor development. They remain in the tentative stage of verbal or written language, or otherwise exhibit an arrested, abortive state. Such are plans which remain in the realm of sentimentality or those which the fickle character of the individual or society leaves partially completed. Where the idea or rational system of

[1] J. R. Angell, *Psychology*, p. 355.

IDEAS AND RELIGIOUS EXPERIENCE

ideas is not inhibited or deserted through weakness and perversity of will, the unity and continuity of idea and act are evident.

Not only are ideas determinate forms of consciousness springing from impulsive activity, but they are also the explicit developments of unanalyzed, confused emotional states which result from conflicting tendencies to action. This vague emotional consciousness is a highly important factor in human experience. In making his way into the human social world, the child is not so much directly confronted by objects in the first hand use of which he gains perceptual and conceptual notions of them, but he is surrounded by social activities, customs, and ideals, within which these objects float. The objects about him do not mean therefore merely certain hand-eye sensations and adjustments, but they also signify indescribable attitudes and expressions of the persons who use them. The child often catches the attitude of persons toward objects first, and is thus introduced to the object as a phase of another person's experience. A younger child, for example, is likely to take the attitude of an older child toward new kinds of food rather than to act for himself toward them as impersonal things. The individual's reactions are so much conditioned by the social environment that it might be said he seldom or never comes into direct immediate contact with physical things. Between him and objects, taking the latter in the abstract sense of material things, there intervenes a medium of social customs, opinions, suggestions, fashions, and taboos. At the point of uncertainty in face of a novel situation the process of deliberation is in large part that of recalling concrete social experiences, and thus attempting to formulate into clearness an appropriate idea of the best conduct for the present emergency. Professor Cooley has shown that all thinking takes place in this social medium and is conditioned by it. "In fact, thought and personal intercourse may be regarded as merely aspects of the same thing; we call it personal intercourse when the suggestions that keep it going are received through faces or other symbols present to the senses; reflection when the personal suggestions come through memory and are more elaborately worked over in thought. Both are mental, both are personal." [1]

Ideas or concepts may be regarded, then, as abbreviated shorthand symbols of the longer, more complete systems of motor activities and adjustments. Biologically and genetically they are late and secondary developments. It is particularly important to note here that so long as they remain normal and fulfill their true and proper functions, these ideas retain their dynamic character. So long as they have the tendency to initiate their accustomed attitudes and to project themselves to the full measure of the conduct implicit in them; so long, that is, as they are vital and have a felt value or meaning, so long are they live ideas and belong to live propositions and to actual, practical interests. Recent psychology recognizes this motor phase of consciousness in the changes which ideas undergo. Concepts are regarded as in constant flux, with the actual life of the individ-

[1] C. H. Cooley, *Human Nature and the Social Order*, p. 61.

IDEAS AND RELIGIOUS EXPERIENCE

ual and of society. The meanings of words change. They change as occupations, customs, and environment change; that is, they vary as the activities or habits which they signify are altered. They consequently have different meanings for different individuals, and for the same person in various stages of development. Before the days of machinery the term "manufacturer" held its original etymological meaning, and designated the individual who made things with his own hands. In the eighteenth century, with the development of machines, the factory system removed the laborers from their homes into shops, under the employment and direction of capitalists. Since the capitalists controlled the system, determining the processes employed and possessing ownership of the output of the shops, they came to be known as the manufacturers, although they no longer worked with their hands. Those who had formerly been called manufacturers came to be known simply as workmen or laborers. The gradual development of new social institutions and business customs registered themselves in this new growth of the concept. In a similar way the concept of "courage" has changed in dependence upon the underlying, controlling forces of social habit and readjustment. In simple social conditions, when the will to live involved personal, physical conflict with human beings and the elements of nature, courage designated the willingness to face enemies and obstacles in reliance upon one's own strength and prowess. In organized societies courage means devotion to the common good with the prompt and patient readiness to suffer various private ills for the public welfare. In modern life men who follow scientific inquiries or deal with changing social interests are often called upon to advocate ideals in opposition to the customs and opinions of their friends more than to resist the attacks of enemies. The idea of courage which results includes this positive constructive attitude of intellectual and moral fearlessness in the face of both friends and foes. Illustrations might be indefinitely multiplied to show that ideas are in this respect secondary phenomena, and that they serve to register experience. The experience itself arises from the propulsive, instinctive tendencies of the organism. When once attained such ideas serve the invaluable purpose of controlling and directing further effort. There is consequently a constant interaction between impulses and ideas, between new demands for adjustment and the established habits represented by developed ideas or concepts.

Sabatier has applied this principle to the estimate of theological ideas. To feel the vital meaning of the theological terms and to see the process by which they are modified one must take them in actual use. "Just as the life of a language does not lie in the sonorousness of words or in the correctness of phrases, but only in the secret energy of the thought and in the genius of the people who speak it, so the principle of the life of dogmas must not be sought in the logic of ideas or in the more or less exact theoretic formulas, but only in the religious life itself, that is to say, in the practical piety of the church which professes them." [1] This writer represents the authors of the historic dogmas of

[1] Auguste Sabatier, *The Vitality of Christian Dogmas*, pp. 21 f.

IDEAS AND RELIGIOUS EXPERIENCE

the church not "as theorists, or even as theologians by profession, gathered together solely by the impulse of speculative zeal to resolve metaphysical enigmas. They were men of action and not of speculation." In order therefore to understand their ideas, it is necessary to appreciate the practical activities and tendencies with which they were engaged.

The place and function of theological ideas in the religious consciousness may be further developed in terms of the idea of God, which is the central and determining conception in most theological systems. We have seen that among primitive peoples the gods are the central objects in the life processes of man. In the more developed civilizations the gods become quite exclusively anthropomorphic and reflect increasingly the social and political experiences of the people. Thus Robertson Smith observes: "What is often described as the natural tendency of Semitic religion toward ethical monotheism, is in the main nothing more than a consequence of the alliance of religion with monarchy." The relation is still more immediate than this. The forms of religious thought are the direct reflection of the political and social organization. The characteristics of monarchical government are reflected in the transcendence and in the paternalism of the Deity. The king lives apart from his people. He is surrounded by many couriers and guards. His edicts are issued through a series of subordinates. He is approached with difficulty and by various intermediaries. What he does for his subjects is done under seemingly arbitrary laws. On occasion he may act by special dispensation. But whether he acts by law or by grace his gifts are the favors of a superior being bestowed upon those who could not demand them. He keeps his own counsels, working secretly and mysteriously. Whatever he deigns to reveal of his nature and wisdom is his own free act.

Contrast this idea of God with that which expresses democratic social conditions. Here individuals assert themselves with freedom and initiative. They possess sovereignty in their own right and power. Their representatives in government are like themselves. They are exalted to office by the popular will and are held accountable to their fellow citizens. In the same manner, the relations between individuals in private life are theoretically and ideally, at least, determined by mutual agreements, by free contracts and voluntary choice. The appeal from the judgment of an individual or of a class must be made to other individuals and to all the members of the community, as represented in the processes of the creation and administration of popular government. The ideal demanded is not that of special favor, which characterizes a paternal order of society; but it is rather the ideal of justice and equality. The final tribunal is the intelligence, experience, and sense of fair play in the masses of the people. When such a social order projects itself in the form of conscious and comprehensive ideas it results in a conception of God as immanent. The inner reason and conscience of society, by which justice is sought, defended, and avenged, now appears as the central factor in the idea of God. The idea which was formerly dominated by the functions of the sovereign and the parent now embodies the spirit

IDEAS AND RELIGIOUS EXPERIENCE

of justice and equity manifested in the aspiring social consciousness of the classes and masses of mankind.

The idea of God, in so far as it is a live idea in consciousness, carries with it this dynamic character. The attitudes and tendencies which it sets up when brought to the focus of attention depend upon the social relations and processes which operated in the formation of the idea in the individual or in the group from which he derived it. A person's idea of God may be taken as comprehending the highest ideal interests known or felt by him. It stands therefore for concrete purposeful activity and effort in those directions. Calling this idea to mind means putting one's self in an attitude consistent with the interests which controlled its formation. Therefore in a despotic society where sovereignty is idealized, to think of God means to humble one's self, to take on the postures and employ the phrases which a menial uses in the presence of his lord. The ritual and psalms of many oriental peoples illustrate this type of reverence and worship. But where the idea of God is the embodiment of ideals arising from democratic social movements, its presence in the mind expresses itself in motor reactions indicative of respect for the welfare of all members of society. The thought of God is then accompanied by impulses toward social conduct. In other words the idea of God, like any other general idea, signifies a system of habits, and in this case, as elsewhere, the presence of the idea has for its normal effect the initiation of those habitual attitudes and endeavors.

This fact concerning the idea of God has been put

in a striking way by Professor Leuba. Upon the basis of his investigation of the religious experience of various persons he concludes: "If we are to judge by our records, it would seem that the God who rises up before the Protestant Anglo-Saxon in his religious moods does not ordinarily throw him on his knees. That stage appears now transcended. God has remained for him the bestower of the things he wants, but the belief that adoration is an effective means of obtaining satisfaction has been to a very large extent forgotten. Could this be the result of experience? However that may be, the fact is that when God, conjured up by his needs, appears before him, his hands stretch forth in request for power or mercy, not in adoration. And, preposterous as it may seem, it is yet true that he cares very little who God is, or even whether He is at all. But *he uses Him*, instinctively, from habit if not from a rational conviction in His existence, for the satisfaction of his better desires, and this he does ordinarily with the directness and the bluntness of the aggressive child of a domineering century, well-nigh stranger to the emotions of fear, of awe, and of reverence. The truth of the matter may be put this way: *God is not known, He is not understood; He is used* — used a good deal and with an admirable disregard of logical consistency, sometimes as meat purveyor, sometimes as moral support, sometimes as friend, sometimes as an object of love." [1]

In this discovery that the idea of God is not so much known as used there is brought to light that

[1] James H. Leuba, "Contents of the Religious Consciousness," *Monist*, vol. xi, p. 571.

IDEAS AND RELIGIOUS EXPERIENCE

which this idea possesses in common with all other ideas. It is true also of the idea of the "desk" and of the idea of the "city" that they are not so much known as used. The knowing process, wherever it is alive and urgent, is concerned with action, with the adjustment of means to ends. Mere contemplation or analysis or syllogistic manipulation of ideas is empty and unsatisfying when divorced from practical interests. It is in their use, in the interplay of cognition and action, that ideas have any meaning or can be understood. It is in this living process also that both ideas and habits change. When these no longer satisfy the felt needs of society they are transformed. Old customs and their corresponding modes of thought are constantly being discarded under the influence of new shifts of interest. Nowhere is this more apparent than in the great massive movements of society and in the comprehensive ideas of God in which these movements are symbolized. This active, functional aspect of the idea of God is thus described by Professor James: [1] "The deity to whom the prophets, seers, and devotees who founded the particular cult bore witness was worth something to them personally. They could use him. He guided their imagination, warranted their hopes and controlled their will; or else they required him as a safeguard against the demon and a curber of other people's crimes. In any case they chose him for the value of the fruits he seemed to them to yield. So soon as the fruits began to seem quite worthless; so soon as they conflicted with indispensable human ideals, or thwarted too

[1] William James, *Varieties of Religious Experience*, p. 329.

extensively other values; so soon as they appeared childish, contemptible, or immoral when reflected on, the deity grew discredited and was ere long neglected and forgotten. When we cease to admire or approve what the definition of a deity implies we end by deeming that deity incredible."

It would be possible to go through the various theological ideas and doctrines and show in detail how they are determined in form and content by the experience of the individual or the society in which they arise. The Christian doctrines of the atonement are clearly illustrative of the principle. Anselm took the relation of the debtor and creditor, and in these terms elaborated the commercial theory. Grotius, himself a distinguished jurist, started from the presuppositions of the legal institutions of his time, and developed the governmental theory of the atonement. In the same manner, in more recent times, have appeared the modern "penal satisfaction theory," "the ethical satisfaction theory" and "the moral influence theory." It is not to be thought that this process is complete. Many new forms of social organization and regulation might be taken as the basis for other doctrines of the atonement. Modern missionary enterprises, labor unions, scientific experimentation and exploration might afford outlines upon which selected scripture passages could be arrayed with genuine and convincing arguments. They might also penetrate as deeply into the mystery of the problems as any historic theories have done.

The psychology of ideation appears from this to have important bearing upon the meaning of the truth

IDEAS AND RELIGIOUS EXPERIENCE

of ideas. So long as the idea is held closely to the habit or system of conduct which it signifies, then its truth is that of a record of experience or of a plan of action. It is true as a symbol of past experience, or it is true as a guide for further adjustment. The chief difficulties concerning the truth of ideas arise from attempts to estimate their validity out of relation to the only situations in which they can be true or false, that is the situations involving conduct. The idea of God has been treated in this way. It has been taken apart from the social experiences and the genetic processes in which it arose, and then has been subjected to various ingenious manipulations to determine whether it be true! It is somewhat comparable to seeking the meaning of a word after removing it from any context by repeating the sound, counting the letters, or analyzing the ink with which it is written. The mediæval and Cartesian arguments for the "being of God" are largely just such inapt endeavors. As Kant demonstrated, they are full of fallacies and labor in vain to produce the desired results. No such static, transcendent, non-empirical reality is conceivable by us: much less are its existence and nature demonstrable. The psychological solution of the difficulty lies in another direction, as already indicated. Perhaps the case is analogous to the experience of a child who looks behind the mirror for the reality answering to the image which he sees. Before he can solve the puzzle of the reflected image he must seek for it in another place and by a different method. The reality to which the image leads is not within the image alone, as phenomenalism might say; neither is it behind and beyond the mirror as the realist and the absolute idealist might say; but it lies on this side of the mirror, within the actual world of men and things. The idea of God, when seriously employed, serves to generalize and to idealize all the values one knows. Our actual interests move in the social world and within the vast order of nature. In the simplest reflections upon the facts of life one is led deep into the labyrinth of the natural and of the human worlds. The idea which gathers into itself the interests and values of our daily concerns must therefore signify what are for us the greatest realities in nature and in human experience. To the plain man as he uses the idea of God, in contrast with a passive formal attitude toward it, the idea involves a living process, law or movement, in the working of which human needs are satisfied, justice and truth established, and distant ideals attained. Even the oath of the profane man has an echo of the tremendous dynamic force of the word. It is the biggest word he knows. The reality answering to the idea of God, it may be said, must include, at its best, all that is involved in the deep instinctive historical and social consciousness of the race. It signifies the justice which government symbolizes, the truth which science unfolds, and the beauty which art strives to express. The "attributes" in the conception of God are as numerous as the ideal interests of those who use it, for it signifies the totality of our purposes and values.

It is sometimes said that the God-idea belongs peculiarly to the realm of values rather than designating factual reality. But the distinction between value-judgments and factual-judgments is not absolute. That it is a relative distinction may be seen in the universal and inherently teleological character of thought. All thinking is normally purposive. Only when extremely abstract and partial can it be characterized as merely descriptive and factual. Again the God-idea is formed in terms of personality. And the conception of personality involves primarily purposive action, not static being. The character of a person cannot be thought of except in terms of what he does. The idea of a supreme Person necessarily involves in the highest degree the element of will, of purpose and of movement toward great goals. It is a contradiction in terms to conceive a person as mere existence, that is, as fact simply. The historic attempts to think the God-idea in this way have resulted in abundant inconsistencies. But the readiness to think of a dualistic world in which a realm of purpose and a realm of fact exist together is also prolific of contradictions. The only kind of thinking of which human beings are capable is that which refers to ends, to needs, to values. The God-idea is a teleological idea, and in being such it shares fundamentally in the nature of all ideas. For actual human experience there are no other normal ideational processes than those which involve value.[1]

The nature and place of ideas in the religious consciousness include the question of the relation of theory and practice, of doctrine and life. After what has been said of the reciprocal relation of conduct and

[1] A. K. Rogers, *The Religious Conception of the World*, p. 117. The whole chapter on "The Argument for Purpose" bears upon this point.

ideas it is not necessary to add much here. The effective criticism of doctrine as abstruse, academic, and fruitless is valid chiefly against obsolete or otherwise irrelevant doctrines. All efficient practice, on the contrary, if it is anything more than rule-of-thumb custom, requires a clear and well articulated body of principles or doctrines. The scientific developments of this age and the increasingly successful application of theory in practice of all kinds are rapidly compelling theory and practice to recognize each other as indispensable. This is recognized in the realms of moral conduct and social progress with deeper insight than formerly. Religion has greater difficulty here than other forms of social experience because in Christianity at least, doctrines have been supposed to partake more rigidly of the nature of fixed and final truths. The Church cannot be said to have yet accepted with any thoroughness the scientific and psychological view of all doctrines, namely, that they are working hypotheses, subject to constant modification and revision in the light of further experience and reflection. But not until such a view is accepted can religion become domesticated in the modern world and overcome the inner conflict which now crassly separates faith and knowledge from each other and in large measure separates both from concrete experience.

CHAPTER XVII

FEELING AND RELIGIOUS EXPERIENCE

IN the reaction from intellectualism with its machinery of concepts and syllogisms there has been a remarkable insistence that feeling is the central factor of religious experience. Professors Starbuck and Pratt, developing certain suggestions of Professor James, have attempted to give scientific justification to this point of view.

Professor Starbuck[1] sets the affective life in opposition to the cognitive processes, and makes feeling a direct source of knowledge, independent of intellectual cognition. His position may be summarized as follows. Knowledge has to do with objective facts and relations. In religion the intellectual, ideational, rational cognitive processes perform only a mere by-play. These means of knowledge, in all science and philosophy, are finally subjected to a sort of intuition or feeling of worth. It is natural therefore that in religion also the final appeal should be to feeling. Religion is a feeling adjustment to the deeper things of life, and to the larger reality that encompasses the personal life. There can be, however, no statement of the nature of this larger reality in cognitive terms. It is necessary to trust the reports of

[1] E. D. Starbuck, "The Feelings and their Place in Religion," *The American Journal of Religious Psychology and Education*, vol. i, 1904, pp. 168-186.

PSYCHOLOGY OF RELIGIOUS EXPERIENCE

religion within the affective experience itself, for it is not pertinent to ask for any cognitive description of it.

The nervous mechanisms of the cognitive and affective processes are different. The mechanism for the cognitive-intellectual group of activities is the central nervous system and that of feeling is the sympathetic nervous system. This accounts for the fact that the individual is liable to be torn between two contending worlds, between science and religion, between mysticism and worldly wisdom, that is, between the lower and external world and the inward spiritual life.

Professor Pratt[1] accepts this opposition of the cognitive and feeling elements in consciousness, but does not go so far as to assign to each a special nervous mechanism. Starting with the distinction between the "centre" and "fringe" of consciousness as described by James, the author finds in them two chief divisions of consciousness, two principal kinds of psychic stuff. One of these consists of the definite, describable, communicable elements of consciousness; the rational, the cognitive, the representative; the material which may be made public property by means of scientific and exact description. The other class is made up of the indefinite, the indescribable, the peculiarly private mass of subjective experiences which by their very nature are not susceptible of communication, and which to be exactly described must be made over so as to lose their characteristic quality and cease to be what they were; the conscious material that refers to nothing but it-

[1] James B. Pratt, *The Psychology of Religious Belief*, chapter i.

FEELING AND RELIGIOUS EXPERIENCE

self, has no outer reference, does not pretend to be representative, stands for itself alone. In further characterization of the fringe or feeling background it is said to be in intimate and direct relation to the life of the organism. The instinctive desires and impulses have their roots in this feeling background. This is the primary, elementary form of consciousness and is the original continuum or matrix out of which the various forms of sensation and ideation arise. Yet Professor Pratt admits some hesitancy in this contrast and hastens to add that he is really contending that the whole man must be trusted as against any small portion of his nature, such as reason or perception. The contrast is true only in analytic abstraction. In actual experience ideation and sensory experience and the feeling background are never found isolated from each other, but together they form a unity which is our conscious life.

This affective consciousness appears in three characteristic stages, primitive credulity, intellectual belief, and emotional belief. These the author seeks to illustrate from various types of historical religious development. Within mature minds of the Christian faith he finds the three stages. Primitive credulity is represented by those who accept unquestioningly the authority of the Bible or of their religious instructors without hesitancy. Intellectual belief occurs in those who flatter themselves that they have arguments and reasons for what they believe, even if the arguments are specious and extremely fallacious. These persons are likely to decry all emotionalism and to insist upon a matter-of-fact, literal, and rationalistic demonstration. The third type, according to Professor Pratt, is dominated and controlled by a touch of mysticism. Belief in God and devotion to the religious life is here ascribed to experience of God's presence, to the revival of childhood impressions, to one's immediate consciousness of God, to the illumination, assurance, and quickening of energy which one feels in moments of stress or exaltation. It is this type of person in which the author finds the highest and truest form of religious consciousness. In them the affective, mystical experience greatly preponderates over reason and authority and is felt by many to be in sharp contrast to any intellectual or institutional interests.

In criticism of the main contention of these authors it will be sufficient to summarize the assumption and inconsistencies of their position. This negative criticism will be followed by a constructive statement of the place and significance of feeling in the total religious experience.

The assumption of Starbuck that the central nervous system and the sympathetic nervous system are quite distinct in their structure and function is not supported by the investigations of neurologists. "We now know," writes one of these authorities, "that this (sympathetic) system consists of a series of ganglia or collections of nerve cells connected with each other and connected also with the spinal nerves."[1] The exact relation between them and the problem of their interaction is not understood. But there is no

[1] W. H. Howell, *Text-book of Physiology*, p. 231. Cf. C. S. Sherrington, *The Integrative Action of the Nervous System*, pp. 255-268.

FEELING AND RELIGIOUS EXPERIENCE

basis for the assumption that they function separately. Much less is this assumption justified when the alleged facts which it is invoked to explain are themselves in doubt.

Both Starbuck and Pratt hesitate to commit themselves to the view that the facts introspectively considered show that feeling and cognition are entirely distinct. The latter refers to ideation as developing out of the feeling background, and to this background as being affected by all our thoughts. Starbuck holds that ideation must be tested by a feeling or intuition of value and that the "knowledge" derived from the affective life must be submitted to the criticism of reason. Both fail to discriminate between feeling and the subconscious, although there is evidence that the subconscious cannot properly be taken as identical with affective experience. Both admit quite explicitly that feeling is itself secondary and derivative with reference to the "tendency toward reaction," or as the other states it, the "hereditary and instinctive tendencies." That which they characterize as the background, the hidden depths, the organic activity, is rightly admitted now and then by both to be the underlying unity within which, upon reflective analysis, feeling and ideation are discriminated. This, however, is far from establishing any final alienation between the affective and cognitive processes, and from proving the superiority of the former.

This admission of dynamic, instinctive adjustment as the most original and fundamental characteristic of human life is the principle upon which modern psychologists increasingly agree. From this standpoint a statement of the place and function of the affective processes is possible without confusing them with the total instinctive nature and without subordinating them to intellectual functions. The reaction from the older rationalism is shared by all parties. But the alternative is not the adoption of the view that the feelings are the most basic and important factors in experience. All that is said concerning the small part which clear ideas have in conduct as compared with habit, impulse, instinct, and the subconscious may be accepted. But this does not necessarily lead to the conclusion that feeling is the proper term to apply to all that is non-ideational. What, then, is the relation of feeling to the total human experience?

The James-Lange theory of the emotions, with the further developments suggested by its critics, affords an illuminating answer to this question. According to this theory, the emotion is the feeling involved in the different types of action elicited in a given situation or with reference to a certain object. According to James "we feel sorry because we cry, angry because we strike, afraid because we tremble." The emotion therefore follows upon the activity and is the feeling of the bodily changes involved in the activity. Professor Dewey has pointed out that the case is more complex than this, being complicated by incipient tendencies to react in different ways in a given situation. The inherited nervous mechanism of man is the carrier of various organized systems of reaction formed in the long struggle for existence. On occasion of meeting a bear there are tendencies to run away and

FEELING AND RELIGIOUS EXPERIENCE

also to stand and fight. These tendencies conflict and thus inhibit or hinder each other. In other words, there is uncertainty and hesitation in the execution of any one reaction. This vacillation and inner tension is felt as the emotion of fear or of courage according to the course of action which predominates. In grief the disintegrating, dissolving relaxations are met by the returning sense that the evil condition cannot be real and by the momentary disposition to act in accordance with the happier conditions which one cannot now believe are impossible. The emotion of joy likewise is the accompaniment of activities which alternate with the rise and resurgence of their dread opposites. It is the victory narrowly achieved which gives greatest satisfaction. Even the memory of a triumph is pale unless set off against the distressing possibilities which defeat would have made real.

In all such experiences it is plain that feeling depends upon activities of the organism. The activities themselves are instinctive and organic. They arise within the life process in the course of the adjustment which it involves. Feeling is secondary to these. The "background" out of which the clearer ideas are generated and which constitutes so large a part of all experience, is a background of impulsive, instinctive, habitual, and teleological activity. In its most thoroughly organized and harmonious movements it may be characterized as a vegetative-motor adjustment, accompanied only by sense-feelings. With the advance of experience into novel and complex situations, the adjustment becomes more intricate and the conflict of various types of action produces the class of feelings designated as emotions. And further, in the terminology of Professor Dewey,[1] when action is unified and undisturbed in the realization of a given end, the feeling involved may be designated as interest. In every case, whatever type of feeling is experienced, it involves and is conditioned by activity.

The function of feeling in the total experience may be stated as that of a sign of the value of the activity in which the organism is engaged. Feeling is either agreeable or disagreeable or a mixture of both, as in emotion. Agreeable feelings attend the successful, life-fulfilling operations of the organism. Under normal conditions, eating food when hungry, exercising well-toned muscles, pursuing one's chosen occupation afford pleasure. Disagreeable feelings accompany inhibiting, disintegrating, unsuccessful experiences. Extreme hunger, over-fatigue, loss of business or prestige, produce the danger signal of pain. The emotions, as has been shown, belong to experiences in which there is confusion, hesitance, and conflict of tendencies to action. They demand energy, reflection, and further action to eliminate the disturbance and to attain control of the situation in which the tension arose. Feeling is not, then, an independent, original factor of experience, nor is it a proper end in itself. It has its place within the larger process of activity and adjustment. Like the ideational phases of conduct it springs from and points forward to movement. Feeling discloses the harmony or discord of movement

[1] John Dewey, "Theory of the Emotions," *Psychological Review*, vol. i, p. 553; vol. ii, p. 13.

FEELING AND RELIGIOUS EXPERIENCE

and properly tends to facilitate pleasurable and to inhibit painful movements. It is not therefore a legitimate objective of conduct. The critics of hedonism have sufficiently displayed the paradox that pleasure cannot be gained by any direct effort to secure it. It is always found as an accompaniment. He who plays the game for pleasure, introspectively appraising his satisfaction at every point, is likely to lose both the game and the fun. It is only when the activity is self-forgetting in its harmonized and unified expression that it affords the quality of pleasurable feeling. The attempt to seize the pleasure and to prolong it on its own account eventually destroys the conditioning process from which alone it can arise. The natural issue of sensualism and sentimentalism is therefore the ultimate corruption and devitalization of the organism or institution which practices them. Wherever feeling is consciously or unconsciously made the uppermost factor in conduct, it defeats itself by the deterioration of the structures and functions employed to produce it.

It is evident that the most intense feelings accompany the most vital experiences. The pleasures of food and the pains of hunger or other bodily distress are rudimentary and acute. Likewise the joy of social approval in one's set and the sting of disgrace among one's peers have great biological depths and dimensions. Those social functions in which these interests are projected upon a vast scale and with corresponding intensity are therefore calculated to produce extreme phenomena of an affective character. And it is just because religion involves these immense concerns of

PSYCHOLOGY OF RELIGIOUS EXPERIENCE

individual and social welfare that it is characterized by intense feeling, particularly of the emotional type. These central interests of the individual and of society are not the result of intellectual activity. They do not issue from doctrinal systems. Thus far the critics of rationalism and intellectualism are right. It is true that as compared to the total religious experience of mankind, the clear theological ideas and doctrines are but as the peak of the iceberg to the vast bulk hidden beneath the surface. But it is a mistaken conclusion that the non-intellectual factors of religion are chiefly the feelings, or that the feelings are original and basic among these non-rational factors. Both intellectual and affective elements in religious experience are secondary to and conditioned upon instinctive activity, — habit, custom, imitation, — and the interplay of various types of such activity. This may be clearly seen in the development of religious phenomena under the influence of suggestion, especially in the excitement of the crowd. The method of awakening the crowd is certainly not that of reasoning, argumentation, analysis, and systematic thinking. But neither is it that of transferring or eliciting feeling without an intermediate process. That mediating, conditioning process is the awakening of instinctive, deep-seated impulses. The stirring, inciting means of arousing the crowd are suggestive, dynamic representations of the attitudes and experiences with which the crowd is to be inoculated. If the mass can be stimulated to certain rudimentary reactions, then they share in the accompanying states of feeling. It is a matter of common observation that the extreme emotionalism of the

FEELING AND RELIGIOUS EXPERIENCE

modern religious revival is caused by fascinating the attention with certain dynamic images which necessarily result in tensions and reactions of a violent nature. The phenomena are simplest and crudest among primitive peoples and among children between ten and twenty. But the principle operates in the same manner among civilized persons and with those of mature years. Thinking of the dentist boring into one's teeth sets one's muscles and puts one "on edge" generally. The sight of luscious fruit, when one has an appetite for it, makes the mouth water. Similarly the symbols of infinity may increase the heart-beat and deepen the breathing, while pictures of suffering innocence throw one into attitudes of open-handed helpfulness. In all such experiences the central fact is the imitation of action and therewith of the states of feeling. Emotions commonly aroused in the revivals are those of fear, pity, and love.

The means of arousing fear are those of stimulating shrinking, trembling, cowering reactions over against the stubborn resistance of the "natural man" in his attempts to be brave and firm. He is given a vivid picture of the distress of a lost soul. The familiar figure of the prodigal son, famished, sleepless, and weeping in his gnawing misery as he sits shivering and foul among the filthy swine will wrench the nervous system and excite disturbing motor responses in any person who will concentrate his mind upon it and elaborate the excruciating details with sustained imagination. The pictures of damned souls shut out from paradise, wailing and gnashing their teeth, is capable of endless variation in terms of social disgrace, ostracism, and punishment. It allows numberless statements from the standpoint of actual social experience, such as that of business failure, disease, and loss of opportunity. The greater the lifelikeness and sense of reality in the description of the torments of the wicked, the more certainly will it set up neural and muscular excitations in those whose consciences are pricked, and therefore the greater will be the emotion of fear for one's personal safety.

The emotion of pity has been one of the most prominent feelings in the Christian religion. The supreme instrument for producing it is the image of the innocent Christ upon the cross set round with all his previous experience of suffering, torture, betrayal, desertion, and mockery. "All these events copiously amplified in detail, set in scene by the most realistic imagination until it stood out with an almost scarifying and sometimes actually stigmatic effect in the psycho-physic organism of the believer, appeal as nothing else has ever done to the sentiments of sympathy and pity, the foundations of which strike to the very roots of man's gregarious nature." [1] It is only necessary to image a single detail, such as that of the nails being driven through the quivering flesh of the palms, to realize something of the motor reaction it produces. It soon creates an itching in the palms, a tendency to withdraw the hands as from the piercing points of the nails, and a general sinking and sensation of nausea. Rightly induced such activities of the organism are the occasion of the most intense pity,

[1] G. Stanley Hall, "The Jesus of History and of the Passion," *The American Journal of Religious Psychology and Education*, vol. i, 1904.

FEELING AND RELIGIOUS EXPERIENCE

and may easily lead one to take sides with the sufferer.

The emotion of love is derived in a similar way. It comes by attitudes of gratitude and tendencies to sympathetic helpfulness. In this way one might survey the entire list of emotions prominent in religion, and show that they are all dependent upon the arousal of complex, variant tendencies to instinctive and imitative conduct. The same relation between action and feeling holds true in the more refined and ideal types of religious experience. Feeling is never communicable or transferable by a direct process. It is the nature of affective consciousness to be individual and subjective. The means of communication is that of sense perceptions and thought symbols. These operate by arousing neural and motor processes having their attendant affective qualities. The refinement and cultivation of the emotional nature must therefore necessarily be accomplished indirectly by the control of the attention and by directing it to the symbols and models of ideal forms of conduct, and by securing the natural expression of such direction of attention into its appropriate activities.

The advance from lower to higher types of experience may be measured in terms of the fullness and wealth of the experience, in the degree to which it is illuminated and controlled by intelligence, and in the flexibility and adaptation which it displays. Religion, as we have conceived it, is the deepest phase of the social consciousness. The higher types of religion are therefore those in which this inmost social consciousness is varied and comprehensive, illuminated and guided by intelligence, and subject to constant revision with the changing and growing life of man. In religion thus conceived there is that constant interplay of habit and attention, of the old and the new which belongs necessarily and inherently to vital processes. Such a movement is precisely that in which modern society finds itself. It is compelled to change its social methods and customs as it changes its machines, until it is coming to be characteristic to expect changes and improvements and to look forward confidently to such readjustments. The satisfying faith and trust which formerly centred in the static unchangeability of the world is shifting to the conception of the law of movement and development. The reverence for custom gives way to reliance upon intelligence, operating through criticism and experimentation. Professor Pratt has expressed this necessity of constant rational reconstruction in religion as follows: "Among every people that *thinks* religion must always be at a crisis; for progress is the life of thought and crisis is essential to the life of religion. It must forever be sloughing off an old shell and growing a new one. It must be broad and great enough to accept all that science and criticism have to say and brave enough to face the whole truth and the whole future without fear. In short, the very life of religion depends upon its being able to distinguish between those things which for its age are essentials and those which may be parted with as non-essentials; upon its being able to adapt itself to the ever advancing thought of its time. In thus formulating and reformulating the conceptions of religion in conformity with the pro-

FEELING AND RELIGIOUS EXPERIENCE

gress of human knowledge and reflection, reason will ever find a most useful sphere in the service of religion." [1]

In the light of these general principles, it is possible to see how feeling, like ideation, becomes abnormal and inconsequential the moment it loses touch with reality and action. Just as ideas have been mistakenly believed to have value on their own account and have therefore been manipulated in abstract formulæ to discover their truth, in a corresponding way the feelings have been artificially stimulated by unreal tensions and fictitious relationships to produce sentiments of piety and the conviction of contact with the unseen. It is commonly recognized that music and other arts may be cultivated in parlor-soldier fashion so that they result in emotional dissipation. One also has frequent occasion to observe that the care of a brute pet may develop anxieties and tears on its behalf beyond all comparison with those bestowed upon suffering human beings. From the standpoint of social values and ideals such misdirection of energy and affection is pathological and despicable. But such perversions have not been wanting in religion. The survivals of those primitive cults in which the cow or the monkey is revered as a sacred being afford pathetic illustration of the way in which feeling may cling to conduct which in a civilized age is worse than absurd. But the higher religions often suffer from perversions within particular sects and individuals. Calvinistic Christianity, for example, has in many instances resulted in morbid

[1] James B. Pratt, *The Psychology of Religious Belief*, pp. 287 f.

brooding over the question as to whether one belongs to the number of the elect, whether one has committed the unpardonable sin, whether one has scrupulously observed some ordinance, performed the proper works, and experienced the necessary degree and type of faith. The corrective for such perversions of feeling lies in an objective and critical estimate of the conduct with which they are involved, and in the substitution for such conduct of other activities more serviceable in the furtherance of human social interests. Feeling depends upon action. The fundamental motive to action is fuller living, and the keenest satisfactions belong to those acts which minister to the highest form of life craved by the normal individual for himself and others. The most ideal affections and emotions are therefore those which spring from efforts to make actual and secure a thoroughly socialized human life constantly moving forward through the free and harmonized activity of the individual members of the society. Here is involved the highest practical task and the ultimate satisfaction of both religion and morality. It is just this task and its accompanying feeling which makes morality religious and religion moral. Professor Dewey, writing of the quality of happiness which is morally most important, says: "That quality which is most important is the peace and joy of mind that accompanies the abiding and equable maintenance of socialized interests as central springs of action. To one in whom these interests live (and they live to some extent in every individual not completely pathological) their exercise brings happiness because it fulfills his life. To

FEELING AND RELIGIOUS EXPERIENCE

those in whom it is the supreme interest it brings supreme or final happiness. It is not preferred because it is the greater happiness, but in being preferred as expressing the only kind of self which the agent fundamentally wishes himself to be, it constitutes a kind of happiness with which others cannot be compared. It is unique, final, invaluable." [1]

[1] Dewey and Tufts, *Ethics*, p. 301.

CHAPTER XVIII

THE PSYCHOLOGY OF RELIGIOUS GENIUS AND INSPIRATION

WE have seen that for primitive thought all strange things are regarded as partaking of a divine or demoniacal life. Exceptional persons are viewed in the same way. They possess magical properties and are taboo. The primitive, undeveloped mind in every period of history to the present time has been disposed to consider all peculiarities and exceptional traits as signifying spirit possession, using this expression in a free sense. This is abundantly illustrated by the attitude of the masses of unscientific people toward dwarfs, giants, albinos, cripples, the insane, and criminals. There is felt to be something queer and uncanny about them. Similarly a very old person or a very precocious child attracts attention. There is also a sense of awe in the presence of any person of exalted rank or authority or of notable achievement. The great artists, musicians, orators, and poets always have been popularly regarded as receiving special gifts or visitations from the muses. There is a haunting and insatiable sense of something in them over and above the laws of common experience. The unusual individual has "luck" or "divine guidance" of a supernatural and unique character. Such special favors or endowments have not been supposed to be the sole possession of religious teachers and leaders. Great

PSYCHOLOGY OF RELIGIOUS GENIUS

warriors, hunters, artisans, athletes, as well as philosophers, lawgivers and poets, priests and prophets of all races have been thought to be recipients of the favors of the gods. Even among the Hebrew people, where the phenomena of inspiration are commonly said to distinguish a special class of men, the facts show no such limitation. All of the great men of Israel, whether warriors, lawgivers, judges, poets, prophets, priests, or kings, were understood to be inspired in the sense of receiving communications and direction from Jehovah. The view which conceives inspiration to be restricted to the Hebrew people and to a special group of men within that nation is historically late, and is not in keeping with the feeling of the Hebrews themselves nor with that of any other race. All great men of all races are popularly believed to be inspired.

The term genius has gradually come into quite common use to denote remarkable ability and achievement. It has greater comprehensiveness than the word inspiration. We speak of a scientific, political, literary, or musical genius, and also of a great religious leader or teacher as a religious genius. This word has some advantage for scientific purposes in that it is freer from superstition and from the confusions of controversy. But it has not always been used with scientific care and precision. It has often designated an assumed irreducible and unanalyzable factor in human nature, a kind of given endowment which the science of psychology cannot legitimately adopt. It is a part of the scientific attitude to insist upon the application of analysis and interpretation to all factors and functions of the mental life. It is too much to expect that scientific explanations will not be undertaken simply because the phenomena involved are complex and obscure, or because some persons insist that they are wholly inscrutable. The results of the investigation may be negative or meagre and only partially sustained, but no phenomena of human experience can lay claim to immunity from at least the attempt to understand them. Therefore any statement of genius which assumes it to involve factors radically different from those of ordinary experience is vitiated at the outset by that assumption.

The legitimacy and practicability of subjecting the mind of genius to the same methods and standards that are applied to ordinary men are supported by the discovery that great men are not so isolated from their fellows as has been supposed. The more intimate knowledge of history does not make it appear as the work of a comparatively few great men of extraordinary endowments. It is becoming clear that the ideas and inventions by which progress comes are the culmination of the work of many men of different grades of talent. "The popular mind spares itself effort by crediting the house to the man who lays the last tile and allowing his co-workers to drop out of view. History, however, far from gratifying these hero-worshiping propensities, shows that nearly every truth or mechanism is the fusion of a large number of original ideas proceeding from numerous collaborators, most of whom have been forgotten." [1]

[1] E. A. Ross, *Foundations of Sociology*, p. 227.

PSYCHOLOGY OF RELIGIOUS GENIUS

Francis Galton's account of genius seems to make it a matter of race. Various races produce a number of extraordinarily great men, and that number is the measure of the quality of the race. These individuals, through the inherited combination of the temperaments and capacities of many ancestors, attain greatness and distinction quite independent of the historical, social situation. The social conditions may be disturbing factors, facilitating or augmenting the career of the genius, but natural capacity is the important thing. Those who possess great abilities almost always rise to eminence over all obstacles.

Professor Cooley effectively criticises this theory, particularly with respect to the unimportant place it assigns to education and to social environment.[1] He accepts Galton's main thesis that genius may be transmitted by heredity, but holds that absence of education and social advantages may act as a bar against genius attaining recognition. This manner of distinguishing sharply between the natural endowment and the environment introduces an unfortunate dualism which Cooley does not altogether overcome. He appears to accept the distinction and to differ from Galton chiefly in making favorable environment essential to the development of nature's gifts. Still he approaches a more organic conception of the relation of genius and circumstances when he admits that we cannot know what greatness is in a man unless it comes out. "If genius does not become fame we cannot be sure it was genius."

[1] C. H. Cooley, "Genius, Fame and the Comparison of Races," *Annals of the American Academy*, vol. ix, 1897, pp. 317 ff.

PSYCHOLOGY OF RELIGIOUS EXPERIENCE

In his contention that genius cannot develop without support from a favoring environment, Professor Cooley really accomplishes more than he claims to do, for not only is he justified in concluding that education and opportunity and an atmosphere are necessary to enable the genius to attain recognition, but he might well insist that such circumstances are essential factors in the creation and growth of the powers, capacity, and skill of great men. He shows with convincing evidence that lack of early education is an effectual bar to literary genius. There is proof that Burns and Bunyan were sent to school when children. They escaped the illiteracy which characterized their class and the great mass of the population of Europe and Great Britain down to the nineteenth century. Other hindrances to the development of genius are unfavorable economic and social conditions which result in physical defects and arrested development. Among these influences are the underfeeding of children and child labor. The great majority of the famous European men of letters came from the upper classes of society, in which there is no distressing want. "It would seem, then," writes Cooley, "that if we divide mankind into these three classes (upper, lower-middle, and peasantry), the number of famous men produced by each class is in something like inverse proportion to the total number in the class." He concludes that the few individuals among the peasantry and proletariat having had the aid of education who have achieved fame make it reasonable to infer that if instruction and opportunity had been general the number of geniuses would have been correspondingly increased. The fact that democracy seems to favor the development of genius points in the same direction.

But perhaps the most telling feature in Cooley's article, for the present discussion, is the disclosure of the fallacy of Galton's view that the production of geniuses is a matter of race rather than of history and social environment; that there is something final as to the quality of a given race which is indicated by the number of its great men almost without reference to economic or cultural influences. A very striking argument is based on the distribution of famous painters in Italy. "Previous to the thirteenth century Italy produced no great painters. In the thirteenth century seven were born; in the fourteenth, seven; in the fifteenth thirty-eight; in the sixteenth, twenty-three; of whom fourteen fall in the first half. In the seventeenth, eighteenth, and nineteenth centuries a few scattered painters, none of them of very high merit." This appearance of genius in certain periods and its absence at others is held to be capable of explanation at least in broad outlines. First, it involves the development of a technique through the personal contact and training of masters from childhood. Probably this technique of art needs also to rest upon handicraft. "The great painters and sculptors were first of all craftsmen." They were apprenticed very early, and thus had the full force of the best tradition and opportunity for imitation and refinement of technique. A second condition is that of "atmosphere," a social environment in which appreciation, sympathy, and friendly criticism play about the individual in his most sensitive and formative years. A third factor is that of "an aspiring and successful general life, furnishing symbols" for a common enthusiasm. This general life and its symbols may be religious or political, or conceivably it may be industrial or scientific. In the Italy of the mediæval period it was predominantly religious.

If these principles are freed and given application to genius in various lines, it becomes clear that they express the social and functional conception of the development of consciousness. The underlying condition is the one mentioned last, that of a vital, urgent life for the whole social group. Great men have arisen in crises when the nation or race felt the stress of unusual tension and opportunity. At such times the currents of thought and feeling are deepened and quickened. Not only are unusual men demanded by the situation, but they are created by it, through the stress and stimulation and experience which it furnishes. Such epochs in the history of nations and of social classes develop more or less gradually and are realized with increasing might and power by multitudes of men. Thus an atmosphere and a technique are generated. The direction of attention is fixed. Facility and mastery are attained. Models, types, patterns, and records are produced and the individuals of remarkable capacity and skill are given full opportunity as well as the high pressure of a most educative and disciplining social consciousness.

How widely applicable these principles are is suggested by Galton's inclusion of distinguished English oarsmen among his men of genius, and by Cooley's

PSYCHOLOGY OF RELIGIOUS GENIUS

reference to the American game of baseball. "It is as difficult," says the latter, "for an American brought up in the western part of our country to become a good painter as it is for a Parisian to become a good baseball player, and for similar reasons. Baseball is a social institution with us; every vacant lot is a school, every boy an aspirant for success. The technique of the game is acquired in childhood, and every appearance of talent meets with enthusiastic appreciation. Hence we have many good players and a few great ones. Now it is probable that Frenchmen are from time to time born with a genius for this game, but how can it be developed? What chance do they have to achieve excellence or acquire fame?"

The appearance of scientific geniuses suggests a still clearer operation of cultural influences independently of race and of local centres. Scientific men in all countries, by the aid of books and easy inter-communication, have established a group relationship and consciousness quite superior to geographical and racial limitations. The rapidly developing scientific spirit in all civilized countries furnishes cumulative evidence that great men are products of something more than original native endowment or racial inheritance. They come with the confluence of great economic and social interests which give a set to attention and furnish intense stimulation and a wealth of suggestion. This is illustrated in the work of inventors, whose devices often spring from a sense of urgent need guided by a sensitive and disciplined knowledge of other kindred achievements. "An effective invention," Baldwin remarks, "is always rooted in the knowledge already possessed by society. No effective invention ever makes an absolute break with the culture, tradition, fund of knowledge treasured up from the past." [1]

The relation of the individual and the social group is liable to overstatement on either side. In the older view the great individual was regarded as coming in some quite marvelous way, bringing a nature and an equipment so much superior to his contemporaries that he needed little if any aid from them. At the other extreme is the theory that the race or society is everything and that the individual is shaped and played upon by the mass mechanically and externally. There is, however, another conception. It is that which finds the springs and the channels of social life in the impulses and habits of the individual and at the same time recognizes that these are expressed, stimulated, inhibited, and operated through a living social organism. The great individuals, the geniuses, are those who possess fully the social consciousness and at the same time contribute to its development. They furnish additional impulse and momentum to ideals which have been dimly felt or feebly supported. They act as reagents to precipitate ideas and policies already in solution in the popular mind. Such persons represent, as Baldwin puts it, "a variation toward suggestibility of the most delicate and singular kind. They surpass the teachers from whom they learn." "Now," he continues, "let a man combine with this insight — this extraordinary sanity of social judgment — the power of great inventive and constructive

[1] J. M. Baldwin, *Social and Ethical Interpretations*, p. 180.

PSYCHOLOGY OF RELIGIOUS GENIUS

thought, and then, at last, we have our genius, our hero, and one that we well may worship." [1]

Such an account of genius affords an illuminating interpretation of the great prophetic leaders in Hebrew history. They appeared at times of great national tension and of the most acute material and political struggles for existence. The great writing prophets accumulated a literature which furnished models, a technique and an atmosphere. These prophets were in close and sympathetic relation with the currents of the social and political life. They were in touch with the masses of the people and they were familiar with affairs at court. They knew the situation in their own nation and were informed concerning the attitudes and conflicts of the great empires around them. These facts are better recognized with reference to the later writing prophets, Isaiah, Jeremiah, and Deutero-Isaiah, and therefore it may be more serviceable to make a fuller statement concerning the earlier prophet Amos.

The time at which Amos appeared was one in which the vices and corruptions of the despotism introduced by Solomon had become most flagrant, the ancient laws and customs had been set aside, the freedom of the people had been crushed by forced labor, and there had been wars, famines, and plagues.[2] The court was luxurious and licentious, while the masses were hopelessly impoverished. The class distinctions between the aristocracy and the people, between the rich and the poor, were aggravated by rampant op-

[1] J. M. Baldwin, *Social and Ethical Interpretations*, p. 173.
[2] William Robertson Smith, *The Prophets of Israel*, Lecture III.

pression and fraud. The officials of religion shared in the degeneracy of the court and of the rich. The sanctuaries were degraded by idolatry and by licentiousness aided by the mercenary priesthood, which encouraged lavish gifts and offerings for their own selfish ends. The priests also acted as judges and appropriated the fines and the spoils of neglected justice for their own indulgence. "The strangest scenes of lawlessness were seen in the sanctuaries — revels where the fines paid to the priestly judges were spent in wine-drinking, ministers of the altars stretched for these carousals on garments taken in pledge in defiance of sacred law." The professional prophets also had sunk to the level of the priests, prostituting their sacred function for the sake of gain. Amos saw that the priests and prophets were allied with the court and with the corrupt aristocracy. Over against these he appealed to those of the nation yet sensitive to the old ideals of religion and to the rights and needs of the masses. He became the exponent of the deeper conscience and the outraged social justice of the "remnant." He voiced the impending judgment which Jehovah would visit upon Israel for its sins. "Behold I set the plumb-line — the rule of divine righteousness — in the midst of Israel; I will not pass them by any more; and the high places of Isaac shall be desolate, and the sanctuaries of Israel shall be laid waste, and I will rise against the house of Jeroboam with the sword."

Amos appealed to the traditions and ideals current among the people of Northern Israel in the stories of the patriarchs, of Moses, of the Judges, of Saul, and of

PSYCHOLOGY OF RELIGIOUS GENIUS

David. At every sanctuary was heard the recital of Jehovah's great and loving deeds which had consecrated these holy places from the days of the patriarchs down. Deep in the consciousness of the people to whom Amos spoke was the sense of Jehovah's holiness and jealous care, of the sanctity of the priestly office, and of the dangers of departing from the ways of righteousness and justice. These were familiar in the popular traditions and in written documents.

There is also evidence that Amos was not without the education and culture which his time afforded. William Robertson Smith says: "The humble condition of a shepherd following his flock on the bare mountains of Tekoa has tempted many commentators, from Jerome downwards, to think of Amos as an unlettered clown, and to trace his 'rusticity' in the language of his book. To the unprejudiced judgment, however, the prophecy of Amos appears one of the best examples of pure Hebrew style. The language, the images, the grouping are alike admirable; and the simplicity of the diction, obscured only in one or two passages by the fault of transcribers, is a token, not of rusticity, but of perfect mastery over a language which, though unfit for the expression of abstract ideas, is unsurpassed as a vehicle for impassioned speech. To associate inferior culture with the simplicity and poverty of pastoral life is totally to mistake the conditions of Eastern society. At the courts of the Caliphs and their Emirs the rude Arabs of the desert were wont to appear without any feeling of awkwardness, and to surprise the courtiers by the finish of their impromptu verses, the fluent eloquence of their oratory, and the range of subjects on which they could speak with knowledge and discrimination." The same author also notes the prophet's width of human interest based on a remarkable range of observation, and insists that it is illegitimate to ascribe this knowledge to special revelation. It can be accounted for on the ground that Amos was an observer of social and political life in his own and other countries. "Long journeys are easy to one bred in the frugality of the wilderness, and either on military duty, such as all Hebrews were liable to, or in the service of trading caravans, the shepherd of Tekoa might naturally have found occasion to wander far from his home." It is still more obvious in the case of the successors of Amos that their prophetic genius was developed by the aid of stirring public events, personal experience, great teachers, and many other influences which stimulated and aroused their sensitive natures.

There is one other characteristic which is constantly in evidence in the experience of the prophets. They refer to their message as coming to them from a source quite outside themselves. They appear to be the passive recipients of the words they utter, and this phenomenon is frequently cited as conclusive evidence that they receive supernatural inspiration or revelation. The formula is, "The word of the Lord came unto me"; or "Thus saith the Lord." There is the sense of a direct communication, sometimes with an accompanying vision of the speaker in the form of an angel or messenger. At other times the scenes described

PSYCHOLOGY OF RELIGIOUS GENIUS

appear in a kind of dream panorama with a vividness and detail which the prophet interprets as meaning that they are sent from God.

It is not difficult to show that this type of experience was not peculiar to the Hebrew prophets and that it had no significance in discriminating between true and false prophets, or between the great and the ordinary prophets. We have seen that it was universal among primitive religions for individuals to experience the phenomena of possession. All automatisms, trances, dreams, ecstasies, deliriums, and the like were attributed to possession by spirits. The Hebrew was no exception. "Peculiar mental and physical conditions which were inexplicable to him easily passed for the states in which the god was giving his special communications."[1] It was the custom among the prophets of the more primitive type to employ certain exercises, such as processions and dancing, accompanied by the music of drums and pipes, to induce states of trance and frenzy.[2] By such means Saul and Elisha were said to have been enabled to prophesy. When Elisha desired a message he commanded a minstrel to be brought. "And it came to pass, when the minstrel played, that the hand of the Lord came upon him."[3] This conviction of the prophet that God spoke to him, or in some direct manner conveyed a revelation, has never been of itself the sole or chief guarantee of the value of the prophecy. The distinction between true and false prophets or between

---

[1] Irving Wood, *The Spirit of God in Biblical Literature*, p. 28.
[2] William Robertson Smith, *The Prophets of Israel*, p. 391.
[3] 2 Kings, iii, 15.

important and insignificant prophets was never determined alone by the psychological processes which they experienced. The value of the prophet's word has been measured rather by its ethical significance, by its appeal to the historic social judgment and conscience. In the greatest of the prophets, the cruder phenomena of frenzy and ecstasy disappear. They speak in a quite natural manner, and scarcely claim for themselves any greater sense of passivity and subordination to external influence than do many modern writers.

Modern psychology has classified, described, and to some extent explained the various phenomena exhibited in cases of inspiration. It finds that such phenomena appear in every age down to the present. The cruder, more primitive type is represented by our whirling dervishes, medicine men, trance mediums. There are also those who claim direct communication from a supernatural source by an inner mysterious illumination of the mind. This has been characteristic of various sects of pietists and theosophists. There is a third class of leaders and writers who regard their activity in quite a natural way, but who recognize in their experiences a certain passive attitude and a seeming external control. This has been frequently reflected upon and described by authors of other than religious literature. One student of the subject of genius has collected statements from various eminent authors concerning this phase of their work.[1] Goethe spoke of writing "Werther" "somewhat unconsciously like a sleepwalker." He says in another connection:

[1] William Hirsch, *Genius and Degeneration*, pp. 32 ff.

PSYCHOLOGY OF RELIGIOUS GENIUS

"It had happened to me so often that I would repeat a song to myself and then be unable to recollect it, that sometimes I would run to my desk and, without taking time to lay my paper straight, would without stirring from my place write out the poem from beginning to end, slopingly. For the same reason I always preferred to write with a pencil, on account of its marking so readily. On several occasions, indeed, the scratching and spluttering of my pen awoke me from my somnambulistic poetizing and distracted me so that it suffocated a little product in the birth." Lamartine said, "It is not I who think, but my ideas which think for me." Bettinelli said, "The happy moment for the poet may be called a dream — dreamed in the presence of the intellect, which stands by and gazes with open eyes at the performance." Valuable suggestions have often come to the subject in dreams during sleep. Klopstock gives that account of many of the ideas for his Messiah. Robert Louis Stevenson, writing of depending upon the Brownies of both his sleeping and his waking dreams, says: "I am an excellent adviser, something like Molière's servant; I pull back and I cut down; and I dress the whole in the best words and sentences that I can find and make; I hold the pen, too; and I do the sitting at the table, which is about the worst of it; and when all is done, I make up the manuscript and pay for the registration; so that, on the whole, I have some claim to share, though not so largely as I do, in the profits of our common enterprise."

The common factor in all these cases, including those of the prophetic experience, is the consciousness of being the more or less passive instrument or agent of forces outside one's conscious self. This consciousness cannot be any proof that one is really subject to influences of a supernatural kind, for such consciousness is often induced by known causes arbitrarily, as in hypnotism and in various forms of suggestion. It is also a familiar feature of habitual activity, and we have already noted that this feeling of externality and urgency is no guarantee of the superior quality or wisdom of the message which it accompanies, since it is often found in connection with most trivial and absurd deliverances. It may therefore be regarded as an incidental and negligible phenomenon. The truth and value of any message must rest upon more objective and verifiable grounds. It must justify itself to other minds by its intrinsic merit and by its serviceability for consistent action. The inevitable conclusion is that the distinguishing marks of great religious teachers and leaders, so far as psychology can determine, are no different from those of other geniuses. Like these other geniuses they are evidently men of extraordinary mental capacity who appropriate the materials at hand with facility, interpret them with illuminating insight, and employ them as guides to higher standards of appreciation and to new lines of conduct. The genius, whatever the sphere of his activity, is an individual of remarkable native ability profoundly saturated with the social consciousness, and operating effectively to bring that consciousness to greater clearness and efficiency.

CHAPTER XIX

NONRELIGIOUS PERSONS

THERE is ordinarily little question as to what is meant by nonscientific, nonmusical, or nonsocial persons. And there is no doubt that many individuals belong to each of these classes. There are also numbers of people who are nonreligious as judged by conventional standards. They belong to no ecclesiastical organization, they profess no creed, and disavow having had any personal "experience" of religion. The practical religious worker usually does not hesitate to designate them as nonreligious or as positively irreligious. The modern theologians and psychologists, however, have been slower to commit themselves to that position. The theologians of the newer school often assert that man is by nature religious, "incurably religious," in Sabatier's much quoted phrase. They sometimes mean that the race has been endowed with a "sense of the infinite," with a religious faculty or instinct, which craves expression and makes one restless until it is given satisfaction. This religious endowment or experience is frequently regarded as something distinct from the moral nature or ethical character and as the fundamental condition of morality. With the psychologists there is more of a tendency to the view that man possesses no special instinct or endowment which makes him religious, but that he is capable of developing the attitudes and habits which are religious. Such varying conceptions require a more careful analysis of the phenomena and more definite use of terms.

In primitive groups there could be no nonreligious persons. The customs were imperative and inexorable. Any one who would not conform was punished or expelled from the group and not infrequently was put to death. Even in the high civilizations of Greece and Rome whoever did not observe the prevailing rites was considered impious and dangerous. It has required a long and troubled history to develop any degree of tolerance for the dissenter and the nonconformist, for the free-thinker and the heretic. But with the individualism of the modern world there has come a loosening of the old group morality and religion until there are many persons in every civilized community who are not religious in the conventional sense of the term. Are such persons actually nonreligious; and, if so, what are the psychological characteristics which they manifest?

Taking religion as we have defined it, the answer is not difficult. If religion is viewed as participation in the ideal values of the social consciousness, then those who do not share in this social consciousness are non-religious. The psychological criterion of a man's religion is the degree and range of his social consciousness.

It is of course often true that this participation is not direct. It is not always conscious of itself. It may nevertheless be real and powerful. The great majority of persons doubtless develop their social conscience, their patriotism, sense of justice, and vision of the fu-

NONRELIGIOUS PERSONS

ture of society under the influence of custom and institutional authority. They could not explain why they are so deeply moved by the symbols of the aspiring national life. The flag, a popular song, or the name of one of their heroes stirs them to enthusiasm and self-sacrifice. The symbol has become identical with the reality, and the popular mind has little disposition to distinguish the hero from the cause he represents, or to analyze just how he is identified with it. The depth and urgency of a great national ideal are undoubtedly vaster than the achievement or intention of the persons who advocate and enact it, but for the mass of men the leaders are the embodiment of it. Professor Cooley has stated this with suggestive insight. He says, "To think of love, gratitude, pity, grief, honor, courage, justice, and the like, it is necessary to think of people by whom or toward whom these sentiments may be entertained. Thus justice may be recalled by thinking of Washington, kindness by Lincoln, honor by Sir Philip Sidney, and so on. The reason for this, as already intimated, is that sentiment and imagination are generated, for the most part, in the life of communication, and so belong with personal images by original and necessary association, having no separate existence except in our forms of speech."[1]

It is natural and quite indispensable that social ideals should be felt in this way. If one approves a leader who is vitally representative of his group, one thereby shares in the inmost life of that group, though he may appear to himself to be devoted directly and solely to the individual leader alone. He who prides

[1] Cooley, *Human Nature and the Social Order*, p. 83.

PSYCHOLOGY OF RELIGIOUS EXPERIENCE

himself on following his own conscience or obeying a certain law of external authority may also in reality be accepting the standards of his immediate social environment or those remote in time and space which yet are vivid in his imagination. One's conscience or one's external authority is necessarily the living embodiment of some social system. The symbols which appeal to a man so powerfully may seem to him entirely beyond and above any human social origin. He perhaps resents the scientific conclusion that they are really products of the historical, social life of the race. He may conceive that his religious consciousness is significant just because it has no such natural origin and history. But to the psychologist it remains clear that the man is genuinely religious in so far as his symbols, ceremonials, institutions, and heroes enable him to share in a social life. It is also psychologically evident that the man who tries to maintain religious sentiment apart from social experience is to that extent irreligious, whatever he may claim for himself; while the man who enters thoroughly into the social movements of his time is to that extent genuinely religious, though he may characterize himself quite otherwise. Again a psychological estimate of a given person may show that the interests and activities on account of which he considers himself religious do not in fact make him religious so much as do the benevolent, philanthropic, and civic concerns in which he engages without ascribing to them any religious values. From this standpoint the classification of persons as religious or nonreligious would not coincide with conventional distinctions. It would follow more closely the socio-

NONRELIGIOUS PERSONS

logist's grouping of persons according to their social attitudes and habits.

Nonreligious persons are accordingly those who fail to enter vitally into a world of social activities and feelings. They remain unresponsive to the obligations and the incentives of the social order. They are lacking in the sense of ideal values which constitutes the social conscience. It is not possible to draw the lines of separation with great precision, and it may not be easy to determine individual cases. But there are two or three classes of nonreligious persons not difficult to describe in the main features. One class includes those who lack the mentality or the organization of impulses necessary to enable them to share in the appreciation and effective pursuit of ideals. No one can doubt that this is the case with the defective and delinquent classes. Idiots, imbeciles, the insane, many paupers and persons suffering from hysteria and certain other diseases are of this type. They are too unstable and inchoate to appreciate even in a formal, conventional manner the customs and controlling sentiments of society. The social life is a work of the imagination through which one is able to enter sensitively and intelligently into the experience of other persons and to maintain toward them consistent and dependable relations. This requires adjustment to many individuals, not only to those who live immediately within one's sense perception, but also to those who move in memory and those who dwell in the realms of fancy. It is the imagination which makes any of these real to us. In this social world of the imagination exist the real commandments of the moral law and the duties of the spiritual life. To be a part of this society one must be able to form efficient habits, employ memory and foresight, and hold with some tenacity to ideal purposes. Without these qualities one cannot belong to the political state, to the company of artists, to the schools of the scientists, to unions of labor, to the corporations of business men, nor to the clubs of the professional classes. For the same reason whoever is incapable of such reactions cannot be religious. The sociologists have not hesitated to draw this conclusion with reference to other social activities, and the same considerations make it pertinent to religion. "Men and women who are physically diseased cannot, as a rule, perform their social tasks efficiently.... Weak-willed, slothful, intemperate, passionate, depraved persons cannot be combined into normal families, and although some of them may perform certain tasks well, on the whole, these classes impair the health of all groups and organs to which they belong, and help to form and maintain institutions which are a constant menace to society."[1]

A second class of nonreligious persons consists of those who are not defective or diseased, but whose mental life is not organized in accordance with the scale of values which is recognized by the morally mature and efficient persons of the community. These are the irresponsible, inconsequential individuals who live in the present, largely controlled by their sensuous impulses, without comprehensive purposes or standards. They are found at all levels of the social world, not only among the idle rich, but also among the im-

[1] Small and Vincent, *Introduction to the Study of Society*, p. 269.

NONRELIGIOUS PERSONS

provident poor and the delinquents. The sporting element of the community as described by Veblen belongs here. He shows that habitual sportsmen represent "an archaic spiritual constitution," and "an arrested development of the man's moral nature." Sportsmen are likely to credit themselves with a love of nature, a need of recreation, and to hide from themselves the real purposelessness of their sport. By these reflections and by other illusory impressions they convince themselves that there is some genuine purpose in their "dexterous or emulative exertion." Veblen states it thus: "Sports — hunting, angling, athletic games, and the like — afford an exercise for dexterity and for the emulative ferocity and astuteness characteristic of predatory life. So long as the individual is but slightly gifted with reflection or with a sense of the ulterior trend of his actions, — so long as his life is substantially a life of naïve impulsive action, — so long the immediate and unreflected purposefulness of sports, in the way of an expression of dominance, will measurably satisfy his instinct of workmanship. This is especially true if his dominant impulses are unreflecting emulative propensities of the predaceous temperament."[1]

Others of this class represent, if possible, still less organization of impulses than the sportsmen. Where the natural means of developing instincts through the customary responsibilities of real tasks are absent, the instincts are apt to appear in crude, unregulated excesses. This is seen in those individuals who by inheritance of wealth or sudden success in securing it

[1] T. Veblen, *Theory of the Leisure Class*, p. 260.

seem to lose control and direction of their powers. The modern woman is frequently cited in illustration of the effect of withdrawing human nature from the restraining, supporting influence of real work and serious enterprises. Thomas shows that because man controls wealth and the substantial interests of society, woman is left to gratify her instinctive interest in display. She may even make marriage an occasion of more elaborate display, insisting on the employment of sufficient servants and other aids to make this possible. "The American woman of the better classes has superior rights and no duties, and yet she is worrying herself to death — not over specific troubles, but because she has lost her connection with reality. Many women, more intelligent and energetic than their husbands and brothers, have no more serious occupations than to play the house-cat with or without ornament."[1] It is these women who are the habitués of the matinée and the afternoon musical and are the devotees of card clubs. They occasionally allow themselves the further diversion of charity balls and the prevailing "devout observances."

A third class of the nonreligious includes those who have more definite intellectual and habitual organization, and are consequently more powerful. These are the criminal classes, whose chief psychological characteristic is that they conceive other persons and society in such ways as to subordinate all other interests to some one or few desires which are low and narrow. The confirmed thief, for example, regards individuals and communities with reference to the one point of

[1] W. I. Thomas, *Sex and Society*, p. 240.

NONRELIGIOUS PERSONS

the spoil they may afford. He becomes extremely clever in constructing in imagination the personal traits, habits, and surroundings of the victim. But instead of using this insight for social coöperation and for sympathetic devotion to objective interests, he subverts it to private ends. His knowledge of men becomes his strongest weapon against them. Such exploitation appears in its most appreciable form where the outrage is committed against the person of individuals with violence and blood. But the psychological abnormality is seen on a grand scale where the thief operates more indirectly and insidiously with the vast and complex social relations represented by the highly organized industrial and financial systems of the modern world. Such a robber, to be successful, requires even greater imagination for the motives and mentality of other persons than does the honest capitalist or manager: for he must not only use the legitimate methods of business, but at certain points he must divert them from the proper channels and at the same time avoid detection. To escape with the plunder may require more brains than to seize it.

In the confessions of criminals this perverse manner of apperceiving persons is apparent. To the highwayman the citizen on the street is simply an object with a purse, and with more or less elaborate equipment for protecting the purse by resistance, flight, and outcries. The plans which the citizen may have for using the money to buy food for his children or to aid the unemployed are totally discounted by the robber and have no place in his image of the case. Even the pain incident to the "hold-up" is ignored through eagerness for the pelf. A thief recounting how he had told a society lady the method by which he might get her diamond pin, said: "It was fastened in such a way that to get it, strong arm work would be necessary. I explained how I would 'put the mug on her' while my husky pal went through her. 'But,' she said, 'that would hurt me.' As if the grafters cared! What a selfish lady to be always thinking of herself!"[1] The same criminal, as he lay on his cot in prison, reflected: "Yes, I have stripes on. When I am released perhaps some one will pity me, particularly the women. They may despise and avoid me, most likely they will. But I don't care. All I want is to get their wad of money."[2]

The studies of criminals show that such a rigid mental state, convergent upon some inadequate end or disproportionate desire is their chief psychical trait. Along with this there is naturally found less sensibility, fewer ideas, and lower intelligence than in normal persons.[3] Crime is rare among scientists, and in general a developed mind, being better able to take in the various phases of the whole situation and possessing greater foresight, is restrained from such unsocial conduct. Or, on the positive side, an educated, cultivated normal mind is usually more aware of the ideal claims of the human world and more sensitive to their appeal. The trained socially sane individual is therefore best able to construct in his own imagina-

[1] Hutchins Hapgood, *Autobiography of a Thief*, p. 71.
[2] See Giddings' description of the "anti-social class," *Principles of Sociology*, p. 127.
[3] Havelock Ellis, *The Criminal*, chapter iv, 130 ff.; MacDonald, *Criminology*, chapter iv.

NONRELIGIOUS PERSONS

tion the interplay of motives and purposes in the members of the race at a given point and throughout history, and to hold tenaciously to those moral standards with which the highest religious life is bound up. Those who do not, either by reflective imitation and assent, or by conscious volition, support and further these ideal ends are nonreligious.

It follows from this functional manner of conceiving the matter that the religious consciousness is subject to the same variations, alterations, complications, and abnormalities as other forms of consciousness. It is marked by the same indefiniteness in estimating individual cases, and yet in the average and on the whole it is no more difficult to determine. It is frequently very puzzling to decide whether a certain person is sane or insane, whether he is a genius or a crank. But in general our working standards are sufficient. Religion, like art, science, and statesmanship, is a matter of degree and of variation. Like other attitudes it is subject to cultivation and to increment, and also to neglect and degeneration. It is dependent upon attention, association, and habit, and in a growing social order a process of readjustment and adaptation is as necessary in religion as in any other interest. The "final perseverance of the saints" cannot possibly signify any greater stability than that represented by the persistence of habit and custom and by the ability to readapt habit and custom to meet the new demands of the changing social order.

The most intense and closely articulated expressions of the religious consciousness undergo radical modifications under the stress of new economic and social forces. Witness the rise of Protestantism, and, more recently, the appearance of Modernism within Catholic Christianity. Still more crucial is the development of rationalistic and liberal social tendencies within Protestantism. New industrial conditions, new scientific and historical conceptions of nature and of human life, and manifold agencies, coöperating to expand knowledge, to furnish new measures of freedom and responsibility to the individual, are creating new types of value, different ideals of conduct, and unaccustomed goals of endeavor. The religious symbols of Dante and Milton belonged to the Ptolemaic order, but their incongruity with the Copernican universe is just being felt with full force by the popular mind. The result is that there is great confusion on every hand with reference to religious experience. The old forms and symbols possess an attractive familiarity and seeming simplicity. They appear so immediate and so venerable that it is with the greatest difficulty that those who have employed them can give them the critical analysis and historical setting which is necessary to realize that they are the products of a passing social system. On the contrary, the emerging world order is so vast and intricate, so much a thing of cloistered specialists and of undisciplined democratic enthusiasts, that it is yet vague and crude, without adequate prophets in literature or art, to provide expressive and convincing symbols.

This transition period produces a variety of types of religious consciousness. Among the most characteristic are those who live in the new world of business and social concerns but cling to the old religious terms

NONRELIGIOUS PERSONS

and notions. They simply illustrate the dual personality which modern psychology has found to be frequent even among normal people. Two or more sets of habits and mental reactions are kept quite distinct. This dualism is aided by the fact that religious observances are so much given over to special days, separate institutions, and socially segregated functionaries. The isolation of religion is also effected by the use of a special literature from a foreign age and people, translated into archaic forms of speech. This literature, elaborated in numberless commentaries and devotional books, supplies its own unique historic background, its familiar human characters and vivid incidents which furnish endless subjects for reflection and entertainment without necessitating any reference to the facts and problems of contemporaneous experience. It is therefore quite possible for a man, without conscious inconsistency, to be devoutly religious in the churchly sense, and at the same time to pursue his business or profession as if it belonged to another sphere. He may even employ methods which his religion does not sanction, and justify it on the ground that "business is business." Or he may be honorable in his dealings and charitably disposed to the community without considering such labor and charity among his religious virtues. He may not regard work on the board of the town library or hospital as part of his religious activity.

A second type resulting from the present situation is represented by many school-teachers, settlement workers, philanthropists, and patriots who devote themselves assiduously to the relief of human suffering and to the betterment of the conditions of life, but who stand outside the existing ecclesiastical institutions. Accepting the narrow, traditional notion of religion, they allow themselves to be considered nonreligious, although their feeling for the big human situations is sometimes keen and heroic enough to constitute them a new order of saints. It would scarcely alter the fact that they are genuinely and practically religious, if they were openly opposed to the conventional beliefs and ceremonies. Religion, in a psychical, as well as a scriptural sense, is a matter of the spirit rather than of the letter. The tithing of mint, anise, and cummin are not so important that their performance or their neglect is of much consequence. It is the weightier matters of justice, of sympathy, and of intelligence which determine whether one is religious in a vital sense. As a result of the prevailing confusion many persons are really religious who think themselves either indifferent to religion or positively opposed to it.

There is yet another type of mind which attains with difficulty, if at all, a thoroughly socialized consciousness. There is a tendency for specialists in highly organized occupations to work within their chosen limits and to lose sight of community interests. It is not alone the operator of a machine, or the workman who performs monotonously the same movements day after day who is in danger of losing appreciation of the larger task to which he contributes. His work is perhaps the most deadening just because it is so largely a matter of recurring, invariable physical reactions. But the scientific specialist

NONRELIGIOUS PERSONS

and technical expert who exercises a highly developed mind may also absorb himself in his task and take no serious account of the community life which sustains him in the pursuit of his specialty. It is doubtful whether any justifiable labor does not somehow have such reference to the interests of others that it may be more effectively carried on with awareness of such implications. In any case the individual who does concentrate upon a specialty to the neglect of social duties to that extent narrows his world of personal relations and reduces his sensitiveness with reference to the common ends of the social body. If the motor phases of consciousness have a determining effect upon ideational processes, then the very fact of limiting one's self to the work-bench or the laboratory will limit the perspective of one's outlook and of one's social imagination. This may account to some extent for the present indifference among large classes of workmen, scientists, and artists to the problems of religion.

In one form or another the difficulty for most earnest persons with reference to religion is that the symbols and imagery which are at hand are not satisfying because they belong to an outgrown order; while the activities and conceptions which engage attention are not yet expressed in sufficiently definite and familiar ideals. Our modern ideals have not yet developed a sufficient history, richness, sanctity, and authority to give them religious value. They are not commonly enough recognized and accepted to furnish an outline and scaffolding in which the thought of men is organized with the objectivity and insistence of the old forms. "In times of intellectual unsettlement, like the present, the ideal may become disorganized and scattered, the face of God blurred to the view, like the reflection of the sun in troubled waters. And at the same time the creeds become incredible, so that, until new ones can be worked out and diffused, each man must either make one for himself — a task to which few are equal — or undergo distraction, or cease to think about such matters if he can."

The most casual inquiry among thoughtful people confirms this. In the questionnaire already referred to, one of the questions was, Do you consider yourself religious, and why? About one fourth of the respondents answered either that they did not consider themselves religious, or that they did not know whether or not they were religious. In nearly every instance the reasons given were that some traditional belief had been discarded or public worship discontinued. For example, one says: "I presume I am nonreligious because I cannot agree with any sect I know of and I have nothing definite to offer instead." Another replies: "I have for the past ten years considered myself nonreligious, or rather this has been a growing conviction, because: 1. I am not interested in church activities of an intra-church kind; 2. I get no pleasant emotional reaction of a religious kind from attendance at church or from commingling with worshipers at church."

In the two following experiences there is definite renunciation of some central beliefs of the orthodox faith and yet an inclination to take the side of religion: "I honor Jesus Christ as a beautiful inspiring example,

NONRELIGIOUS PERSONS

but it seems impossible for me to think of him as divinity. I like to go to church because I believe that the influence of all working towards the right and the moral is good. I like the thoughtful atmosphere. I consider myself religious because I think seriously of religious and ultimate problems. I do not believe in a personal God. Such a conception to me is illogical. I think that religious belief should be the natural growth of a man's experience." This statement is from an active church worker and Sunday-school teacher: "I do not know whether I am religious or not. I have no practical faith in God. I get no strength outside of myself — except from human beings; and I have no desire for a personal life after death. On the other hand, I believe that a moral life is the only thing worth while. I desire to work out my own salvation, here and now; and I wish (in a half-hearted way) to see all people know the joy of right living. That seems to be religious — in theory."

Two who are doubtful about their being religious suggest the explanation that it is probably due to lack of attention to the subject. One of them says: "Do not know whether I am religious or not, as I have never been able to define the term. Religion has never taken a deep hold of me, and what has at times stirred this emotion in friends most violently has usually lacked point for me. I have given religious matters very little attention." The other experience is this: "No, I do not think I am religious. I have never taken any interest in any church life nor have I ever done any work for the church — I have had no time for any religious work."

PSYCHOLOGY OF RELIGIOUS EXPERIENCE

The three cases which follow indicate that the persons have worked their way further through the problem and have nearly reached the point of calling themselves religious, but from a radically different standpoint than that of orthodox teaching. "Since becoming a member of the church I have attended quite regularly, but my faith in the church as an institution and in the Bible as the work of God, has steadily decreased. I have tried to study honestly and fair-mindedly, and my studies lead me steadily farther away from those beliefs. In other fields, the only instance I can suggest is in the matter of my profession. From childhood I was possessed of the desire to be a physician, and all my early work was toward that end. If by the term 'religious' we mean a belief in the Bible and its teachings, a belief in God and in the church, then I am not religious. If by religion we mean a sincere endeavor to live up to a code of morals, to do right as we see it, to play the man in relation to our fellow men, then I am at least trying to be religious."

"If the standard of religion includes simply the idea of futurity and God, with its practical social application through the church, I consider myself religious. But according to my former standard before being influenced by modern teaching, I should not now consider myself religious, — e. g. implicit belief in the infallibility of the Bible, the virtue of belief, and the idea of redemption through vicarious suffering would be essential."

"Do not know about being religious, but do know that there is a sincere desire to follow the highest

NONRELIGIOUS PERSONS

ideals and do the most good one can in the world, for it is only this that makes life truly worth while. I believe in a religion of helpfulness and cheerfulness, trusting the Divine Spirit which is surely in his world and will somehow bring things around right."

The following experience is suggestive of a large class who incline to identify the religious and the esthetic consciousness. There is little sympathy here for either orthodoxy or social interests. "The more I think about it, the more I have found it impossible to say whether I am religious or not. I have always felt a deep interest and a strong desire to support any movement towards breadth of interpretation, but this is due merely to a dislike of dogma. Personally I get no inspiration or religious value from Unitarianism or any religion which stresses the moral or rational side of religion. As far as I can see, I have absolutely no needs which cannot be satisfied better outside religion than in it. Apart from its dogmatism, the personal, pragmatic attitude of all evangelical protestant churches I have known, arouses instinctive prejudices in me. On the other hand, participation in a service of an Episcopal or Anglican Church puts me in a mood that might perhaps be called religious. The service impresses me as voicing but one need, and that an impersonal one, the need of worship. Sometimes the mood becomes definite enough to centre around my own ideals; more often it is vague and without a definite object. In no case do I make any effort at reinterpretation of the ideas involved in the service. In my happiest times, they cease to be facts or dogmas and become real in the same way as the ideas of a beautiful poem. This value seems to me a little different from a purely esthetic value. I do not know whether it is religious or not."

It may be of interest to note that two clergymen in an orthodox denomination, themselves liberal men, however, gave the following reasons for considering themselves religious: "A conscience that makes me trouble and a love of the right and the truth." The other's reason was, "An abiding desire for the best in life."

This experience of a scientist is included because it describes so well the process through which many minds are finding their way to a constructive religious faith after the new order. It is a fair illustration of the religious consciousness of those who are yet too often considered nonreligious. "I think most of us have passed through very much the same general experience regarding religious matters. As boys we were taught the elements of Christianity; were brought up in one or another of the Christian sects; were told of God and of heaven and of hell, and generally given the idea that this was religion and the basis of morality. I think most of us accepted this as we accepted other things told us, or that we learned in childhood without reasoning or thinking about it at all, and that though it lay there in our minds as we matured, we paid small attention to it, finding it really touched our lives but little. We took our place in the world of men and facts around us, and our work and duties absorbed us more and more till this early religious training was quite overlaid. To the extent that we later thought of it we found it primitive and unsatisfactory.

NONRELIGIOUS PERSONS

It was neither the basis of our own lives nor of the lives of those we met. Our code was not this code, our ethics not founded on any such system of future rewards and punishments. These things might be, — but we, and others, acted as though they were not. Our lives were simpler, more direct and material. Certain things we felt right and did, certain other things wrong and tried to avoid. If we questioned the origin of these feelings there seemed to be a more immediate rational explanation of them than that they were taught two thousand years ago, or that the one way led to hell and the other to heaven. In short, we had outgrown the forms of our childhood, and religion and conduct were for us divorced.

"But while we were outgrowing certain forms we were growing into certain perceptions and feelings. We were studying nature or life itself, and the immensity and grandeur of *what is* were laying their hold upon us. The immeasurable lapse of time, the infinitude of space, the mighty rush and swirl of cosmic energy, the infinite richness and variety of nature, the myriad forms of organic life, and, perhaps more than all else, the slow, sure march of evolution and the immobility of law, were opening our consciousness to new perceptions and emotions. It is these emotions which typify for me to-day religious feeling, as I think they do for many other scientific men, and I offer as my definition of religion what Haeckel has called 'cosmic emotion.'"[1]

If this experience had continued on to an appreciation of the social world, as viewed from the standpoint

[1] H. B. Mitchell, *Talks on Religion*, pp. 15 f.

PSYCHOLOGY OF RELIGIOUS EXPERIENCE

of the evolutionary processes and the immanent ideals of the human moral order, it would have expressed in fairly adequate terms the feeling for reality and experience which is coming to be recognized as the substance of modern religious faith.

CHAPTER XX

THE PSYCHOLOGY OF RELIGIOUS SECTS

IN the foregoing discussion the conclusion has been reached from several standpoints that the social consciousness, in its most intimate and vital phases, is identical with religion. In primitive society this relation is more obvious because it is more simple and direct. Since there is little freedom for the individual, his habits and superstitions are fairly typical for all his kin. Even there, however, in spite of all rigidity, there are slow currents and occasional crises, which effect some modification of myth and ceremonial, and not infrequently impose new or foreign customs and traditions upon older formations. These changes in the life of the tribe operate through the activities and minds of individuals, such as the head men or other leaders of the group. In the Australian tribes the authority of the old men to institute slight changes is definitely established.[1] The individual, at this low stage, is therefore not merely the passive medium of the common life, but also experiences and contributes actively to its readjustments. His mind is the living expression of the social mind, and the social mind in turn is none other than the minds of the individuals bound together in the common life.

In highly developed societies the same general relation exists, only here the activities are more varied

[1] Spencer and Gillen, *The Native Tribes of Central Australia*, p. 272.

and more difficult to trace. The social groupings are more numerous, complex, and subtle. It is difficult to determine by casual observation what particular persons constitute a man's social *milieu*. The educated, widely experienced man mingles with many classes, and is identified with various groups in business, professional, and neighborhood life. Yet the standards of his ideal interests may be those of still another set. In a cosmopolitan community a person may be held within family and race associations to such an extent that he is relatively insensible to the inner life of other circles into which his trade or profession frequently carries him. In any great American city, where immigrants are colonized, there are many who live outwardly with the world around them, while within they maintain a constant reference to their own racial, family ideals and social customs. Hutchins Hapgood has vividly described this in the case of the Russian Jew. "When the Jew comes to America he remains, if he is old, essentially the same as he was in Russia. His deeply rooted habits and the 'worry of daily bread' make him but little sensitive to the conditions of his new home. His imagination lives in the old country and he gets his consolation in the old religion."[1]

One may thus by training and by prolonged exercise of the imagination identify himself with select companies of a distant time and place, for example, with the Greek Stoics or the primitive Christians. By intimate familiarity with their habits, temper, and ideals it is possible to derive from them spiritual

[1] *The Spirit of the Ghetto*, p. 10.

THE PSYCHOLOGY OF RELIGIOUS SECTS

companionships, controlling tastes, and regulative practices. A similar selection and identification may be made with the widely scattered members of one's profession or party. It is by this imaginative vividness and intellectual sympathy that the cautious, sensitive scientific temper fortifies itself. The scientist is more mindful of the masters in his specialty than of all the world beside. It is the opinion of that particular company, however small and scattered, which expands or contracts his ego, while to the judgments of others he is relatively indifferent. Every person of normal mind and action appeals to his set, — to his club, his family, his church, his union, his fellow scientists, with a sensitivity which is entirely beyond any rational intent or calculation. The individual consciousness is thus embedded in a kind of social protoplasm, of which it is so intimately and organically a part that the changes and adjustments in either radiate into and affect the other most vitally. Just what elements of the social protoplasm, that is, what particular social organizations, sustain the most immediate and controlling relations to a given individual it may be difficult to determine. But since there is this connection for every sane, efficient person, the social psychology of particular groups is an aid in the interpretation of individual minds. And in periods of change and transition, the perception of this relationship may afford illumination for many difficulties. At the present time there is a notable movement in the whole social system toward a larger and more closely articulated human life. The profound changes which are involved for religion may be indicated in reference to the development of the various denominations of Christianity and the tendencies now operating to transcend these historic formations and to produce a new alignment of religious bodies.

A psychological interpretation of the different Christian sects requires that they be regarded as social organisms whose life history is much fuller and richer than can be measured by their intellectual doctrines. In fact such doctrines may be viewed as phases of the whole development. They are products and results of social movements, as well as means of control and guidance. Each denomination represents a type of personality, a social stratification, which is determined in its original pattern by the economic forces and the personal leadership which fashioned it. Afterwards it aggregates like-minded people to itself and stamps its members with its own marks. All protestant bodies have common characteristics, within which there are differentiations and lesser organic growths of great variety. The main features of the leading sects are easily detected in comparison with each other, but the subdivisions often rest upon differences and involve distinctions scarcely appreciable to any but those of their own number.

Protestantism itself represents the disintegration of the mediæval social unity and the assertion of national and community, as well as personal, individualism. The protestant type is therefore marked by initiative, aggression, and loyalty to personal leaders. Its parties are given to emphasis upon special reforms and to the elaboration of single principles, or half-truths. Its name describes its spirit of revolt and

THE PSYCHOLOGY OF RELIGIOUS SECTS

dissent. This tendency was curiously favored by the circumstances under which the Bible was put forward as the authority of protestants. It was the invention of printing which facilitated its circulation, and the fact that the Bible was the book most commonly printed may be regarded as the cause almost as much as the result of its authority. "It became at once a primer, a history, and a law book."

The Bible was well adapted to serve as the instrument of the protestant spirit. It gave the semblance of an external authority which the long-accustomed subservience of the human mind required. It was a standard having age, universality, and adaptability sufficient to offset the corresponding claims of the Catholic Church. The ease with which the Bible yielded itself, by means of its rich, figurative, human contents, to the purposes of different national temperaments and widely variant classes of society gave a certain unity to protestant sects while affording free play for their differences. Each party found that the Bible taught the doctrines which its own culture and needs demanded. Each selected proof texts suitable to its purposes and usually believed its own subjective ideas were the objective and literal meaning of the sacred book itself. In spite of this one-sided doctrinal interpretation of the theologians, the masses of the people found also a vivid, appealing, and stimulating literature.

The Bible was thus the convenient material from which the different movements supplied their filling, while the molds into which this material was shaped were supplied by the rising genius and institutions of the different nationalities, cultures, and classes. These controlling forces were represented by great personalities who embodied and expressed the will of the people. Luther was the incarnation of the free Teutonic spirit, with its independence, spontaneity, and moral earnestness. The people for whom he was spokesman were overburdened by papal taxation to aid in building St. Peter's at Rome and to maintain there an extravagant and luxurious court. Luther's visit to Italy prepared him to realize to the full the immorality of the sale of indulgences in his own province. This vicious development of the practice of meritorious "works," aggravated by the effrontery of the papal agents and supported by the superstitious credulity of his countrymen, produced a profound revulsion in Luther's deep moral nature. It found expression in the text, "The just shall live by faith."

Calvinism, even more than Lutheranism, is an expression of the mental traits of its founder. Calvin was a lawyer and a man of books. He expounded religion in terms of law and in the form of final and inflexible authority. The Bible is a law book containing a complete code and affording direction for every phase of conduct. The elect constitute the spiritual aristocracy. The individual is not dependent upon his own nature or effort, but is part of a chosen company, a settled order. Participation in this order is a gift or endowment. In this way Calvinism comes to the aid of the individual to relieve him of the authority and oppression exercised by the Church and the State.

THE PSYCHOLOGY OF RELIGIOUS SECTS

In this sense Calvinism is democratic. Man is in his higher nature related to a nobler authority — that of the infinite, eternal God, between whom and the soul of man no human agency should interfere. But this view allowed small place to man's initiative and individual volition. This character of Calvinism is indicated by the classes to whom it appealed. It won those in whom there was a strong sense of solidarity, such as the clannish Scotch and the English artisan classes with their guilds and corporate interests. In such groups the individual had a sense of dependence and yet of superior strength and merit through the power of the body to which he belonged. He received much which he did not earn and his acts in turn reached farther than himself. Calvinism gave men that sense of security in spiritual relationships which they already experienced in earthly affairs through their family and guild. With this feeling of special privilege as elect members of the divine kingdom, Calvinism developed a scorn of all things earthly, human, and papal. The Puritans, especially, displayed this contempt for the natural man and for mere human authority of king and pope. They devoted themselves to an austere and strenuous conception of duty with the utmost conscientiousness in opposition to the worldliness and sensual indulgence of the time. They despised the life of nature, whether this meant sensual indulgence or thoughtful regard for the welfare of the body. Their self-restraint and cleanliness preserved the Puritans from the plagues which carried off the improvident and indulgent classes; but their neglect of the physical comforts and their overwork and exposure brought their own disease. It has been said that the Puritans died of consumption![1]

The Puritans contended for a more pronounced protestantism than was congenial to the Anglican Church. That church never shared fully in the theology of the reformation. It remained true for the most part to the old type. The Anglican divines never favored rigid Calvinism, but "tended more and more to blunt the sharpness of doctrinal statements on this subject." Indeed, it was the insistent contention of the Puritans that the Anglican Church remained essentially Catholic, keeping as it did the old ceremonial, the vestments, and the general attitude and spirit of the sensuous, liturgical form of religion. Such a religion was suited to the court circle, to the aristocratic and esthetic type of mind. It was fitted to a ruling and a leisure class, possessing freedom and disposition for the pleasures which wealth and station afford. This class experienced the consciousness of long established privilege and of a security as firm as the state itself. It therefore naturally found satisfaction in a religion which embodied the proprieties of long usage in stately ceremonials, sufficiently objective to carry the mind out of itself through sensuous symbolism, and involving no novel or strenuous duties in opposition to the tastes and enjoyments of the natural man.

The Wesleyan movement was primarily a religious development among the masses which emphasized freedom of individual action and the possibility of

[1] Simon Patten, *Development of English Thought*, p. 140.

THE PSYCHOLOGY OF RELIGIOUS SECTS

immediate experience in every soul of the greatest spiritual realities. Reaction against both the formalism of the established church and the predestinarianism of Calvinism was characteristic of Methodism. Those who accepted it prove what it was. They also helped to fix the type. A new industrial class had developed in England, the laborers employed in factories and in other new and unaccustomed occupations. The routine and drudgery were exhausting, particularly to those classes previously devoted to less exacting pursuits. Puritanism had suppressed the popular amusements and had made Sunday a quiet and difficult day. Methodism offered a means of self-expression, of emotional excitement and of stirring demonstration through a free and unrestrained religious service. The great religious revivals furnished genuine and valuable recreation of more than passing moment. They attached great importance to outward manifestations of feeling. Change of heart showed itself in a demonstrative conversion and in visible signs. The newly awakened mental state and the intense emotion were the inner evidences of genuine religion, but these expressed themselves in powerful and quite involuntary motor reactions. Such phenomena, partly because they were so largely involuntary, were "signs of grace" as the familiar "works" could not be. Good deeds, such as participation in formal worship, acts of penance, alms or pilgrimages, which were the familiar and conventionally accepted evidences of salvation, were as nothing for the Methodists, compared to the direct and unpremeditated expressions of emotion. These experiences were most easily obtained in the crowd, and Wesley "shrewdly utilized social customs for religious ends by encouraging large gatherings. In the place of fairs, May days, and other sensual events, he introduced religious organizations, which gave the same activity and satisfied the natural cravings for society. Wakes, revivals, and love feasts broke up the monotony of family life and made outside interests once more supreme." [1] In all this, Methodism presented the emotional experience as something within the range of all persons and in comparison with which all other attainments were insignificant. Learning, creeds, and doctrines; social station, wealth, and achievement, counted for nothing against this immediate sense and evidence of the presence of God. Here was found a new social bond. All who possessed this experience understood each other and felt themselves the fortunate members of a mystic company.

When these great social organisms, the religious denominations, pass beyond their experimental stages, they develop a structure and a momentum which enable them to persist. They continue to assimilate people of their class and type, spreading over all social areas where there is favorable soil. In their later development, less is said with reference to particular doctrines which were originally distinctive, and progress is continued through social influence, family ties, prestige, and the inertia characteristic of older growths. Emphasis upon doctrine is more marked in new cults or in those whose place is still in doubt. The proselytes to such bodies are likely to be most

[1] Simon Patten, *Development of English Thought*, p. 258.

THE PSYCHOLOGY OF RELIGIOUS SECTS

interested in the creed and in general to be more conscious of the forms and customs, whereas those who have grown up in a faith are held to it by less conscious and by deeper ties. They experience the profounder human qualities in the living associations of kinsmen and comrades, in comparison with which the doctrinal statements and theoretical implications are relatively formal and superfluous. The creed is for them no longer a matter for justification and discussion but a symbol of social realities and ideals. It is something to be employed in a ritual, a comforting and elevating form of words to be read or intoned with feeling and devotion rather than a set of propositions submitted to critical analysis or rational affirmation. The casual observer of religious services frequently fails to realize this fact. He may think that people do or should take their creeds and hymns very literally and discriminatingly, whereas they oftener employ them quite naturally as ready and familiar symbols of ideal values. Even the sermon is usually more significant in its general tone and earnestness than in its information and logic, if the latter are present at all!

The development of the various denominations in America affords interesting illustration of the persistence of these social organisms and of their limitation to the nationalities and classes to which they are by nature adapted. Calvinism is represented by the Congregationalists, the descendants of the English Puritans who were strong in New England; by the Presbyterians, who are Scotch and Irish, and are most numerous in Pennsylvania and New York; and by the

Baptists, widely scattered through the States, and representing the popular extension of Congregationalism. The Episcopalians are also mainly English, and are most numerous in New York, where is found one fourth of their total number. Methodism may be considered as a form of Episcopalianism well adapted to reach the masses of people. Like the Baptists, the Methodists are strong throughout the country. Both denominations found in America much vaster numbers of people of their class and type than in England. Of the Lutherans in this country, one half are Germans and one quarter are Scandinavians. The Catholics, like the others, remain much the same in their spirit and temper, and, through their attraction for the masses, are everywhere numerous.

The fact that different denominations tend to operate among populations according to social classes is interestingly illustrated by a recent investigation of a certain American community in New York State.[1] In the first period of its history the whole community was pervaded by simple rural conditions. Religion in all the churches was very little a matter of doctrine and almost wholly of the nature of custom and superstition. The emphasis fell on Sabbath observance and austere self-denial. This self-denial meant abstinence from the popular amusements, card-playing, theatre-going, dancing, and conviviality. That Sabbath observance was prompted by simple primitive attitudes toward nature is seen in the fact that in unfavorable seasons there was an increase of religious fear. It was felt that they were the judg-

[1] J. M. Williams, *An American Town*.

ments of an angry God. Sunday was the day when the people attempted to win the favor of God by abstaining from work. A record was found stating that the minister was once explicitly urged to "be more earnest at the throne of grace that the seasons be ordered in mercy." Self-denial in gifts of money was practiced in the same spirit. One man said that his reason for increasing his contributions to the church was that in the past every time he had increased his gifts "the Lord had prospered him." In this earlier period there were no sharp differences noticeable between the various denominations. All of the people were dependent quite directly on the soil, and there was little opportunity for the play of social distinctions or for indulgence in amusements. About 1874 the economic conditions of the community were radically changed, owing largely to marked development in the hop industry. In the periods of its greatest prosperity significant changes took place. There was considerable migration from the surrounding rural districts into the town, the comforts and pleasures of more expensive modes of life developed, better houses and stores were built, travel increased, and the patronage of summer resorts grew. In general, amusements of "receptive sensation" increased. These included card games, music, theatres, conviviality, and horse-racing. In the churches, after the new economic conditions began, revivals became ineffective, none arousing any excitement after 1879. With prosperity there was a marked increase in church expenditures. They paid more for music, for ministers, and for missions. But a process of selection was operating among the different denominations. "Just as the rural districts selected the austere characters and the village the convivial, so the Baptist and Methodist churches, the membership of which has been more largely from the rural districts, have selected the austere from among the entire population, village and rural, while the Presbyterian and Episcopal churches, the membership of which has been more largely from the village, have selected the convivial characters. Since 1893, the Methodists have become convivial, and have selected the convivial characters of the lower classes of the village population." The change in the character of religion in the second period is indicated in the different type of minister demanded. "The minister of the early days must, in his personal appearance, walk, and conversation, as we have seen, be a perfect example of self-denial. The successful minister of the later period was the handsome, well-dressed, sociable man who had traveled extensively, read widely, and could be entertaining at all times, in sermons as well as in social functions."

The subdivisions of these main forms of Protestant Christianity have become numerous under the influences of pioneer conditions which have developed local characteristics and afforded many new movements. More sporadic and unique cults have also arisen quite independently of any old-world precedents. Among these are the Mormons, Adventists, Spiritualists, and Christian Scientists. Particular motives, special doctrines, and controlling individuals furnish abundant material for a psychological account of their history. Christian Science represents

THE PSYCHOLOGY OF RELIGIOUS SECTS

the latest and in many ways most significant of these contemporaneous religious cults. The healing art is its chief feature. The class to whom it appeals is largely of the well-to-do city dwellers who have a competence or salary sufficient to bring them within the taxing stimuli of the artificial community life. These people are accustomed to seek their own comfort, and yet at the same time are often the victims of the imaginary or real ills which those removed from simpler, sterner tasks and homelier circumstances are apt to experience. Nervous diseases are common among them, and these may often be cured by suggestion. Mrs. Eddy's belief in her own recovery from sickness by mental healing proved to be a belief in which many others could participate for themselves. Her belief expressed itself in a strange mixture of Biblical texts and pseudo-philosophical optimism and voluntarism suited to uncritical minds worried by pain, languor, and other unpleasant forms of self-consciousness. It appeals also to the mystical and superstitious elements of the traditional religion, using the Bible in a quite allegorical manner while professing to be thoroughly scientific. That it is, however, lacking in the scientific temper is seen in the fact that it has no attractions for genuinely scientific men. An important part of its capital may be said to consist in the popular distrust of scientific medicine. Christian Science has also been fortunate in several features which give it prestige among the classes indicated. It has exalted the feminine factor in the conception of the "Mother-God," and in having an attractive woman "reader" equally prominent with the male

PSYCHOLOGY OF RELIGIOUS EXPERIENCE

reader in the conduct of the public service. This introduces in an unobtrusive and effective manner the powerful sex influence. It has been shrewdly organized and administered. It has provided elaborate buildings and keeps up all appearances of the prosperity and outward success so attractive in a commercial age. That this movement appeals to those disposed to seek and to pay for their own comfort is evident in the fact that its organizations participate in no charities or philanthropies, and thus far have coöperated little, if any, in the wide-spread efforts on behalf of better social conditions, such as legislation for the protection and elevation of dependent, educable classes. Both in its clannish spirit and in its non-rational attitudes it is still at the level of the older religious sects which are fundamentally controlled by relatively unconscious economic and social conditions, operating by the controlling force of custom, imitation, and prestige.

But just on this account Christian Science reveals, in a striking manner, the nature of religious brotherhoods in their historic development. They arise as results of complex and more or less profound social influences, and have their nucleus in a few strong personalities who become the organizing and radiating centres. Claim of some objective, external authority is made — the Bible, direct revelations by visions or voices, or the sense of the authority of the body of believers itself. At last it is the claim of custom or tradition or the exigency of some pressing necessity. For Lutheranism the immediate pressure was the sale of indulgences; for Calvinism it was the compulsion

THE PSYCHOLOGY OF RELIGIOUS SECTS

of the papal system; for Puritanism it was the plagues and the license of the time; for Wesleyanism it was the craving for motor expressions and the cry of the masses for an assurance of salvation within their comprehension; for Christian Science it is the desire for personal comfort in a tense and nervous age. In their later development these religious sects gain a sense of individuality and a pride of life and growth which operate with the force of primitive custom and tribal conquest. The different religious bodies are in effect so many social clans. Their loyalties, antipathies, and methods are based upon race and class inheritances and prejudices, merged with the fine idealism of the central Christian faith. Under the influences of modern life these clans feel drawn or driven together for mutual defense, but they are suspicious and awkward in actual attempts at union. While theoretically admitting that the things in which they agree are more numerous and more vital than those in which they differ, yet they continue under the influence of deep-seated instincts and habits to magnify incidental differences. They are under the control of the ancient biological, primitive, clan impulse to preserve the identity and integrity of the organism. The desire of the Young People's Societies of Christian Endeavor to become an interdenominational organization was met by the preference of the most numerous denominations to have their own separate institutions for their young people. While the young, freer, and broader minds of all denominations favor such coalitions, the clan spirit remains strong in the official representatives of missionary agencies, and among those who have become most identified with the practical administration of institutional interests.

The conflict, however, which is coming to consciousness in modern society is no longer that between clan and clan, or between the clan and complete social detachment, but rather a conflict between the lesser and the larger social whole. Devotion to institutions, to powerful social structures, is a necessity. But this devotion inverts the scale of values when it puts provincialism above nationalism, or local sectarian loyalties above the common welfare. In religion, as in the state, no single virtue or theory can be adequate to the needs of the whole many-sided social life. "Much energy has been wasted or nearly wasted," remarks Professor Cooley, "in the exclusive and intolerant advocacy of special schemes — single tax, prohibition, state socialism and the like — each of which was imagined by its adherents to be the key to millennial conditions. Every year, however, makes converts to the truth that no isolated scheme can be a good scheme, and that real progress must be an advance all along the line." The same is true in religion. The religious group, like the family, cannot fulfill its largest function by being self-centered and exclusive. It is possible that all family and group attachments should lead outward into comprehensive and expansive relationships. When this is accomplished the tension between them, for example, between the family and the state, is overcome, and gives way to the finest, widest-reaching patriotism and social idealism. The modern spirit may be said to be contrasted with the traditional, tribal character chiefly in these two respects: in the vastness and symmetry of its ideal of human society and in the conscious, critical methods of experimentation and practical endeavor by which it strives to make this ideal actual. The various denominations possess genuine social consciousness. That is their strength. But that consciousness is too much restricted both in outlook and in methods. What is now demanded by the spirit of the age is that they shall overcome their partial and limited historical functions and participate more fully and with scientific awareness and efficiency in the highest ideals for the whole race.

CHAPTER XXI

THE RELIGIOUS CONSCIOUSNESS IN RELATION TO DEMOCRACY AND SCIENCE

It is scarcely necessary to cite proof that the two most characteristic features of the aspiring life of the present period are the democratic and scientific tendencies. Attention is more and more centred in them, and there is a determination to make them pervasive and controlling. The signs of the growth of democracy are greater popular interest in humanizing the ends and processes of government, the efforts to enable all to share in education and opportunity, the breaking down of class distinctions through the recognition of their historical relativity, and the creation of the facilities for interchange of experience and ideals. The progress of science is evidenced by increasing invention, by the control of disease, by the development of natural resources, and by the better knowledge of the human mind, of the conditions of human training and of efficient action. Democracy and science are thus remaking the whole social order. Religion does not escape their influence. Like government and education, religion in its conventional forms feels itself confronted with the most extreme alternatives. It must undergo reconstruction or perish. The history of religion shows that it has never failed to attain reconstruction where the general social life was organized and commanding. Whether the forces

DEMOCRACY AND SCIENCE

which now operate in the newer social movements have positive religious significance can be fully determined only with their future development, but the psychological point of view employed in the preceding pages suggests that the rising, expanding life of the present era is gradually attaining a consciousness of social ideals and values which is genuinely religious.

Democracy, stated in psychological terms, is a matter of mental attitudes and habits. It means breadth of sympathy, interaction of individuals, and imaginative coöperation of personal wills. These states may, perhaps, be most easily understood in connection with the concrete experiences in which they arise. Wide-reaching sympathy and the sense of a vast human order in which the individual is an active, organizing factor, as well as a recipient of great influences, have developed along with modern facilities for communication. The telegraph, the printing press, the railroad, and the postal system are among the structures whose rise has been accompanied by a marvelous growth of the social mind. These have expanded human nature by interchange of ideas, by easy contact of distant groups, and by affording the organization of great social wholes.[1] From this enlivening of thought by novel and varied stimulation arises not only a larger intellectual outlook but a quickening of feeling. The conditions of other classes and races than our own are brought vividly into consciousness, and make their appeal with startling directness and familiarity. Contact with people reveals eventually their likeness to ourselves. "Even

[1] C. H. Cooley, *Social Organization*, chapter viii.

the animosities of modern nations are of a human and imaginative sort, not the blind animal hostility of a more primitive age." International commerce, travel, and migration have led to such constructive feeling for the rights and welfare of all concerned that war is increasingly viewed as a horrible crime against humanity, and "the newer ideals of peace" rest upon mutual acquaintance through common needs. It was fine insight into the big world problems presented by the contact of foreign populations in her own city which enabled Miss Jane Addams [1] to see amicable international relations attained in a single neighborhood by the same experiences which are also creating such relations on a vaster scale. Sympathy, respect, and regard for common purposes spring from the same tasks and difficulties, and this law holds good for the world as well as for a given city.

The industrial development also contributes to the enlargement of human brotherhood, especially among the classes which have been regarded as participating least in that brotherhood. The sense of common needs and of the value of concerted action have produced organization and mutual loyalty to an unexpected degree. By these agencies, the individual feels the power of his whole order. He learns to consider others and to subordinate mere personal interests to a larger welfare. This movement tends to fulfill itself in the attainment of a still wider outlook upon mutual interests with other classes, and by the utilization of industrial education and various other means, it gives individuals efficiency and appreciation of the inclusive

[1] *Newer Ideals of Peace.*

DEMOCRACY AND SCIENCE

total life. All class organizations are liable to formalism and to a certain blindness to fine interests, but it may be possible to preserve united effort while preventing its evils. The same influences which result in modern class consciousness are powerful factors in bringing classes into harmony, and the ultimate issue of the process should be recognition of the inclusive social order. Classes are not in themselves necessarily undemocratic. Where they are not based upon artificial or extraneous conditions, they are capable of contributing diversity without endangering social unity. They may effect specialization, intensity of interest, and high stimulation to achievement, and yet preserve sympathetic understanding. The greater diffusion of education and the shrinking dimensions of the human world keep classes open which formerly were closed to each other. All types of association and of experience give larger attention to the human element in life. Labor has more regard for the safety and fullness of life. Industrialism is compelled to count the cost in terms not only of the number of men but in the quality of manhood. Democracy makes progress in so far as it proves advantageous to human nature, not in reference to extraneous circumstances such as rank, heredity, and wealth, but in reference to intelligence, serviceability, and function as tested by the welfare of all members of society.

Modern society has been characterized by this freeing and revaluation of human nature in all its forms. Industry and commerce have awakened and given scope to the man who possessed no hereditary privileges; the diffusion of knowledge has trained his mind;

the rise of free states has given him the task and opportunity of self-government; and a humanitarian idealism thus generated and actualized has begun to take possession of his will. This idealism radiates with growing consciousness and definiteness. At its best it seeks to put into the hands of all members of society the instruments of a free and full life, and it recognizes that partially developed or suppressed personalities are not only abnormal in themselves, but weaken and depress the entire social organism. It has been discovered that slavery is not only injurious to slaves but to their masters. The extension of the ideal involved in this insight is being felt in reference to many other groups. The education of woman and her incorporation into the intellectual practical life of the race are justified both by her own growth under such conditions and by her contributions to an ideal society. This motive expresses itself in various "reform" movements dealing with temperance, child labor, prison reform, social hygiene, juvenile crime, poverty, foreign immigration, peace movements, race problems, congestion of population in cities, administration of charity, and many other causes of ill-conditioned humanity. Such reforms are not merely sentimental, abstractly altruistic efforts, but are grounded upon the conviction that the persons affected deserve better things from society and that society deserves from them more than they are able to render under present conditions. There is doubtless much confused, impulsive "social service," and the evils of particular groups, for example, the "slums" or the "fast set," are at times grotesquely exaggerated and undiscriminatingly denounced. Perhaps the growth of the spirit of democracy is best represented by those who realize that most of the crime and misfortune of society are not due to conscious, malicious intent, but to habits and environment which can be corrected only by modifying the conditions which lie beneath them. Philanthropists now devote their energy more to the understanding and removal of conditioning causes, maintaining genuine sympathy and generous attitudes toward the individuals involved. Not that individual responsibility is thus replaced by attention to external facts, but there is an attempt to take persons in relation to their concrete, complex experiences. Only then can their wills be stimulated to affirmative, constructive decisions and to gradual readjustment and moral control.

This progress of imaginative insight into the nature of the mental life of various classes is as important as the extension of the great social structures of the modern world. No mechanical unification of the world can satisfy the ideals of democracy, but the social mind, like the individual mind, does require a structure. The growth of this structure is impressive on its own account, but it becomes doubly significant when viewed as the carrier of the spirit of coöperation and mutual interdependence for the whole world of human beings.

In contrast to the small social groups which characterize the lower stages of human development, the vast coöperative communities of civilization indicate a structural development which requires for its counterpart an equally sensitive and reliable social consciousness. This emerging conception of a comprehensive human order, a world society, in which all nations and races coöperate for essential human ends, is not now merely the possession of a few imaginative minds. For many centuries, individuals here and there have possessed the vision of such an ideal, but it is now clear to multitudes and is consciously chosen by them as a controlling goal of endeavor. Nor is this stupendous yet fine-textured democracy conceived simply in a naïve, utopian manner, as something belonging to a distant day and place, but as a concrete, natural, voluntary development, effective both locally and universally with as much reality as the postal system which operates from one's door to every inhabited spot on the entire earth. One author cites the fact that the progress of the race is reflected in a constantly enlarging social sympathy, represented by ever widening circles woven thick with interlacing lines of mutual interest. He shows that whereas the average social group of lower savagery numbers only 40 persons, and the lower barbarians 6500, yet the lower civilized races form unions averaging 4,200,000 with cities of 250,000, while the lower cultured races effect unions of population numbering 30,000,000 with cities of 6,000,000. In this highest stage yet reached, "their cities present incomparably the most wonderful social life that the world has ever witnessed. London with nearly 6,000,000, Paris and New York with 2,500,000 each, their orderly populations living in a harmony from which internal warfare is utterly absent; all working into each other's hands; all fed, clothed, educated, amused, and provided with a

DEMOCRACY AND SCIENCE

thousand comforts and conveniences by the easy play of coöperative forces; these are as yet the triumphs of social sympathies. In these races of the lower culture no less than 30,000,000 people dwell in cities of over 250,000 each, there being fifty-three such cities which average 623,000 inhabitants apiece. The centuries that are coming are sure to witness associations to which these will seem but small concerns, for still the empires grow, and still do the instincts of people lead them to mass themselves in ever larger cities, thereby to reap in the fullest measure all those advantages of social sympathy which arise when man dwells beside man to comfort and be comforted."[1] It is only necessary to reflect similarly on the growing organization of international relations to complete the impression of the developing structural unity of mankind.

That the outward form and the inner spirit of democracy have direct religious significance may be seen in the widely felt need of reorganizing religious institutions, both in their spirit and methods, to conform to and express this democratic temper. The critics of the church — and it is significant that these are often members of it — insist that it has in large part become identified with certain classes, that it draws its financial support and its view of life from the rich and from the scholastic circles. As a consequence, it is said, the church has little hold upon the industrial classes and other groups of plain people. It continues to maintain ideas of God drawn from patriarchal and monarchical types of life. Consequently

[1] Sutherland, *The Origin and Growth of the Moral Instinct*, vol. i, p. 365.

it interprets spiritual relations in terms of princely favors which are bestowed upon men through grace and as free gifts. But the laborer and the voter have come to prefer to think of themselves as earning what they get. They are even more anxious to receive what they believe they deserve than to gain favors through charitable benevolence, even if it be represented as divine.[1]

The church also appears to be controlled by an individualistic type of religious experience. It sets up a task and a salvation for the individual which attach too great importance to personal will and sentiment. But people find themselves in social conditions which they are unable, single-handed, to overcome. They feel the need of alliances able to cope with the whole intricate system to which they belong. Their sins are no longer their own alone, and they have not learned the means of corporate repentance. The evil things are not so much personal habits, but belong to methods of business, to wage systems, to tenement methods of housing. These are matters of the collective body.[2] To change them, concerted, intelligent, patriotic action is necessary. For this the church has not yet the habits or the expert knowledge. The general idea of the evil and of the remedy is clearer than the means for its application. Programs of reform are numerous, and occasional experiments appear, but it is a large task for which there really are no precedents in history or in other contemporaneous institutions.

[1] J. H. Tufts, "The Adjustment of the Church to the Psychological Conditions of the Present," *American Journal of Theology*, vol. xii, 1908.
[2] E. A. Ross, *Sin and Society*, pp. 122 f.

DEMOCRACY AND SCIENCE

These criticisms of existing institutions are cited as evidence that democracy feels itself to be religious, and makes a claim for recognition in the organizations and methods of religion. The frequent condemnation of the church for lethargy and blindness with respect to existing conditions and opportunities would not be so vital if it were not clear proof that these concerns are felt to be the central interests of religion. Since the church assumes to represent and interpret religion, the democratic spirit demands to know how she can be so unresponsive to these vast human aspirations. The inner identity of democratic and religious interests is witnessed by the confessions and endeavors of an increasing number of leaders in the church. The literature produced by her scholars and ministers in the last decade centres in these social ideals.[1]

The scientific temper of the age is not so easily seen to contribute to the religious consciousness as is democracy. Many reasons may be given in explanation of this fact. The scientific attitude is a newer achievement of the human mind. By its nature it is yet the possession of fewer persons. It requires a training and general standpoint which have not been accessible to the masses of men until recently. Science does not

[1] A few of the books of this character are: Francis G. Peabody, *Jesus Christ and the Social Question;* Shailer Mathews, *Social Teachings of Jesus;* also *The Church and the Changing Social Order;* Walter Rauschenbusch, *Christianity and the Social Crisis;* Washington Gladden, *Social Salvation;* R. J. Campbell, *Christianity and the Social Order;* cf. A. C. McGiffert, "Was Jesus or Paul the Founder of Christianity?" *American Journal of Theology*, January, 1909; "How may Christianity be Defended To-day?" *Hibbert Journal*, October, 1908; Charles Zeublin, *The Religion of a Democrat.*

lend itself to popular statement so readily as does democracy, and the latter gives the impression of being more directly important for the masses of people. Democratic ideas seem to express immediately the grievances and the hopes of the plain man, while science confronts him with a technique of concepts and methods which require effort and persistent thought. A fact of great significance is that the ideal of democratic freedom, equality, and greater participation in goods does not at first sight involve any radical break with accustomed modes of thought. It appears as only the natural demand of all classes for a share in what has previously been the lot of a few. The representatives of the conventional religion feel that they are here aiding in the full development of the impulses and tendencies which are really intrinsic and central in their faith, but whose fulfillment the circumstances of the historical development have prevented. They are able to reinforce the present awakening of the social conscience by many words of their ancient teachers and by many examples of their saints and reformers. The abstract idea of a spiritual brotherhood, of an inclusive fraternity, is old and familiar, and appears like a long-cherished faith only now attaining realization.

But there is little if any such familiar background for the appreciation of the religious significance of science. It has been the cause of grave apprehension among religionists. It has dealt largely with natural, material phenomena. The method it employs is that of fallible reason, and its results, laboriously attained, are held tentatively, ever subject to revision. Men

DEMOCRACY AND SCIENCE

have not been used to qualified and hesitant authority. They have been subject to absolute commands, to urgent necessity, which offered little option. Obedience and submission to the dictation of the past and of mysterious power have been the prevalent attitudes. In religion, especially, the interests at stake were too urgent and essential to be submitted to man's choice or inquiry. They possessed sanctions and demanded assent of quite a different type from those which belong to science. Science further has seemed to put stress upon knowledge for its own sake, subordinating its practical and useful application to the discovery and systematization of facts and principles on their own account. Religion in its normal forms has emphasized in contrast great historical, practical ideals. It has moved in the sphere of urgent purposes. Action, drama, tragedy, have been its expressions. Even the practice of mystical contemplation was chosen for its saving power. The correct control of vital processes was its aim.

No opposition could then seem greater than that between the intense, hot action of the reforming, heaven-building saint or the passionate mystic, and the dispassionate, critical, tread-mill scientific observer of facts. The faith of the forward-reaching religionist and the knowledge of the poised scholar seem to belong to different orders of experience, and the difference has often been accepted as radical and uncompromising by both sides. Systems of psychology and philosophy have been developed under this conception, and in support of it.

But in spite of all such theories of its friends and

foes alike, science has moved quietly and steadily forward, extending its minute, detailed description of facts and organizing these under hypotheses. Here and there it has discovered fruitful application of its methods to the most vital practical concerns. Increasingly it is apparent that science does not select its problems arbitrarily, but finds them in the tasks incident to the production of food, the invention of devices for transportation and communication, the control of disease, and in the determination and direction of the central human interests. It is true many discoveries of science have been quite accidental, but in the main lines of its development it is more and more consciously set for the solution of questions of tremendous human significance. The success of wireless telegraphy and aërial navigation have not been accidental. They resulted from long and patient observation and experimentation. The history of medicine affords even more striking illustration of the solution of most vital practical problems by the use of scientific methods. Experts definitely set out to find the bacteria which produce malaria and other fevers, tuberculosis, sleeping sickness, syphilis, and other dread diseases. Having found these, they went on to secure preventives and cures. It has come to be the confident expectation of scientists that infectious diseases may be entirely robbed of their power if society will unite in the support of the undertaking.[1] Even those branches of science which have not always been able to give obvious and significant demonstration of their utility have come to share in the practical

[1] E. Ray Lankester, *The Kingdom of Man*, p. 36.

DEMOCRACY AND SCIENCE

results. "The zoölogist thus comes into closer touch than ever with the profession of medicine, and the time has arrived when the professional students of disease fully admit that they must bring to their great and hopeful task of abolishing the diseases of man the fullest aid from every branch of biological science. I need not say how great is the contentment of those who have long worked at apparently useless branches of science — such as are the careful and elaborate distinction of every separate kind of animal and the life-history and structure peculiar to each — in the belief that all knowledge is good, to find that the science they have cultivated has become suddenly and urgently of the highest practical value."[1]

The application of scientific methods to the investigation and correction of crime, pauperism, and juvenile delinquency brings science into even more immediate relation to ideal spiritual interests. Psychology and education here take their place among the great agencies for the development of human life; while the new science of eugenics sets for itself the task of controlling the production of men by heredity and training. In the social sciences, knowledge appears less and less abstract and remote. It is here under the leadership of great social ideals, and in the most intimate relation to the progress and fulfillment of the hopes of democracy.

The scientific development of machinery has transformed the world of labor and of transportation. In agriculture and horticulture it has gone far in the recovery of waste lands by engineering, by chemical

[1] E. Ray Lankester, *The Kingdom of Man*, p. 147.

treatment of soils, and by selection and culture of grains and fruits. The results are already sufficient to subvert the older doctrines of Malthus with reference to the fixed limit of the population which the earth can maintain. On every side the confidence of man in the control of natural forces for his own welfare has been placed upon more intelligible and appreciable grounds than ever in its history. This has given to science a practical aspect even in the eyes of those who do not understand its methods. The masses of laboring men are constantly in the presence of machines, and work under the control of elaborate engineering plans, enabling them to construct with precision and facility the greatest public and private utilities. They are called upon to direct the forces of steam, compressed air, electricity, and gas, and their minds are influenced by the training of their hands in these occupations. The farmer and the stock breeder are also brought under greater necessity to employ the knowledge and skill of the expert. They see that such expert wisdom is profitable, and that it is indispensable in keeping up with competition and in gaining the largest possible returns from their labor. It is in these immediate and marvelously efficient operations of science that the rank and file see its power and value. The physician, the machinist, the sales agent, with the illustrated periodical and the trade journal, bring the keen edge of the new knowledge home to the spot where it is able to enter the consciousness of the average man.

The mental traits which are created by science in its inner circles, and to some appreciable degree wher-

DEMOCRACY AND SCIENCE

ever its effects are felt, are of a clearly defined character. The scientific mind respects facts and is wary of fancies and guesses. It seeks actual experience. It works under a closely articulated procedure, with an organized technique. Complex phenomena are analyzed into simpler elements and systematized under tested principles and formulæ. Openness of mind, readiness to verify conclusions and to adopt qualifying factors are notable. The frequent reorganization of accumulated material under new points of view, such as that introduced into many fields by modern biology, has contributed powerfully to an expectant, inquiring, adapting attitude. New angles of observation and persistent experimentation are ever bringing up familiar and long-established theories for reëxamination. Therefore one of the most impressive characteristics of the mental type which science creates is its search for novelty in what is old. At the same time it maintains a sensitive and delicate regard for the results which have been reached by previous conscientious investigation. The restatements of science are usually revolutionary only with reference to prescientific attitudes, as where chemistry supersedes alchemy or astronomy supplants astrology. But within the scientific period of a given area of knowledge, change is of the nature of enlargement, of new perspective and additional material and methods. The sense of continuity is strong, and the acknowledgment of previous achievements is frank and generous. This kind of docility and reverence are united with courage and initiative. What has been achieved is felt to be but a stage in an ever-unfolding process. The doubt which is engendered is not merely negative or destructive, but is essentially positive in its ultimate reference and function. The new is expected to relate itself to the old, and to aid in establishing a broader organization of experience.

This confidence in its method, in the necessity of constant analysis and experimentation, and in the possibility of bringing most mysterious, variant phenomena under laws and to this extent explaining them, is the factor which at first makes science appear to be lacking in religious quality. In several other respects the virtues of the scientific mind seem inherently religious in the familiar sense. For example, science requires patience, diligence, accuracy, honesty, self-control, self-forgetfulness, willingness to take risks and to endure. But in this devotion to inquiry, to doubt, to reconstruction, to experimentation, in this unwillingness to be quiescent under mystery or authority, in this, the scientific mind seems fundamentally opposed to the prevalent, conventional religious mind. Dissent from the external authority of custom or precedent is insubordination which the accepted religious type cannot tolerate. Permanent compromise or evasion is impossible here. Science recognizes only the authority of experience. Its principles must be intelligible and its results verifiable. It cannot remain true to itself and surrender the right to question, to doubt, to reinvestigate any problem. Any assent to the occurrence of events in essentially mysterious and unknowable ways is impossible. Belief in miracles as contraventions of law — the only meaning of miracles which has ever occasioned any significant discussion — is therefore diametrically opposed to the mind of science. Less bluntly, it may be said that such a belief lies entirely beyond the sphere of science, or that it is psychologically incompatible with scientific mental habits.

Probably the difficulty is exaggerated by an unfortunate partiality in the terminology employed. Science has arrogated to itself the claim of knowledge, taking the term as meaning an exclusively intellectual, emotionless affair; while religion has magnified faith, giving it the significance of an emotional, volitional state of a unique type. Faith has thus come to be regarded as the test of religion, as knowledge is the organ and the sphere of science. Religion as faith then involves submission to authority, and its test is sometimes represented as the willingness to accept that which is intellectually inconsistent in itself, but which is presented as the dictate of conscience or of the Divine Being. Knowledge, at the other extreme, has been held to possess absolute certainty and final truth. In such a view, it is obvious that no reconciliation of faith and knowledge is possible. But psychology does not support such a dualism of experience. When both terms are related to action, to purposive will, they become reconciled in a vital way. Then knowledge appears as instrumental, provisional, and practical; while faith becomes the attitude of confidence and expectation in reference to the further progress of experience. Knowledge, in actual, vital operation, is accompanied by the glow of interest in the concrete process and outcome which is faith; and faith, in its hope and trust, relies upon knowledge and tested experience. Faith, unrelated to such knowledge and experience, becomes wholly sentimental and fatuous. Experimentation involves both faith and knowledge. It could not exist if either were absent. And successful experiment increases both.

That the scientific temper is rapidly establishing itself in the modern consciousness, there can be no doubt. With its growth superstition, belief in miracles, subjection to the authority of custom and tradition are disappearing. Is religion also being destroyed in this revolution? Or is the new social order, marked as it undoubtedly is by the rise of democracy and science, creating values and ideals which are genuinely religious?

Here the view that the religious consciousness is identical with the core of the social consciousness — with the inner soul of conscience, of duty, of patriotism, of social righteousness — affords valuable aid. Religion becomes as natural and vital in a democratic and scientific age as in a patriarchal, custom-ruled era. The same will-to-live, to lay hold upon life-giving powers, which in primitive groups fashions ceremonials, with their dramatic action, myth, magic, and emotion, may operate also in modern life through the sense of a far vaster social whole. Why should not the latter also produce pageants, festivals, poetry, and music, uttering and elevating its ideal life in powerful forms of art? The ideals of welfare have become more explicit, and the means for their attainment are better discriminated, but they are no less urgent. Indeed the consciousness of the values involved in the new social conceptions seems incalculably greater, both extensively and intensively, than that of earlier stages of development.

Democracy and science thus come into harmonious coöperation and mutual support by something more than the accidents of history. Democracy emphasizes personal responsibility, eliciting initiative and reflection in all its members. All are confronted with the tensions and conflicts which under other forms of society are borne by the few. It is under such conflict and individual obligations that careful, systematic observation and constructive thinking, or scientific knowledge, arise. In the submission of all fundamental issues to a popular vote, every citizen is summoned to share in the policies and functions of the state. To do this effectively he is required to inform himself and to act in the light of his judgment. It is of course just this process which makes real democracy so difficult to achieve. It is a slow and vast undertaking to get all voters to act intelligently. There is constant temptation to make programs for them, to influence them by "bosses," and to treat them patronizingly. Democracy can therefore only become real and operative through a universal and efficient system of public education. This means in the end the diffusion of the scientific spirit, of its method and results. Democracy thus leads naturally and inevitably to science.

On the other hand, science is in its spirit and function democratic. It employs impersonal methods, and its results stand on their own intrinsic merits. In the end it is, however, a human interest, a function of the mind. It cannot be indifferent to the instrument upon which it depends. The mind, viewed biologically, is a means of adaptation, an organ of adjustment, a servant of its possessor. In its higher processes, it requires relative detachment for its greatest efficiency, but the final test of what it achieves in comparative isolation is found in the advantage such achievements afford to the concrete, practical life of the whole human organism, individual and collective. Intellectual activity which does not finally complete the circuit and advance conduct and fullness of living is condemned as useless and injurious. Here the popular mind and the spirit of the specialist may seem to be widely separated, but the populace are impatient and hasty in their demand for the fruits of science. The scholars, knowing the necessity of quiet, undistracted inquiry, often seem to resent entirely the natural and ultimately irrepressible insistence that knowledge shall bake bread. A survey of the last fifty years of scientific advancement affords sufficient proof that in the main the carefully established knowledge of the various branches of science has genuine human value, and that it contributes in appreciable ways to the comfort, efficiency, and richness of a democratic social humanity.

The religious significance of democracy and science becomes apparent as they are more thoroughly established.[1] Their constructive character is evident when they are sufficiently advanced to work out their impli-

[1] It may be said that these two tendencies express in ideal and powerful forms the elemental, primitive life-interests, — democracy embodying the sympathetic, socializing quality of the sexual life, and science exemplifying the insight and mastery worked out in connection with the food process. In the new social order there is increasing reciprocity and fusion, as well as idealization, of these interests.

cations freely and with less opposition from conventional types of organization and intellectual procedure. In the minds of many leaders of social reconstruction and critical idealism the religious quality of the new social order is already realized and expressed. They recognize that the old creeds and symbols are now inadequate and disadvantageous, but they also have confidence that the new forces will create doctrines and symbols for themselves, by which the new spiritual values may be brought home to the heart and conscience of the times. "There will be creeds, but they will affirm no more than is really helpful to believe, ritual, but only what is beautiful or edifying; everything must justify itself by function." [1]

A notable expression of the difference between the new and the old cultures is stated by Professor Dewey in an argument for the omission of religious instruction from the public schools until the new religion of democracy and science is sufficiently developed to take its place in the educational system naturally and in accordance with the type of mind which the schools normally develop. He says: "We need to accept the responsibilities of living in an age marked by the greatest intellectual readjustment history records. There is undoubted loss of joy, of consolation, of some types of strength, and of some sources of inspiration in the change. There is a manifest increase of uncertainty; there is some paralysis of energy, and much excessive application of energy in materialistic directions. Yet nothing is gained by moves which will increase confusion and obscurity, which tend to an

[1] C. H. Cooley, *Social Organization*, p. 418.

emotional hypocrisy and to a phrasemongering of formulæ which seem to mean one thing and really import the opposite. Bearing the losses and inconveniences of our time as best we may, it is the part of men to labour persistently and patiently for the clarification and development of the positive creed of life implicit in democracy and science, and to work for the transformation of all practical instrumentalities of education till they are in harmony with these ideas. Till these ends are further along than we can honestly claim them to be at present, it is better that our schools should do nothing than that they should do wrong things. It is better for them to confine themselves to their obviously urgent tasks than that they should, under the name of spiritual culture, form habits of mind which are at war with the habits of mind congruous with democracy and with science."[1]

Another significant indication of the religious implications of modern progress is the attempt to rewrite the Book of Common Prayer in terms of ethical and social idealism.[2] This courageous effort to reconstruct the familiar ceremonials and symbols of the Anglican Church is undertaken with a sense of the historical tendencies of the last three centuries toward a democratic and rational order of society and its religious evaluation. It recognizes the propriety of admitting the indigenous and contemporaneous factors of our civilization into a share in the religious consciousness, and draws upon the poets and moralists of the modern world for the enrichment of the litera-

[1] *Hibbert Journal,* "Religion and Our Schools," vol. vi, 1907–08.
[2] Stanton Coit, *National Idealism and the Book of Common Prayer.*

ture of piety and devotion. Such attempts to give artistic, imaginative form to the consciousness of the individual in relation to a complete whole are likely to become more frequent. They will furnish additional, illuminating testimony that the human spirit has gained a new height in its ascent, and has become possessed of an outlook and a perspective in which there is intelligible order together with opportunity for limitless progress.

INDEX

ACT, practical character of the religious, 110.
Addams, Jane, 398.
Adolescence, Religion and, Ch. XII; preëminently the period for the rise of religious consciousness, 214; conversion a phenomenon of, 215-216; confirmation and initiatory rites during, 217-218; physiological changes as affording an explanation of the new social attitude in, 218-219; appearance and maturing of sexual instinct the central factor in, 219; inadequate expression of the relation between sex and religion in, 220-221; religion neither a perversion of, nor antagonistic to, sex, 221; social character of sex instinct makes it directly the source of religion, 222; illustrations of new social interests during this period, 224-227; technique of sexual life employed in highly developed social groups, 227-228; awakening of mental life along with sexual impulse, 229; adolescent idealism, 230-233; repression of religious impulse through conflict of social interests, 233-234; summary on, 235.
Angell, J. R., 19, 24, 306.
Animism and Spiritism, see under Spirits.
Anthropology related to psychology, 6-7.
Atonement, sacrifice as, 136; influence of social setting on Christian doctrines of, 316.
Australian tribes, various religious observances of, 47-49, 55, 61, 85-87, 91, 118, 121, 124, 142.
Awe, not the distinguishing mark of religion, 109-110.

Baldwin, J. M., 197, 346, 347.
Barnes, Earl, 230.
Barton, G. A., 174, 178.
Brinton, D. G., 49, 149.
Budde, K., 177, 178, 182.

Campbell, R. J., 405.
Ceremonials, and Magic, Ch. V; as reflecting both masculine and feminine elements, 43-45; masculine control of, 44; as reflecting activities essential to tribal welfare, 47-48; hence varying with means of subsistence, 49; definition of, in terms of custom, 71; importance of, for primitive religion, 71; dramatic character of, 72; connected with nature phenomena, 73-74; with birth, initiation, and marriage, 74; with death and burial, 74; with war and dealings with strangers, 75; relation of, to magic and spirits, 76; views of Frazer, Lang, and Jevons on magic, 76-77; Smith's discrimination of magic from religion, 77-78; definitions and illustrations of collective, individual, imitative, and sympathetic magic, 79-87; names as possessing magic, 87; songs and chants as means of imparting magic, 88; magic ceremonies as means of overcoming taboo or of producing it, 88-91; as elaborate symbolic forms of habitual activities, 91; importance of emotional excitement in ceremonies, 93; educational value of, 94; magic power imparted through sacrifice, 127-130.
Childhood, Religion and, Ch. XI; problem of rise of religion in, that of the rise of the social consciousness, 197; the child in early infancy non-moral

INDEX

and non-social, 198; in early childhood social attitudes but slightly developed, 198-203; some advance in later childhood, 203-206; religion neither an instinct nor a special endowment, 206-207; solution from the functional standpoint of some theological difficulties, 207; meaning of "the sinful and perverse nature of the child," 207; of "impartation of grace" in later childhood, 208; criticism of the view that the child is endowed with a religious instinct, 209; beginnings of religious life in crude coöperative activities often anti-social from the adult standpoint, 209-210; the child in some senses an alien till late in the adolescent period, 210; externality of religion to the child as shown by records, 211-213.

Coe, G. A., 3, 4, 215, 216, 240, 243, 259, 261, 272, 286.

Coit, Stanton, 418.

Consciousness, always specific, 21; as guide of action, 22; the religious, a phase of group consciousness, 49, 110.

Conversion, Ch. XIV; central in protestant Christianity, 5; as a sudden, intense, and extremely emotional experience, 257; different attitudes of various churches towards, 257; dissatisfaction and sense of sin as first stage in the emotional circuit of, 258-260; the turning point, or second stage in, 260-263; reaction, sense of peace and joy as third stage in, 263; variations in, due to sex, age, and temperament, 264-265; as induced by external control, 266; common methods of inducing, 266; preliminary work in the revival, 266-267; the characteristic revival service, 268-269; influence of the crowd, 269-270; efforts directed to insignificant effects, 271; hypnotic phenomena produced, 273; defects of the conversion method, 272-273; secondary results as hurtful, 274-276.

Cooley, C. H., 97, 139, 308, 341, 342, 343, 344, 357, 394, 397, 417.

Crawley, Ernest, 54, 62, 64, 66, 73, 87, 89, 91, 103, 120, 168, 192, 221.

Cushing, Frank H., 150, 156-157.

Custom, important problems concerning primitive, 7; earliest types of religion a matter of social, 33.

Custom and Taboo, Ch. IV; rigidity of primitive customs, and taboo as the negative side of, 51-52; various explanations of the origin of taboo, 53; non-rational origin of custom and taboo, 54-56; explanation in terms of instinct, imitation, etc., 57-59; how habitual actions get their sanction, 59-61; sanctity of customs as proportional to their degree of vital interest for the group, 61-62; psychological explanation of taboo, 62-63; Crawley's limitation because of over-emphasis on ideas, 63-64; taboo as related to natural social divisions, 64; sex taboos, 64-66; taboos of kings, war chiefs, and leaders, 66-67; taboos of the dead, 67-68; primary determinations of taboo in life-processes, 68; secondary development of taboo to associated objects, 68-69; differentiation of taboo into holiness and uncleanness, 69-70.

Daramulun, two interpretations of the worship of, 115.

Davenport, F. M., 165, 270, 272, 276.

Dead, the, as members of the tribe, 104.

Death and burial, importance of ceremonials of, 75.

Democracy and Science, the relation of religious consciousness to, Ch. XXI; as recasting the social order, 396; meaning of democracy stated in psychological terms, 397; development of democracy through invention and travel, 397-398; industrialism as a factor in, 398; ideals of democracy in relation to slaves, women, criminals, and defectives, 400-401; growth of social groups and its significance, 401-403; religious spirit of demo-

INDEX

cracy as shown by its criticism of the church, 403–405; democratic ideals latent in the conventional religion, 406; religious significance of science obscured by conflicting methods in science and religion, 406–407; practical tasks with which science deals, 407; intimate relation of scientific method to the great social ideals, 409; general recognition of the social value of science, 410; mental traits developed by the study of science, 410–412; antagonism between science and religion partly due to a wrong conception of both faith and knowledge, 413; naturalness of religion, when properly defined, in a democratic and scientific age, 414; coöperation of democracy and science, and religious significance of both, 414–416; contrast of old and new culture, 417–418; tendency to create new religious symbols, 418–419.

Development of Religion, Ch. X; origin of religion determined by origin of the social consciousness, 168; first stage of primitive Semitic religion, the polydæmonism of the desert, 171–172; second, the nomadic-shepherd life, with the sheep as totem, 172–173; third, migration into cattle lands and the bull as symbol of Yahweh, 173–174; fourth, conflict between pastoral Hebrews and agricultural Canaanites develops group consciousness and a return towards nomadic ideals, 175; priests, prophets, and kings unify religious and national consciousness, and monarchy gives a new pattern for Yahweh, 175–176; change in customs and ceremonials and elimination of traces of Baal-worship, 176–177; continuation of tension, but now within the nation, 178; economic reasons for loyalty to the simpler type of religion and the moral messages of Amos and Hosea, 178–180; Isaiah as advancing the conception of Yahweh's greatness, 181; adoption of Assyrian and Babylonian myths, 181–182; further purification of worship, 182; Jeremiah as completing the anthropomorphizing and individualizing tendency, 183; fifth stage, the exile, with the work of Ezekiel and the second Isaiah, the former pointing to ceremonial reforms, the latter giving further refinement to idealizing tendencies, 184–185; sixth stage, Christianity purifying and strengthening earlier ideals of a divine kingdom and of inward ethical character, 185–187; social conception of the Kingdom of Heaven, 189; development under new conditions, 190; a parallel development in other peoples through certain stages, 190–191; survivals of early religious customs such as the Passover in the Lord's Supper, baptism as a form of purgation and the use of the name in prayer, 191–192; development of religion in terms of modern science and social progress, 193.

Dewey, John, 28, 40, 41, 98–99, 169, 190, 326, 328, 336, 417.

Dewey and Tufts, 191, 289, 337.

Dorsey, G. A., 151.

Dunlap, Knight, 293.

Ellis, Havelock, 364.

Emotion, rise of, 20; in inverse proportion to ideation, 165–166; importance of, in religious ceremonies, 93. See Feeling.

Epistemology, relation to psychology and logic, 25.

Ethics, an elaboration of psychology, 23.

Faith, 296–300.

Farnell, L. R., 133, 147, 191.

Feeling, and Religious Experience, Ch. XVII; relation of, to volitional activities, 19, 20; emphasis on, as a reaction against intellectualism, 321; views of Starbuck and Pratt on, 321–324; sympathetic nervous system not the unique organ of, 324; inconsistency in the contrast between knowledge

INDEX

and, 325; failure to distinguish between the subconscious and, 325; not all the non-ideational can be classed as, 326; James-Lange theory of, as related to the whole activity, 326–327; as secondary to action, 327–328; as a sign of adjustment, 328; danger of giving the uppermost place to, 329; biological depth of social, 329; intellectual and affective elements secondary to activity, 330; emotion in the crowd, 331; methods of arousing fear, pity, and love, 331–333; feeling and readjustment or social progress, 333–334; abnormal development of feeling, 335; the highest happiness, 336–337.
Fishing and hunting, ceremonies connected with, 84.
Fite, Warner, 33.
Fletcher, Alice, 142.
Food, and sex as central interests, 33–36, 58; importance of, in sacrifice, 116–124.
Frazer, J. G., 52, 53, 54, 61, 76, 78, 81, 82, 83, 84, 85, 91, 92, 124, 149.

Genetic method, why used by functional psychology, 27.
Giddings, F. H., 364.
God, growth and objectification of the, in tribal life, 113.
Granger, F., 265.

Haddon, A. C., 104, 112, 126.
Hall, G. Stanley, 210, 215, 218, 219, 220, 225, 230, 231, 236, 255, 259, 332.
Hapgood, Hutchins, 364, 378.
Harrison, Jane, 159, 191.
Harvest, ceremonials of, 73.
Hebrews, see under Development of Religion.
Hegel, G. W. F., 8, 12.
Hirsch, Wm., 352.
Höffding, Harold, 9.
Holiness, relation of, to taboo, 69–70; sacrificial victim the source of, 131.
Howell, W. H., 324.
Howitt, A., 88, 121, 135, 156, 163.
Hume, David, 21.

Ideas, and Religious Experience, Ch. XVI; general revolt against overemphasis on intellectual elements, 303; genetic account of ideas, 18, 304–305; as presupposing impulses and involuntary activities, 305; dynamic character of, 18, 306; relation of emotional consciousness to, 307; as symbols of motor adjustments, 308; correlative change in the meaning of words with variations in activities signified, 309; interaction of impulses and ideas, 310; meaning of theological ideas must be gathered from actual use, 310; idea of God as changing with advancing civilization, 311–312; function of idea of God in conduct, 313–315; influence of social setting on Christian doctrines of the atonement, 316; ideas true or false only where conduct is involved, 317; dynamic character of the idea of God, 318; criticism of distinction of ideas of value from those of fact, 318–319; application to the question of theory and practice, 319–320.
Ideation, secondary to volition, 19.
Initiation, elaborate ceremonials for, 74; mimetic and sympathetic magic in, 85–86.
Instinct, in animals and man, 16, 17.
Intichiuma ceremonies, 118.

James, William, 9, 12, 13, 28, 96, 107, 113, 116, 238, 256, 257, 262, 288, 289, 292, 305, 315, 326.
Jastrow, Joseph, 246, 295.
Jastrow, Morris, 6, 7.
Jevons, F. B., 53, 54, 56, 76, 77, 78, 87, 119, 134, 150, 167.
Judd, C. H., 305.

Kafirs, origin of customs not known to them, 54; their idea of spirit, 101–104.
Kant, I., 8, 11.
Kidd, Dudley, 55, 56, 101, 103, 140, 141, 211.
King, Irving, 50, 73, 110, 111, 207, 219.

INDEX

Lang, A., 76, 77, 115.
Language, primitive forms of, and their use, 135; as relatively unconscious social habit, 137-139.
Lankester, E. Ray, 408, 409.
Lessing, G. E., 111.
Leuba, J. H., 298, 314.
Locke, John, 17.
Logic, as a differentiation within psychology, 24-25.
Lovejoy, Arthur O., 188.

Magic, see Ceremonials.
Man, as fighter and hunter, 38-40; psychological significance of his occupation, 40-43; as source of authority, 44; attitude toward woman, 66.
Marett, R. R., 82, 88, 102, 106, 107, 108, 109, 112, 115, 140, 143.
Marriage, safeguards of, 75, 89-90.
Mason, Otis T., 35.
Mathews, Shailer, 405.
Mind, as instrument of adjustment, 15, 17; correlation of mental and bodily states, 18-19; fundamental function of mental life, 17; mental life as process, 17-18.
Mitchell, H. B., 375.
Morality, see under Religion as Involving the Entire Psychical Life.
Morgan, Lewis H., 34.
Miller, Max, 149.
Myth, Ch. IX; diverse theories of, and their defects, 149-150; as equivalent to cult-lore, 150; distinguishing characteristics of, 151; relation of, to the motor activities of the ritual, 152-154; topography, plants, animals and heroes as important factors in, 154-157; the hero's increasing prominence in, 157-159; as speech expression of the life-drama, 159-160; more variable than ritual, 160; as dramatic rather than rational and scientific, 161-162; limited character of savage concepts which appear in, 162-164; inverse relation of emotion and ideation in, 165-166; common basis for similarity in those of different peoples, 167.

Nature phenomena, ceremonies connected with, 73-74.
Names, magical quality of, 87.
Non-religious persons, see Persons.

Object, emerges when attention is arrested, 100; as living agents in active process, 100.
Occupation, difference in male and female, 35; significance of, for building up the mental life, 40-43.

Palmer, G. H., 287.
Patten, Simon, 384, 386.
Peabody, Francis G., 282, 405.
Persons, Non-religious, Ch. XIX; common belief that there are such not beyond question, 355; not found in primitive groups, 356; the criterion of, failure to share in the ideal impulses of the social consciousness, 356; such participation not necessarily direct or clearly conscious, 356-358; the mentally diseased and defective as non-religious, 359-360; those lacking real tasks and proper training as, 360-361; the criminal class as, 362-365; changing forms of social consciousness and transition types of religious consciousness, 365-367; the merely conventional type, 367; those deeply religious who in some cases are not consciously so, 368; difficulties on account of outgrown imagery and symbols, 369-370; illustrations of those who consider themselves non-religious, 370; of those who are in doubt as to a proper criterion, 371; of those who judge by a non-conventional criterion, 372-373; of identification of esthetic and religious consciousness, 373-374; typical answer showing advance toward a new constructive faith, 374-375.
Philosophical Studies, as elaborations of psychology, 23-26.
Pratt, J. B., 3, 9, 322, 323, 324, 325, 334, 335.
Prayer, Ch. VIII; place of, in primitive

425

INDEX

religion, 134; study of, through speech phenomena, 134-135; primitive forms of language often used without reference to communication with others, 135; articulate speech not necessarily directed to definitely apprehended persons, 135-136; language as relatively unconscious social habit, 137-139; prayer, as not necessarily involving the conception of a spiritual being, 139; as incidental accompaniment of ceremonial, 139-140; illustrations of exclamatory or descriptive type of, 140-141.

Psychology of Religion; its recent origin, 3; demanded by general scientific advance, 3; value of, for general psychology, 3; religious motive for, 4-5; as supplementary to history of religion, anthropology, and philosophy of religion, 5-11; its problems reflected in definitions of religion, 10; general aim of, 13-14; is here treated from a functional standpoint, 15; from this standpoint mental life is regarded as a means of adjustment, 15-17; activities and processes directed towards ends are emphasized, 17-18; correlation of bodily and mental states accepted, 18; emphasis placed upon will, 19; consciousness is regarded as always specific, 21-22; and philosophical studies as elaborations of psychology, 23-26; psychology of religion as fundamental to theology, 26; why it uses the genetic method, 27.

Psychology of Religious Genius and Inspiration, Ch. XVIII; inspiration attributed to all exceptional persons, 338; meaning of genius, 339; its phenomena subject to psychological investigation, 340; Galton's view of racial quality as the predetermining factor of, 341; Cooley's theory of environment as essential to the development of, 341-343; a stronger conclusion justified, 342; functional view puts emphasis on creative power of social environment, 344; application of these principles to athletes and scientists, 345; to Hebrew prophets, 346-347; illustration from the case of Amos, 347-350; the prophet's sense of passive recipiency, 350-352; parallels from modern literary geniuses, 352-353; significance of the message not determined by its accompanying feeling, 354-355.

Psychology of Religious Sects, Ch. XX; identity of religious and social consciousness in primitive life, 377; individual in higher societies a member of various social groups, 378; may be identified with a remote group through imagination, 378-379; different sects as social organisms with marked individuality, 380; the protestant type and its use of the Bible, 380-381; Lutheranism, 382; Calvinism, Puritanism as a form of, 382-384; Wesleyanism, 384-386; decrease in emphasis on doctrine in developed sects, 386-387; development of protestant sects in America, 388-389; illustration of their identification with certain social classes, 389-390; new cults in America, 390; Christian Science; typical in respect to individuality of organization and spirit, 390-393; strength of sectarian or clan spirit, 393-395; need for a larger social whole, 395.

Rain, magic used to produce, 79, 81.
Ratzel, F., 102, 105, 106.
Religion, as involving the entire psychical life, Ch. XV; tendency of specialized social interests to become isolated, 279; religion as a phase of all socialized human experience, 280; a natural relation of interaction between the social and religious consciousness, 280; religion as both a result and the occasion of social reconstruction, 280-281; need of further reconstruction in religion, 282-283; conflict between different types of religion, 284; naturalness of religion as shown by analy-

INDEX

sis of ideals, 285; unreality of the distinction between the religious and the moral, 285-286; the moral ideal in individual religious experience, 287; contrast of such experience with customary doctrine, 288; difference between mediæval and modern notions of divine service, 289; social conception of religion corrects the view of religion as due to some unique instinct, 289-290; mistake of attempting to explain religion through the subconscious, 290; importance of the subconscious for psychology, 290-292; extreme phenomena of the subconscious similar to common phenomena, 294; no valid support for the subconscious as the peculiar organ of religion, 294-295; faith as viewed from the standpoint of functional psychology, 296; differentiation of religious, from other types of faith, 297; solution of some problems concerning faith, 297-299; naturalness of prayer from the functional standpoint, 300-301; teleological character of the other forms of worship, 301-302.

Religious development, normal type of, Ch. XIII; gradual growth including spontaneous awakening as, 236; instances of gradual form, 237-240; instances of sudden awakening within a gradual process, 241-244; no special psychological significance in such awakening, 244-246; growth never absolutely regular, 247; psychology of growth as implying the educational process, 249; emphasis on conversion tends to hinder this process, 248; fallacy of abstracting the educational process from actual religious experience, 248-249; importance of permanent processes, 250; principles for religious education given by psychology of religion: child not irreligious by nature, 250; education must be more than intellectual, 251; activities and interest in concrete things must be employed, 252-253; epochal yet continuous development of child mind must be recognized, 253-254; education may continue beyond adolescence, 255.

Revivals, see under Conversion.
Ritschl, H., 8.
Rivers, W. H., 48, 92, 93, 140, 141, 160, 164.
Rogers, A. K., 319.
Ross, E. A., 193, 270, 276, 340, 404.
Royse, 265.

Sabatier, A., 8.
Sacrifice, Ch. VII; meaning of, in terms of acts involved, 116; eating food as the central act in, 117; other features, 117; supposed benefits of, 117; sacred objects themselves at first sacrifice, 118; totems originally staple articles of food and totemic ceremonies similar to sacrificial feasts, 118; how taboos against eating the totem arose, 119; mysterious, life-giving power attributed to the totem, 119-120; social nature and religious value of the food process, 121-122; simplest form of sacrificial feast the commensal meal, 122; the divinity appropriated in, 122; transmission of magic power from objects sacrificed, 122-123; other forms of unification through contact, 125-126; sacrifice for immunity from approaching danger, 127; for overcoming taboo already incurred, 128; importance of, and various means used in the second type, 128-129; impartation of sanctity through sacrifice, 130; the god offered to his followers, 131; sacrifice as atonement, 131; only violation of taboo required atonement, 131; purificatory rites sacrificial, not essentially hygienic, 132-133; real value of the sacrifice, 133.

Schleiermacher, F. E. D., 8, 11.
Sects, see Psychology of Religious Sects.
Seed-time, ceremonials of, 73, 80.
Self, man not directly conscious of, as

INDEX

spiritual agent, 95; variety of selves, 96; fused with object, 97; child not a, 97.
Sex, food and, as central interests, 33–34; division of labor dependent upon, 35; woman as social centre, and its significance, 36–38; man as fighter and hunter, 38–40; psychological significance of man's occupation, 40–43; masculine and feminine elements in ceremonies, 43; segregation of sex, 64; taboos of sex determined by customary activities, 64–66.
Sherrington, C. S., 324.
Skeat, W. W., 60, 103, 105.
Small and Vincent, 360.
Smith, H. P., 172, 174.
Smith, W. Robertson, 48, 77, 78, 91, 105, 117, 123, 126, 127, 130, 131, 149, 311, 347, 351.
Snake Indians, radical development of social organization, 170–171.
Social bonds, as centering about woman, 37–38.
Social consciousness, see under Consciousness.
Social development, as dependent upon economic conditions, 170–171.
Spencer, Herbert, 12, 102, 149.
Spencer and Gillen, 46, 47, 55, 61, 85, 86, 118, 124, 142, 143, 155, 163–164, 377.
Spirits, Ch. VI; origin of idea of, usually attributed to man's conception of his own soul, 96; man not directly conscious of himself as soul, or, 97; criticism of Tylor's view of, 99; objects appear to savages as living agents or, 100; vague use of the term, 101; Spencer, Marett, and Ratzel on meaning of, 102–103; Tylor, Skeat, Kidd, and Smith on the corporeal nature of, 103–105; psychological interpretation of, in terms of attention, conception, and habit, 106–108; connection of, with taboo, 108; predominance of those most important for group interests, 109; development of dualism between body and, 111–113; growth and objectification of the god, or 113; as objectification of consciousness of common tasks and ideals, 114.
Starbuck, E. D., 3, 9, 207, 211, 215, 217, 221, 237, 256, 259, 264, 266, 272, 288, 321, 325.
Stevens, G. B., 187, 286.
Sumner, W. G., 59, 60, 63.
Sutherland, Alexander, 403.
Symbolism of ceremonials develops into art, 91, 301.

Taboo, see Custom and.
Tanner, Amy, 236–237.
Theology, depends upon psychology, 7, 8.
Thinking, interlocutory character of, 138–139, 148; as purposive, 319.
Thomas, N. W., 80.
Thomas, W. I., 37, 39, 41, 42, 44, 50, 59, 60, 197, 226, 229, 362.
Todas, relation of ceremonies to food supply, 48; violent emotion and frenzy in ceremonies, 93; ritual of, more persistent than myth, 160.
Totem, see under Ceremonials and Magic.
Tufts, J. H., 190, 404.
Tylor, E. B., 12, 56, 95, 103, 104, 112, 134, 144, 149.

Uncleanness, relation to taboo, 69–70.

Veblen, T. B., 283, 361.

War, ceremonials of, 75; kinds of magic used, 82–83.
Webster, H., 151.
Westermarck, Edward, 144.
Will, primacy of, 19; simplest form of, and relation to habit, feeling, and ideation, 20.
Williams, J. M., 388–390.
Wood, Irving, 351.
Woman, share in primitive culture, 35; significance of, as social centre, 36–40.
Wundt, W., 58, 149.

Zuñis, myths of, 150, 156.

www.ingramcontent.com/pod-product-compliance
Lightning Source LLC
Chambersburg PA
CBHW070057020526
44112CB00034B/1423